Putin's Russia and
the Enlarged Europe

CHATHAM HOUSE PAPERS

Chatham House (the Royal Institute of International Affairs) in London has provided an impartial forum for discussion and debate on current international issues for over eighty-five years. Its resident research fellows, specialized information resources and range of publications, conferences and meetings span the fields of international politics, economics and security. Chatham House is independent of government and other vested interests.

Chatham House Papers address contemporary issues of intellectual importance in a scholarly yet accessible way. In preparing the papers, authors are advised by a study group of experts convened by Chatham House, and publication of a paper indicates that Chatham House regards it as an authoritative contribution to the public debate. The Royal Institute of International Affairs is, however, precluded by its Charter from having an institutional view. Opinions expressed in this publication are the responsibility of the authors.

Already published

Vladimir Putin and the Evolution of Russian Foreign Policy
Bobo Lo

Through the Paper Curtain: Insiders and Outsiders in the New Europe
Julie Smith and Charles Jenkins (eds)

European Migration Policies in Flux: Changing Patterns of Inclusion and Exclusion
Christina Boswell

World Trade Governance and Developing Countries: The GATT/WTO Code Committee System
Kofi Oteng Kufuor

Exit the Dragon? Privatization and State Control in China
Stephen Green and Guy S. Liu (eds)

Divided West: European Security and the Transatlantic Relationship
Tuomas Forsberg and Graeme P. Herd

Forthcoming

The New Atlanticist: Poland's Foreign and Security Priorities
Kerry Longhurst and Marcin Zaborowski

Britain and the Middle East: The Contemporary Policy Agenda
Rosemary Hollis

America at War: US Foreign Policy after 9/11
Michael Cox

Pax Bruxellana: Multilateralism and EU Global Power and Influence
Richard Whitman

Putin's Russia and the Enlarged Europe

Roy Allison, Margot Light and Stephen White

 CHATHAM HOUSE

The Royal Institute of International Affairs
Chatham House
10 St James's Square
London SW1Y 4LE
http://www.chathamhouse.org.uk
(Charity Registration No: 208223)

Blackwell Publishing Ltd
350 Main Street, Malden, MA 02148-5018, USA
9600 Garsington Road, Oxford OX4 2DQ, UK
550 Swanston Street, Carlton South, Melbourne, Victoria 3053, Australia
Kurfürstendamm 57, 10707 Berlin, Germany

First published 2006 by Blackwell Publishing Ltd

Library of Congress Cataloging-in-Publication Data has been applied for.

ISBN 1-4051-2648-5 [ISBN13: 978-1-4051-2648-9] (hardback)
ISBN 1-4051-2647-7 [ISBN13: 978-1-4051-2647-2] (paperback)

A catalogue record for this title is available from the British Library.

Set in 10.5 on 13 pt Caslon with Stone Sans display
by Koinonia, Manchester
Printed and bound in the United Kingdom
by T J International Ltd, Padstow, Cornwall

For further information on
Blackwell Publishing, visit our website:
http://www.blackwellpublishing.com

Contents

Contents

About the authors

Roy Allison is Senior Lecturer in International Relations at the London School of Economics and Political Science. He was Head of the Russia and Eurasia Programme at Chatham House (the Royal Institute of International Affairs) (1993–2005); Senior Research Fellow, Centre for International Studies, University of Oxford (2001–5); and Senior Lecturer, University of Birmingham (1992–9). His editorial board memberships include *International Affairs*. He has previously published, co-authored or edited eight books on Soviet, Russian and CIS foreign and security policies.

Margot Light is Emeritus Professor of International Relations at the London School of Economics. Her recent publications include 'Russia and the West: Is There a Values Gap?' (with Stephen White and Ian McAllister), *International Politics*, September 2005; 'Foreign Policy' in *Developments in Russian Politics 6*, edited by Stephen White, Richard Sakwa and Zvi Gitelman (Palgrave and Duke University Press, 2005); and 'Belarus between East and West' (with Roy Allison and Stephen White), *Journal of Communist Studies and Transition Politics*, December 2005.

Stephen White is Professor of International Politics at the University of Glasgow, and is a Senior Research Associate of its School of Central and East European Studies and of the Institute of Applied Politics in Moscow. He was President of the British Association for Slavonic and East European Studies (1994–7), and is also chief editor of the *Journal of Communist Studies and Transition Politics*. His recent publications include *Developments in Russian Politics 6* (with others, Palgrave and Duke University Press, 2005), and *Politics in Europe* (with others, CQ Press, 2006).

Acknowledgments

This book forms part of a wider project 'Inclusion without Membership? Bringing Russia, Ukraine and Belarus closer to "Europe"', funded by grant RES-000-23-0146 to the three co-authors, for which we gratefully acknowledge the generous support of the UK Economic and Social Research Council. The project addresses a topic of growing significance equally for social science research and policy formation – the risk that new 'dividing lines' may form in Europe on its eastern flanks following the dual enlargements of the European Union and NATO. The project also offers new analysis and data on how far public opinion and elites in Russia, Ukraine and Belarus identify themselves as European and assess the effects of the dual enlargement. A more detailed account of the project as a whole and a list of other publications that have derived from it is available on the project website: *www.lbss. gla.ac.uk/politics/inclusionwithoutmembership/*.

This volume focuses on developments in Russian elite debate, public opinion and official policy formation towards the EU and NATO during the presidency of Vladimir Putin, especially his second presidential term. The extensive agenda of work involved has required us to consult widely, interview extensively and prevail upon officials and specialists too numerous to mention. But our thinking has been enriched in particular by discussions with or comments from Derek Averre, Peter Duncan, Paul Fritch, Bobo Lo, Alex Pravda, and Andrew Wilson. Useful feedback was received at various seminar panels arranged by the project, including one at the VII ICCEES World Congress, Berlin, in July 2005.

Chapter 6 would not have been possible without the assistance commissioned from Russian colleagues, which we explain separately at the end of the book in the note on sources. Special thanks are due in this connection to Dr Olga Kryshtanovskaya, who helped to arrange our focus groups and our extensive programme of interviews. We are also especially grateful to Dr Julia Korosteleva, who was project Research Fellow based at Glasgow University and a highly valued member of the research team, in particular for the data analysis in Chapter 6.

We have benefited from the facilities of three universities, those at Glasgow, Oxford and the London School of Economics and Political Science. The Centre of International Studies of the Department of Politics and International Relations, University of Oxford, kindly provided a congenial intellectual environment for Roy Allison to pursue his research on this book during 2003-05 as a Senior Research Fellow, as did St Antony's College, Oxford.

The Russia and Eurasia Programme (REP) at Chatham House (The Royal Institute of International Affairs) has been a consistent source of encouragement for the publication of this book; the practical assistance of the Programme Manager of REP, James Nixey, and the Programme Head since 2005, Bobo Lo, has been indispensable and much appreciated. A Chatham House Study Group offered constructive suggestions on a draft text and allowed us to explore the impact of our analysis on former senior diplomats and journalists as well as specialists and academics. The text benefited from the valuable suggestions and advice of three readers. Margaret May has steered the publication through with exemplary efficiency and patience. The authors alone are responsible for any remaining errors, but we hope this volume will contribute to understanding and debate on one of the most important issues in contemporary international affairs.

August 2006   R.A.
                                                                           M.L.
                                                                           S.W.

Abbreviations and acronyms

AWACS	Airborne Warning and Control System
CEE	Central and Eastern Europe/Central and East European
CFE	Conventional Forces in Europe
CFSP	Common Foreign and Security Policy (EU)
CIS	Commonwealth of Independent States
CPRF	Communist Party of the Russian Federation
EAPC	Euro-Atlantic Partnership Council
ENP	European Neighbourhood Policy
ESDP	European Security and Defence Policy
FSB	Federal Security Bureau
IFOR	Peace Implementation Force (NATO – Bosnia and Herzegovina)
IPAP	Individual Partnership Action Plan
JHA	Justice and Home Affairs (European Commission)
KFOR	Kosovo Force (NATO)
LDPR	Liberal Democratic Party of Russia
NACC	North Atlantic Cooperation Council
NATO	North Atlantic Treaty Organization
NIS	Newly Independent States
NRC	NATO–Russia Council
OSCE	Organization for Security and Cooperation in Europe
PCA	Partnership and Cooperation Agreement
PfP	Partnership for Peace
PJC	Permanent Joint Council
PPC	Permanent Partnership Council
SFOR	Peace Stabilization Force (NATO – Bosnia and Herzegovina)
SHAPE	Supreme Headquarters Allied Powers Europe
TACIS	Technical Assistance to the CIS
URF	Union of Right Forces (Russia)
WEU	Western European Union

1

The place of Europe in Russian foreign policy

Margot Light with Roy Allison

Russians have always wondered if they are Europeans. Geographically, Russia straddles Europe and Asia; assuming that the Ural Mountains are the border between Europe and Asia (as the 1990 Treaty on Conventional Forces in Europe does), 75 per cent of the Russian population lives on the western side of the border. But the population of Siberia and the Russian Far East is predominantly Russian and the Organization for Security and Cooperation in Europe (OSCE), stretching from Vancouver to Vladivostok, includes all of Russia in Europe.

Since the beginning of the eighteenth century, however, the dominant issue has not been Russia's geographic location, but its identity, or the question of whether Russia shares the culture and values of Europe. Peter the Great built a 'window on Europe' in St Petersburg and imported European habits and technology to Russia. Catherine the Great declared that 'Russia is a European State.'[1] In the nineteenth century there was a debate between 'Westernizers', who believed that Russia's development depended on the adoption of Western technology and liberal government, and Slavophiles, who rejected European liberalism and secularism. They held that Russian civilization was unique and superior to Western culture because it was based on institutions such as the Eastern Orthodox Church, the village community, and the ancient popular assembly, the *zemsky sobor*. At the beginning of the twentieth century the divisions between Slavophiles and Westernizers were reflected in the differences between the Russian Social Revolutionaries and Marxists. In 1917, the Bolsheviks expected that the revolution would spread from Russia to Europe and then the European revolution would come to the rescue of the Russian revolution. Stalin's 'socialism in one country' reversed the direction of this dependence. From then on, the security of the Soviet state, rather than the identity of Russia or the fate of international revolution, became the prime concern of Soviet foreign policy and of the international communist movement.

After the Second World War, the Soviet government was alarmed by those West European regional organizations that were perceived to threaten Soviet security. Its hostility was particularly directed towards the North Atlantic Treaty Organization (NATO), an alliance dedicated to containing the Soviet threat, but the European Economic Community (EEC) was also regarded with suspicion.[2] The Soviet leadership refused to accord the EEC diplomatic recognition and, since it was perceived to operate as the economic arm of NATO, deemed that the inclusion of Finland and Austria was incompatible with their neutral status.[3] Unwilling to accept the supranational authority of the European Commission, the Soviet Union preferred to deal bilaterally with EEC member states. One sign that Mikhail Gorbachev's New Political Thinking represented a radical shift in Soviet policy was his acceptance that the EEC was a political entity. Gorbachev also restated the Soviet claim to a European identity in his call for a Common European Home, but at the same time he was echoing a long-standing Soviet aim to promote a pan-European system of collective security.

When the Soviet Union disintegrated in 1991, the new Russian government believed that conditions were ripe for the abolition of the security institutions that had embodied the Cold War. Both NATO and the Warsaw Pact, Russians thought, would be subsumed within a new European collective security system in which the United States and Canada would play an active part. Western leaders also envisaged a new European order, but they could not conceive of European security without NATO. Moreover, many of the new governments of the Central and East European (CEE) transition states were convinced that NATO membership was the only reliable guarantee of their independence. The CEE governments also believed that accession to the European Union (EU), as the EEC became known in 1992, would ensure their future prosperity. West Europeans began to consider how best to assist them to make the transition to liberal democracy and successful market economies. In 1994 the European Council approved a 'pre-accession strategy' designed to facilitate their eventual accession to the EU, while NATO designed a series of measures to facilitate cooperation with the CEE, the end point of which, it soon became clear, would be incorporation into the alliance.

At first, no one gave much thought to the role that Russia would play in the new European order. When both the EU and NATO began to plan enlargement, however, it became apparent that a necessary and important subsidiary of the process for both organizations was defining and establishing a new relationship with Russia – a relationship which, while not extending membership to either, would ensure that Russia did not obstruct their expansion. This need to engage Russia gave rise to particular challenges after Finland joined the EU in 1995 and the first wave of NATO enlargement took place in 1999, since the expanding Euro-Atlantic community now reached the borders of the Russian Federation. Russians found themselves outsiders in the advancing process of EU and NATO enlargement, and it was far from clear how and whether these organizations could devise the means to promote greater Russian inclusion in European affairs and prevent the entrenchment of new political dividing lines along the eastern borders of the EU and NATO zones.

This book examines the development of Russia's relations with the EU and NATO since that first wave of expansion took place, concentrating particularly on Vladimir Putin's second presidential term, from his re-election in March 2004. It focuses on Russia's relations with the EU and NATO, the two principal international institutions in European affairs, because it is from them, rather than other Euro-Atlantic institutions (for example, the OSCE or the Council of Europe), that Russia has been excluded. And it concentrates on Russian attitudes towards, and relations with, the EU and NATO rather than on its bilateral relations with various EU member states because improving Russia's partnership with these two multilateral institutions is crucial in order to promote Russian engagement in the project of enlargement and to ensure that it is 'a strategy for unifying Europe, not for dividing it'.[4]

Since one of the main objectives of this study is to investigate the extent to which the EU and NATO can act as channels for the greater inclusion of Russia 'into' Europe, in the chapters that follow we concentrate primarily on political and security relations, rather than on economic relations. Moreover, the book is particularly concerned with understanding Russian mass opinion and the perceptions of the informed foreign policy elite, as well as potential Russian policy towards European processes and institutions – and such opinion and debate tend to focus on high politics and not on the substance of economic and trade relations (even though Russia–EU relations at the level of low politics are very active).[5] Furthermore, Russian decision-makers have tended more and more to be drawn from people with a security background and, in Putin's second term in particular, there has been a considerable 'securitization' of Russia's foreign policy agenda. Inevitably, this has been accompanied by a greater emphasis on high politics at the expense of low politics in the Russia–EU relationship. In other words, Russian decision-makers tend to see Russia's interactions with the EU, as well as with NATO in their shared neighbourhood, in geopolitical and security terms. As a result, during Putin's second term, progress at the level of low politics has often been hampered by friction at the level of high politics.[6] As we will see, this has been influenced by perceptions of the 'coloured revolutions' in that neighbourhood and by the fact that the EU has itself become more actively interested in political developments and conflicts in the CIS countries.

This chapter begins by outlining the evolution of Russia's relations with NATO and the EU before Vladimir Putin's election as President of the Russian Federation in March 2000. It then examines the impact on those relations of the terrorist attack on the Twin Towers and the Pentagon on 11 September 2001. The third section assesses the different views that Russian foreign policy elites hold about Russian foreign policy in general, including Russia's relations with NATO and the EU. Finally, we present the structure of the rest of the book and preview the central arguments and research findings of Chapters 2–6.

RUSSIA AND NATO

Although NATO members did not consider Russia eligible for membership of the alliance, they made active efforts over the years to establish a broad framework of institutionalized relations with the Russian government.[7] In March 1992, for example, Russia became a member of the North Atlantic Cooperation Council (NACC), which had been established by the NATO Summit in Rome in 1991 as a forum for consultation between NATO's 16 members, the European neutrals and the CEE. It also became a member of the Euro-Atlantic Partnership Council (EAPC), which succeeded NACC in 1997. The Partnership for Peace (PfP) initiative, launched by NATO in 1994 as a vehicle through which non-members could work alongside the Alliance, was extended to all the members of NACC, including Russia. At the same time as launching the PfP, NATO members began seriously contemplating enlargement. Although the Russian government was unenthusiastic about the PfP initiative, it negotiated a Framework Document, which was initialled on 22 June 1994. Russia's acceptance of a PfP agreement did not, however, denote its approval of NATO enlargement, and when NATO Foreign Ministers announced that they were seriously contemplating enlargement in December 1994, Russia walked out of the PfP signing ceremony. President Yeltsin warned that if NATO enlarged, Europe would be plunged into a 'cold peace', while some Russian analysts advised the Russian government to do its best to hinder NATO expansion.[8]

In an attempt to prevent the Russian government from hindering the enlargement process, NATO began to negotiate a separate charter with Russia once a firm decision had been taken about enlargement. The hope was that Russians would be reassured that cooperation between Russia and the Alliance would continue even if enlargement proceeded. On 27 May 1997 the Founding Act on Mutual Relations, Cooperation and Security between

NATO and the Russian Federation was signed in Paris by the Secretary-General of NATO, Heads of State and Government of NATO and the Russian President. It aimed to enable Russia and NATO to work together to build 'a lasting and inclusive peace in the Euro-Atlantic area on the principles of democracy and cooperative security'. A NATO–Russia Permanent Joint Council was established 'to build increasing levels of trust, unity of purpose and habits of consultation and cooperation'. It would be 'the principal venue of consultation between NATO and Russia in times of crisis or for any other situation affecting peace and stability'.[9]

Many people in the West seemed to think that by signing the Act, the Russian government had signalled its tacit acceptance of NATO expansion. This neither corresponded to the Russian government's interpretation of the significance of the Act nor reflected Russian public opinion. NATO's role in the conflict in Bosnia, and particularly the bombardment of Serb installations in Bosnia in 1995, had already caused great concern in Moscow, re-evoking the hostility towards NATO that had been characteristic of the Soviet era.[10] The adoption of a new strategic concept at the 50th anniversary NATO summit in Washington in 1999, and the announcement that the door to NATO membership remained open, caused further alarm. The strategic concept suggested that NATO would respond with force to regional crises, for example at the periphery of the Alliance, rather than just to threats of an armed attack on member states. Since the periphery of the Alliance would also be the periphery of the Russian Federation once enlargement had taken place, this appeared to imply a direct threat to an area which the Russian government considered to be within its legitimate sphere of influence. The new strategy, according to a Russian analyst, 'gives NATO *carte blanche* to use force on any pretext it chooses'.[11] And NATO's assurance that the 'Alliance remains open to all European democracies, regardless of geography, willing and able to meet the responsibilities of membership' appeared to imply that membership would be further extended to the Soviet successor states, such as the Baltic republics or Ukraine.[12]

By the time the new strategic concept was adopted, it had already been put into practice in the air strikes against Serbia in response to the Kosovo crisis. For Russians, Kosovo was the last straw. Not only had NATO acted without explicit UN approval; it had also failed to take account of Russia's legitimate interests, and it had not consulted the Russian government in the Joint Russia–NATO Council. This seemed to confirm that NATO wanted to exclude Russia from decisions on important European security issues.[13] In Russian eyes, NATO had ceased to be a defence alliance, and the threat implicit in the new strategic doctrine suddenly seemed very real. The Russians responded with 'the loudest, most intemperate and sustained

... protests against the West since the disintegration of the Soviet Union'.[14] On the other hand, Russian support for Milosevic and the 'dash to Pristina' – the unannounced and precipitous dispatch of Russian troops from Bosnia to 'capture' Slatina airport outside Pristina, the capital of Kosovo, before NATO ground troops could reach it – caused NATO members to doubt that Russia was a reliable partner. Except for dealing with matters that arose from the participation of Russian troops in the KFOR peacekeeping operation after Serbia had withdrawn from Kosovo, cooperation within the Joint Council virtually ceased. The Russian government also refused to participate in any PfP activities. Relations were revived in February 2000, when NATO Secretary-General George Robertson was invited to Moscow, but it was only after September 2001 that full cooperation with NATO was resumed.

RUSSIA AND THE EU

Like NATO, the EU tried to ensure that Russia was not marginalized by the enlargement process.[15] It concluded a Partnership and Cooperation Agreement (PCA) with the Russian Federation in June 1994 'founded on shared principles and objectives: the promotion of international peace and security, support for democratic norms and for political and economic freedoms'. Less than the Europe Agreements that were designed to prepare aspirant states for EU membership, the PCA is, nevertheless, far more than an ordinary treaty on political and economic relations. Its aim is to develop closer political links, foster trade and investment, support the reform process in Russia, and create the conditions necessary for the establishment of a future free trade area between the EU and Russia. Ratification of the PCA was delayed, however, as a protest against the first war in Chechnya and the agreement only came into force on 1 December 1997. Since it is a ten-year treaty, it expires in December 2007. A ministerial-level Cooperation Council and a Cooperation Committee at senior civil servant level were established to monitor implementation of the PCA. The PCA also provided for a Parliamentary Cooperation Committee consisting of members of the European Parliament and of the Russian Federal Assembly.[16]

Well before the PCA went into operation, the Russian Federation had begun to receive economic and other forms of support from the EU. The most important vehicle of this support was the TACIS programme (Technical Assistance to the Commonwealth of Independent States), the purpose of which was to support the process of transition to a market economy and democratic society. TACIS committed €1,573.5 million in bilateral aid to the Russian Federation in 1991–2002, which was almost half of its total bilateral aid to the former Soviet states.[17] The EU was also Russia's most important

Table 1.1: Russian trade, by partners (US$ million)

	1995	2000	2001	2002	2003	2004[a]	2005[a]
Exports	82,419	105,033	101,884	107,301	135,929	183,200	241,352
Imports	62,603	44,862	53,764	60,966	75,436	94,800	98,505
Turnover	145,022	149,895	155,648	168,267	211,365	278,000	339,857
including							
EU15,[b]	44,246	47,837	52,150	55,146	69,005	125,507	177,039
% of turnover	31	32	34	33	33	45	52
CECs,	11,530	14,018	13,999	13,685	17,146	–	–
% of turnover	8	9	9	8	8		
CIS countries,	35,317	27,678	28,311	28,526	36,543	47,100	51,519
% of turnover	24	19	18	17	17	17	15
US,	6,963	7,338	7,451	6,969	7,165	9,824	10,881
% of turnover	5	5	5	4	3	4	3
China,	4,236	6,197	7,242	9,238	11,547	14,851	20,298
% of turnover	3	4	5	6	6	5	6

Source: *Rossiiskii statisticheskii ezhegodnik* (Moscow: Goskomstat, 2004), pp. 650, 652–3.
CECs denotes Central European countries.
a. Data for 2004-5 were derived from *www.gks.ru*, accessed 23 February 2006.
b. Data for the EU in 2004–5 comprise 25 country members.

trade partner, accounting for 31 per cent of its foreign trade compared with 5 per cent with the United States and 8 per cent with the CEE states (see Table 1.1).

In June 1997 the EU signed a new intergovernmental treaty, the Amsterdam Treaty, the main purpose of which was to make the EU's Common Foreign and Security Policy (CFSP) more effective. It established a new policy instrument called 'common strategies'. By adopting a common strategy EU members would commit themselves to cooperate on policy towards a particular area or country where the member states had important interests in common. The first such strategy to be elaborated was the Common Strategy on Russia, approved by the Cologne European Council in June 1999. It committed the EU to assist in the establishment of a 'stable, open and pluralistic democracy in Russia', and aimed at 'responding to the common challenges of the continent through intensified cooperation'. It set out four areas of action (consolidation of democracy, the rule of law and public institutions; integration of Russia into a common European economic and social space; stability and security; and common challenges on the European continent) on which the EU would focus in order to 'strengthen the strategic partnership between the Union and Russia'. There were also more particular initiatives in fields such as non-proliferation and organized crime.[18] The Russian government was slightly irritated by the 'apparent tone of condescension and hubris' used in the Common Strategy.[19] It responded by elaborating its own goals for its relationship with the EU, which it presented to the Helsinki European Council in October 1999 as the 'Medium-Term Strategy for the Development of Relations between the Russian Federation and the European Union (2000–2010)'.[20] Apart from setting out ten spheres of cooperation between Russia and the EU, the final section of the Medium-Term Strategy lists a number of ways in which administrative support, coordination and the use of specialist groups will be improved within Russia to facilitate implementation of the Strategy and further the EU–Russia strategic partnership.

Apart from adopting the Common Strategy on Russia, the Cologne European Council also agreed to expand the CFSP so that the EU would 'have the capacity for autonomous action, backed up by credible military forces, the means to decide to use them, and a readiness to do so, in order to respond to international crises without prejudice to actions by NATO'.[21] Russians clearly did not perceive this as a threat to Russian security. Neither the National Security Blueprint, which was drafted and discussed in 1999 and adopted in January 2000, for example, nor the new military doctrine adopted in March 2000, mentions the Common European Security and Defence Policy as a potential threat to Russia.[22] Indeed, the Medium-Term Strategy appears to welcome the plans, since it lists as one of the aims the creation of a reliable pan-European system of collective security and a united Europe 'without dividing lines'. It suggests that the establishment of 'pan-European security by European forces, without isolating the USA or NATO' could be included as one of the stages in the Russia–EU partnership in the next decade. It also proposes practical cooperation with the Western European Union (WEU) in the area of security, 'which could counterbalance ... the NATO-ism in Europe' and enhance the strategic partnership between Russia and the EU.[23]

Although there were a number of disappointments on both sides at the slow pace of progress in implementing these agreements, a dense network of political and economic consultations was established between the EU and Russia. The Cooperation Committee met frequently at the level of senior officials, while various subcommittees brought Russian and EU experts together. At the highest level, EU–Russia summits took place at regular six-monthly intervals, interspersed by meetings between the EU Troika (the head of the country holding the Presidency of the Council, the High Representative for the CFSP and a representative of the EU Commission) and their Russian counterparts. There was also a steady flow of high-level visits between Moscow and various European capitals.

There were important practical reasons for developing the EU–Russia relationship. Between 1995 and 2003, the value of EU–Russia trade increased from €38 billion to €85 billion, making Russia the EU's fifth largest trading partner (after the United States, Switzerland, China and Japan). The EU, for its part, as noted above, was Russia's largest trading partner. Energy supplies predominated in Russia's exports to the EU, accounting for about 57 per cent of exports in 2003. In October 2000 an 'energy dialogue' was instituted on a regular basis which aimed to work towards an EU–Russia Energy Partnership.[24]

Nevertheless, the EU was highly critical of the launch of a second war against Chechnya in 1999. The Council of the EU adopted a declaration condemning the bombardment of Chechen towns and the treatment of internally displaced people, and limiting TACIS assistance to priority areas, including human rights, the rule of law, support for civil society and nuclear safety.[25] Russian officials, in turn, were offended by EU demands that related, in their view, to 'domestic' matters. They perceived EU statements – and sanctions – relating to Chechnya as improper.[26] President Putin appeared, however, to remain committed to a closer relationship with 'Europe' more broadly, and with the European Union in particular, both because of his conviction that Russia is part of a 'greater Europe' and to offset the tensions that had begun to develop in Russia's relations with the US over a range of security issues. In his annual address to the Federal Assembly in April 2001, for example, he listed integration with Europe as 'one of the key areas' of Russian foreign policy.[27]

THE IMPACT OF 9/11 ON RUSSIA'S RELATIONS WITH NATO AND THE EU

After the attacks on the World Trade Center and the Pentagon on 11 September 2001, in the face of the common threat of international terrorism and a united determination to eliminate it, Russia resumed cooperation with the United States and, by extension, with NATO. President Putin signalled Russia's participation in the international coalition against terrorism by promising to increase the supply of weapons to the Northern Alliance fighting the Taliban government in Afghanistan, to open Russian airspace to US airplanes for humanitarian flights, and to participate in 'search and rescue operations' once the attack against Afghanistan began. Putin also gave tacit support to the Central Asian states' offer of logistic support, including bases, to the US military for the operation against Afghanistan. The Russian military objected to Putin's policy and it took a great deal of effort to persuade them that active cooperation was necessary.[28] Russia also supported the UN Security Council resolution that endorsed US military action against the Taliban.

Russian commentators and politicians appeared to expect that Russia would get certain benefits in return for cooperating in the anti-terrorist coalition. First, President Putin had always claimed to be fighting a war against international terrorism in Chechnya and he had insisted that Osama bin Laden was funding Chechen terrorists, many of whom had been trained by Al-Qaeda. He assumed that once the attack against Afghanistan was launched, Western criticism of the war against Chechnya would cease. Second, he hoped to be able to use the leverage of his support for the anti-terrorist coalition to obtain concessions on the security issues that were causing serious strains in Russia's bilateral relations with the United States. Third, he may have hoped that further NATO enlargement might be postponed or even abandoned.[29]

At first the common threat of international terrorism and a united determination to eliminate it appeared to put human rights issues and democratization, previously an active ingredient of EU foreign policy, on the back burner. Western criticism of Russia's policy in Chechnya became far more muted. The final EU–Russia summit statement in October 2001, for example, did not mention Russia's human rights abuses in Chechnya. Instead, the EU expressed its support for the Russian authorities' efforts to reach a political settlement. Moreover, a joint statement was issued on international terrorism and a joint declaration was adopted 'on stepping up dialogue and cooperation on political and security matters', such as 'increasing international security and crisis prevention and management in Europe, non-proliferation and disarmament, conventional weapons exports, the OSCE, the United Nations and combating international terrorism'. In addition to the existing regular consultations, monthly meetings would be held between the EU Political and Security Committee Troika and Russia 'in order to take stock of consultations on crisis prevention and management'. In response to events, other one-off meetings would be organized between the EU's Political and Security Committee and Russia.[30] In November 2002, the EU granted 'market economy status' to the Russian Federation, which substantially increased the ability of Russian exporters to defend their interests in the context of anti-dumping proceedings.

As the enlargement of the EU loomed closer, the European Commission began to give serious thought to the consequences of enlargement for the countries that would find themselves on the external land and sea borders of the enlarged EU, namely the Western Newly Independent States (NIS), as the Commission calls the former Soviet states of Belarus, Moldova, Russia and Ukraine, and the southern Mediterranean. They had no serious prospect of acceding to the EU in the foreseeable future, but they were perceived as 'essential partners'. Indeed, the attainment of security, stability and sustainable development *within* the Union was deemed to require political reform, social cohesion and economic dynamism *outside* it, in particular in the EU's new eastern neighbourhood.[31] The European Commission proposed 'a differentiated, progressive, and benchmarked approach' to the new neighbours. Russians were shocked that the EU's new neighbourhood plans appeared to put Russia in the same category not only as Belarus and Moldova, but also as the states of North Africa. According to Sergei Yastrzhembsky, presidential representative in charge of Russia's EU policy, 'The offered suit is too small for us. It is not the right size for Russia's shoulders.'[32] Russia was duly left out of the European Neighbourhood Policy; instead the EU and Russia decided to develop their strategic partnership through the creation of four common spaces. In effect, this represented the recognition that the European neighbourhood was also Russia's neighbourhood; in other words, it was a shared neighbourhood in which Russia and the EU had to cooperate. As we will see, it is in this shared neighbourhood that some of the most serious difficulties in EU–Russia relations have arisen.

Participation in the coalition against international terrorism did lead to a short-term abatement in public criticism of Russia's policy in Chechnya. It did not, however, lead to concessions on the strategic issues that concerned Russia. Far from abandoning ballistic missile defence (BMD), President George W. Bush reaffirmed his determination to proceed. He rejected Putin's offer to amend the anti-ballistic missile (ABM) treaty and, instead, on 13 December 2001, gave six months' notice that the US intended to abrogate it. And although he agreed to a bilateral arms reduction treaty, he refused to destroy US warheads as part of the agreement. Instead they would be put into store in case of future need. When, in his State of the Union address in January 2002, President Bush identified an 'axis of evil' consisting of Iran, Iraq and North Korea, all three states with which Russia enjoyed good relations, it became apparent that an extension of the war against terrorism would prove divisive to US–Russian relations. In the run-up to the war against Iraq, Russia was critical of US policy and, when the attack began, Putin called it a 'major political mistake', not only in humanitarian terms, but also in the threat it represented to the international order.[33]

Nor were Russian hopes fulfilled that the second round of NATO enlargement would be postponed. Nevertheless, cooperation with NATO in the fight against terrorism proceeded, and it included the regular exchange of information and consultation on non-proliferation and on civil emergency planning.[34] At the same time, negotiations began on a new, deeper institutional relationship between Russia and NATO. On 28 May 2002 Russia and the 19 NATO member countries signed the Rome Declaration, establishing a new mechanism for cooperation, the NATO–Russia Council (NRC), which replaced the Permanent Joint Council. It provided for Russia and the 19 NATO members to work as equal partners in areas of common interest, such as combating international terrorism, crisis management, non-proliferation, civil emergency planning, theatre missile defence, defence modernization, arms control and confidence- and security-building measures, search-and-rescue at sea and identifying new challenges and threats.

The Rome Declaration envisaged active and regular cooperation at various levels. The NRC would meet at the level of Foreign Ministers and at the level of Defence Ministers twice annually, and at the level of Heads of State and Government as appropriate. Meetings at ambassadorial level would be held at least once a month. Under the auspices of the NRC, NATO and Russian Chiefs of Staff would meet at least twice a year, while meetings at military representatives level would take place at least once a month. A Preparatory Committee was established that would meet twice monthly or more frequently to prepare meetings of the NRC. The NRC could also establish committees or working groups for individual subjects or areas of cooperation on an ad hoc or permanent basis.[35]

Despite considerable initial scepticism about the NRC, deemed by some Russians to be symptomatic of NATO's irrelevance after 11 September, early progress appeared promising, even if, in the words of one Russian analyst, NRC activities should be regarded 'as a form of preparatory work, which will enable, when the political will and need arise, Russia and NATO to develop cooperation in essential projects'.[36] If NATO itself expected the NRC to soften the blow of the second round of enlargement, it was moderately successful. Although the Russian government continued to express its opposition to further expansion, it responded with regret rather than anger to the announcement in November 2002 that the Baltic states, together with Slovakia, Slovenia, Bulgaria and Romania, would be admitted to NATO in May 2004.

RUSSIAN ELITES AND THEIR FOREIGN POLICY VIEWS

Broadly, Russian foreign policy elites tend to have more favourable opinions of the EU than of NATO, but their views about Russian foreign policy are by no means monolithic. For analytical convenience, we identify three major trends in foreign policy thinking: liberal westernizer, pragmatic nationalist and fundamentalist nationalist.[37] At one end of the political spectrum are liberal Westernizers who favour a market economy, a democratic political system and a pro-Western foreign policy. Liberal westernizers favour close relations with NATO and the EU and active and cooperative membership of international institutions. They identify with European values and believe that Russia should adopt them. Although they want good-neighbourly relations with the other successor states, they believe that Russia should abandon its historical great-power traditions and any illusions about having a special role as bridge between Europe and Asia in favour of developing its European orientation.[38] As we shall see, although liberal Westernizers are a diminishing minority, their views can still be discerned among foreign policy elites.

Fundamentalist nationalists are at the opposite end of the spectrum of foreign policy beliefs. They combine ardent nationalism and a desire to re-establish Russian hegemony in the former Soviet space with an antipathy towards the market economy. They tend to favour tighter integration of the CIS. Fundamentalist nationalists ground their beliefs in the Eurasianist and geopolitical schools of thought of the nineteenth and early twentieth centuries. They interpret Eurasianism in both geographic and economic terms: Russia's unique and special role implies forging a 'third way' in politics and economics which includes authoritarian government and a corporatist economy. They are hostile to both NATO and the EU.[39]

The views of pragmatic nationalists were developed in the early 1990s as a critique of the unreflective pro-Westernism of Foreign Minister Andrei Kozyrev. Pragmatic nationalism has become the prevailing consensus view of Russian foreign policy. Pragmatic nationalists do not entirely reject liberal Westernist views. In general they favour democracy, for example, although not necessarily 'Western' democracy. They also support a market economy, without rejecting state control of strategic resources. Although they reject the ardent nationalism of the fundamentalist nationalists, there are elements of nationalism in their belief in Russia's great-power status and their view of Russia's role in the former Soviet space. They argue that Russia's vital interests encompass the geopolitical space of the former Soviet Union and believe that the international community should recognize Russia's responsibility for guaranteeing the stability of this area. Although they reject the re-establishment of the USSR, they favour an integrationist policy towards the other successor states. Pragmatic nationalists believe that policy towards the West, including the EU and NATO, should be based on a rational analysis of Russia's national interests. They also favour a diversification of foreign policy. Closer links with former Soviet allies and with the newly industrialized countries of Asia and the Middle East would, for example, give Russia more leverage in its relationship with the West.[40]

ANALYSIS AND ARGUMENTS

During Putin's presidency, the second round of enlargement of the EU and NATO in 2004 has reinforced traditional Russian concerns about the effects of exclusion from the core decision-making processes of these organizations on Russian influence in Europe in general. The Russian leadership is highly sensitive over its status, increasingly insistent that it should be treated as an equal in negotiation processes with European structures and determined that Russia should not assume an 'outsider' status in Europe.

At the same time Moscow does not feel it can count on Russian membership of the Council of Europe and OSCE to influence policies in the EU zone or to counter the risk of new 'dividing lines' in Europe linked to EU and NATO enlargement. Moscow regards the Council of Europe and the OSCE as having little effect on major policy decisions in Europe and as unreasonably focused on political developments in post-Soviet states. Foreign Minister Sergei Lavrov has described the fact that EU law (which Moscow cannot influence) is regarded as higher than the law of the Council of Europe as 'deleterious for the pan-European space'.[41]

This volume explores the extent of Russian 'inclusion' in Europe through the perspectives of the Russian political and foreign policy elite, through the perceptions in Russian public opinion at large and through the policy content of Russian engagement with the EU and NATO. It explores in particular efforts to move Russia 'closer to Europe' and overcome divisions by developing enhanced partner relations and promoting normative and policy convergence between Russia and these core European institutions. Our investigation leads to conclusions as to whether in the medium term Russia is likely to be part of Europe, i.e. Russia *in* Europe, or separate from the architecture and core processes of the enlarged Europe – Russia *and* Europe.

The principal focus of the volume, and hence our contribution to the debate on Russian–European relations, is on Russian policy, policy perspectives and public attitudes. Much less attention is paid to the constraints on Russia's engagement in Europe arising from the evolution of the EU and NATO themselves. Chapter 2 is devoted specifically to an analysis of Russia's domestic political trajectory and influences on foreign and security policy decision-making in Moscow since the State Duma elections at the end of 2003 and the re-election of President Putin in March 2004. Changes in the domestic Russian context underpin shifts in Russian foreign policy, which have become more pronounced during Putin's second presidential term, and are an important focus of investigation elsewhere in the volume.

Chapter 2 charts the transition in Putin's second term to a quasi-authoritarian style of political management in Russia. The consolidation of presidential authority feeds into our analysis of the process of Russian foreign and security policy-making, which has an important impact on foreign policy outputs in general and towards Europe and its institutions in particular. The narrowing of forms of political expression and debate, and the focus on personalized presidential decision-making, accompany problems of coordination of foreign policy positions by agencies engaged in Russian foreign policy-making, along with difficulties in the aggregation and effective use of information. The political trajectory of Putin's Russia is serving to distance the country politically from the EU and NATO zones of states. But in some important respects it also appears to have a dysfunctional effect on Russian efforts to generate a foreign policy that would serve the interest of constructing a Greater Europe in which Russia would be an influential and respected player.

Chapters 3–5 examine Russia's relationship with the EU and NATO since the Duma and presidential elections of 2003–4. Key findings and arguments of this analysis are presented here to help the reader navigate the volume. Chapter 3, which addresses Russian political engagement with the EU, affirms that Russian political elites identify themselves and Russia as European to a significant extent and have predominantly positive perceptions of the EU, though they may not perceive themselves as 'Western'. Regardless of this positive foundation, Russia–EU relations were close to deadlock by mid-2004. They were characterized by ad hoc responses to a series of mini-crises over various controversies rather than by proactive and strategic diplomacy. How can we account for this?

A key theme is the way in which progress with the 'low politics' substance of the Russia–EU partnership, which is characterized by a functional problem-solving framework, has increasingly been hampered by concerns at the level of 'high politics', which require top-level intervention. Chapter 3 demonstrates how a number of significant disputes in Russia–EU relations have reflected practical consequences of EU enlargement eastwards, on issues related to borders, and Russian efforts to counteract or minimize these effects. Moscow has often read security implications into such enlargement issues. For example, the extension of the Schengen regime, which was of less concern to Russian foreign policy elites in 2004 than five years earlier, still symbolized to many the re-division of Europe. The possibility of visa-free travel to the EU zone promises to be a source of rancour in Russia–EU relations for years to come. It was the basis of the acrimonious controversy over access to Kaliningrad during 2001–2 that linked practical issues of Russia–EU low politics to wider geopolitical concerns. Further north, Russian specialists have found it difficult to identify any concrete results from the Northern Dimension – an EU programme specifically aimed to address cross-border issues. There is considerable potential for Russia–EU cooperation over soft security issues, which fall within the remit of Justice and Home Affairs in the European Commission and overlap with cooperation on border and visa issues. But most activity in this category has been in planning rather than implementing policies. Meanwhile EU condemnation of the prosecution of Russia's wars in Chechnya, and Russian criticism in turn of the EU's response to Chechen terrorism, have continued to sour the environment for thriving Russia–EU relations, even if they have had little direct impact on those relations. Most recently, energy security – the nature of EU–Russian mutual dependency on oil and particularly gas (that is, Russian exports and imports by EU states) – has become controversial in the wake of the serious Russian–Ukrainian gas dispute in 2006.

These controversies alone cannot account for the deterioration of the Russia–EU relationship since 2000 to what some Russian analysts have described as a 'systemic crisis'. Chapter 3 highlights contributory factors arising from the *process* of the relationship and *normative expectations*. The complexity and inflexibility of the Brussels bureaucracy coexist with a lack of policy coordination and expertise on the EU in Moscow. Problems are reinforced by the Russian preference to cultivate bilateral relations with key European states rather than interact with EU institutions. In addition, Putin's administration has grown more hostile to the intrusive nature of EU policy, especially the expectation that Russia should adopt EU norms and values, and the Kremlin resists criticism about authoritarian trends in Russian political development. Finally, both sides lack an overall strategic vision of the relationship and this deficiency is not remedied by their tendency to adopt grand programmatic schemes.

Against this background it is hardly surprising that recently few Russian officials or specialists have viewed the visionary idea of Russian accession to the EU, in even the medium term, as a realistic form of inclusion of Russia in Europe. As Chapter 3 observes, for most in Moscow this is precluded by the partial loss of sovereignty that accompanies the requirement to adopt EU rules and standards. But Russian analysts are inclined to accept the possibility of Russian EU membership in the long term, provided that Russian democracy develops.

Chapter 4, which examines Russian security engagement with the EU, confirms the preoccupation of the Russian foreign policy elite with *geopolitical* assessments of the EU and with the high politics of the relationship, even if little substantial cooperation on this level has come about. A focus of Russian debate has been the balance of influence in the EU–NATO relationship and the implications of possible greater EU autonomy for Russia's strategic dialogue with Brussels. The consequences of a more militarily capable and autonomous EU have divided Russian elite opinion. But during Putin's second term the development of European Security and Defence Policy (ESDP) capabilities, and the possibility that its geographic remit might include unstable regions in the CIS (the 'shared neighbourhood'), have been received nervously by most Russian officials and commentators. Moscow's response to the growing EU interest in its new security neighbourhood to the east has become defensive and politically charged. The controversy over the Ukrainian elections in 2004–5 has fuelled Russian suspicions about the possible elaboration of a new 'Eastern Dimension' in EU policy, influenced by new EU member states (particularly Poland), that aims to maintain some kind of geopolitical dividing line between Europe and 'non-Europe' (where Russia is positioned outside Europe). The polarization of views over the Ukrainian leadership contest has also reinforced feelings of rivalry in Moscow over any EU involvement in conflict zones beyond the Balkans on its eastern and south-eastern periphery.

Chapter 4 also confirms that only limited progress has been registered in Russia–EU efforts to coordinate foreign policy positions over crises, to develop a dialogue on conflict prevention and crisis management operations, to pool efforts in combating terrorism, or to develop practical projects for military-technical cooperation. This is unlikely to change in the medium term, since it reflects both structural problems in the relationship of the kind previously outlined and divergent outlooks. There seem to be entrenched difficulties for the EU to interact with the increasingly centralized and defensively sovereign Russian state. Putin, in turn, is inclined to view the EU as a form of Brussels bureaucracy that can be pressured by bilateral treaties with major European states on security as on other areas of policy.

Chapter 5 questions whether NATO, through the NATO–Russia Council or any deeper form of partnership, might provide the institutional setting for a substantive and inclusive security policy engagement with the enlarged Europe. This possibility is suggested by the fact that NATO has considerably more institutional flexibility than the EU. The NRC demonstrates how NATO has been able to blur the line between membership and non-membership, where a non-member state has substantial rights compared with member states. But NATO's potential to go further, to develop a relationship of cooperative security with Russia in Europe, requires a transformation of NATO's traditional adversarial image among Russian elites and society at large. It also depends on an effective dialogue to discuss legitimate Russian concerns, even those that might be misplaced, about the consequences of NATO enlargement.

Chapter 5 identifies a spectrum of opinion in the Russian foreign policy elite on NATO during Putin's second term. Those who seek a convergence with NATO and its leading states based on a value orientation have been marginalized in Russian political life. Those who fundamentally oppose cooperation with NATO and are convinced of its malign intent towards Russia are represented in elite circles, but have not determined Russian policy. The Russian leadership has followed a policy consistent with pragmatic nationalism, which prompts practical collaboration with NATO in defined fields, although this remains vulnerable to the overall state of Russian–Western relations. The chapter argues that this cooperation is tentative and its depth is constrained ultimately by Russia's political evolution; it requires greater pluralism and accountability rather than a reinforcement of statism.

Russia's insistence on developing relations with NATO, as with the EU, on the basis of 'equality' reflects concern about the agendas of these institutions and trepidation that drawing close to them will encourage Western efforts to influence Russian internal politics, possibly leading to explicit policies of conditionality. In this respect, Putin and his entourage view favourably the programme of cooperation under the NRC, since it is not subordinated to any specific process of transformation of Russia politically or economically. True, some of the new NATO members maintain that values and interests should be inseparable in developing the NATO–Russia relationship. But NATO as a body has not insisted that its budding partnership with Moscow in the NRC should have a normative dimension, which might eventually under-write a broader harmonization of policies between NATO states and Russia. This approach indicates that the current form of NATO engagement with Russia is unlikely in the medium term to spill over from security concerns into broader areas of functional integration with the member states of the Alliance that could erode and eventually dispel politico-security dividing lines between Russia and the enlarged Europe.

Chapter 5 reveals that Russia's calm official response to the 2002 NATO enlargement papered over continued conservative threat perceptions in Moscow, especially among senior military officers. These are likely to be rein-forced by the future efforts of CIS states to seek accession to NATO and may also be sustained by 'spoilers' such as clashing Russian and NATO interpreta-tions of interventions in international conflicts, in CIS regions or elsewhere. This is not a promising basis for the creation of a Russia–NATO 'partnership plus' or Russian associate membership of NATO in the future, although an evolution in this direction cannot be precluded. If NATO were to reorient comprehensively from its traditional European focus to global missions, then various new areas of collaboration with Russia might be possible. But by definition NATO could not then provide Russia with a channel for deep engagement in European security policy.

Chapter 6 turns to the domestic implications of Russia's engagement with the EU and NATO, examining, first, the public foreign policy agenda articulated by political parties and election candidates; second, the evidence that emerges from nationally representative surveys of opinion conducted during 2000–2005 on relations with 'Europe', and on Russia's international security more generally; and, third, the views of ordinary citizens as revealed in focus groups during 1999–2000 and 2006. These indicate how far policies aimed at deeper Russian engagement in Europe are reflected in society at large. Public opinion matters, since it provides the broad context for policy-making and for shaping the foreign policy agendas of elites in Russia. Even with the control over policy-making that Putin has acquired, public opinion generates domestic constraints over policy of an informal kind. Broad foreign policy attitudes may also play a role in the electoral competitions for Duma deputies. Moreover, the support of the Russian public would be needed for any possible Russian 'European project' in the future that aims at deeper integration with the EU and that aspires to profit considerably from part-nership with Europe without planning to apply for EU membership. This would require deep reform of the Russian economy and society as well as politics, which could not be implemented without substantial support from the Russian population.

Russia's public foreign policy discourse still lacks any articulate debate on how and to what degree Russia should participate in European integra-tion. However, Chapter 6 reveals a substantial measure of agreement on the public foreign policy agenda across Russian political parties and candidates, though liberals were particularly interested in closer relations with Europe, while nationalists and Communists were particularly keen on relations with Russia's Asian neighbours. Survey data on public opinion revealed that only a quarter of respondents in 2005 thought of themselves 'to a significant extent' or even 'to some extent' as Europeans – levels of European identifica-tion that are substantially lower than those found in 2000. Yet almost half of those surveyed in 2005 described themselves as 'very' or 'rather' positive towards the EU (more than twice as many as in 2000, despite the downturn in Russia–EU relations since then). In 2005, 57 per cent were also strongly or somewhat in favour of hypothetical Russian EU membership (rather more than in 2000).

Survey evidence in 2005 showed that 35 per cent of respondents considered it of the greatest importance to have a partnership with the countries of Western Europe, but only 10 per cent felt the same for the other former Soviet republics. This is more a pragmatic evaluation than one of identity, since the closest and friendliest of states were considered to be the other Slavic republics. But European countries were generally seen in positive terms, if not uniformly. Partnership with Western Europe is assisted by the perception by some 74 per cent (in both 2000 and 2004) that the EU (and by association the ESDP) constitutes 'little' or 'no threat' to Russian secu-rity. The proportion of those who perceived the EU as a 'large' or as 'some' threat fell from 22 per cent (2000) to 10 per cent (2005), despite the growing concern in Russian official and elite circles about the implications of EU policies in the 'shared neighbourhood'.

The surveys showed that the Russian public has a better understanding of NATO than of the EU, and that traditional suspicions and hostility to NATO are far from dominant. Cautious attitudes prevail, but opinion is relatively relaxed or indifferent about the effects of NATO enlargement and the possibility of a closer association with NATO. A clear majority of those surveyed considered that the most sensitive aspect of the 2004 enlargement for Moscow, the entry of the Baltic states into NATO, represented only a slight threat or no threat at all to Russian security. Relatively few Russians perceived NATO as a substantial and immediate threat; far larger numbers regarded a range of new security threats as of more immediate concern. However, if Russians were not much exercised about NATO enlargement, they remained wary about the nature of Moscow's relationship with NATO. The upgrading of Russia–NATO cooperation during 2000–2005 was accompanied by some reduction in the proportion of those surveyed in this period that approved of the principle of Russian membership of NATO. This shift might be linked to findings from focus groups that placed more emphasis on Russia's international isolation.

Chapters 3–6 identify a daunting array of obstacles to a deeper engagement of Russia in the enlarged Europe and to the effective use of the EU and NATO as channels for greater inclusion of Russia in European processes. Chapter 7 brings together a number of themes and extends our analysis by exploring two key influences that are likely to determine the choice of 'Russia in Europe' or 'Russia and Europe': the impact of new foreign policy challenges for Russia since 2004, especially the aftermath of the Orange Revolution in Ukraine, and the tension between the normative and practical aspects of Russia–EU relations – the so-called 'values vs interests' controversy. It concludes with an assessment of scenarios for the medium-term future of Russia–EU and Russia–NATO relations that points to approaching policy dilemmas.

2

The domestic management of Russia's foreign and security policy

Stephen White

Soviet policy-making was nowhere more highly centralized than in foreign and security matters. The Bolsheviks, ironically, had come to power with a commitment to end the 'secret diplomacy' that had plunged the Western nations into the First World War. But they soon became expert practitioners. Without the usual kinds of evidence, outside observers had to base their judgements on public appearances – who sat where, who signed an obituary, who met whom at the airport – and on reading between the lines of newspaper articles. Some of the most important of these – as in the case of the *Pravda* statement that set out a justification of the Warsaw Pact intervention in Czechoslovakia in 1968 – were authored by a pseudonym, which made them even more authoritative, as they could be taken to represent the views of the leadership as a whole. In post-communist Russia, all of this was apparently very different. There were competitive elections to a national parliament. There was a separation of powers and (in principle) a rule of law. There were political parties, and oppositional newspapers. The making of public policy was very different under these new circumstances – or at least it appeared to be. Foreign policy was in the hands of a minister answerable to parliament; security policy was the responsibility of the Ministry of Defence, which had a budget that was approved by elected deputies; and both of them came under the authority of the government as a whole. On the face of it, these were not very different arrangements from those that obtained in the Western democracies.

The first statements of Russia's new leaders, indeed, insisted on these similarities. The Foreign Minister was Andrei Kozyrev, who had been a prominent member of the reform coalition called Democratic Russia and a participant in the meeting that had agreed to dissolve the USSR in December 1991. He directed, as he explained in a New Year's message shortly afterwards, 'not a detachment of revolutionary sword-bearers, but a body of democratically minded individuals who know and well understand the interests and concerns of their people'.[1] Boris Yeltsin, for his part, made clear that the new Russia was no longer the centre of an 'enormous communist empire' that was attempting to 'paint the planet red', but a state that was committed to human rights at home and abroad, and to a 'policy of goodwill' towards the international community.[2] When he addressed the United Nations Security Council at the end of January 1992, he said that he regarded the Western powers 'not just as partners, but as allies', and reiterated the new Russia's commitment to 'freedom, democracy and human rights'.[3] He toured Western countries, addressing parliaments, signing treaties and meeting prime ministers and heads of state. When he visited Britain later in the year and met the Queen they had talked 'like old friends', he told journalists, although it was Yeltsin himself who had authorized the destruction of the house in Ekaterinburg where the Tsarist royal family had met their bloody end.[4] The relationship appeared to be cemented as Russia joined international organizations, agreed to reduce its nuclear arms and ratified the European Convention on Human Rights. ∼ post–CW euphoria.

In the event, the outcome was less a growing convergence with what Kozyrev regarded as Russia's 'natural allies'[5] than an increasingly firm assertion of Russia's distinctive interests in a manner that was often reminiscent of the Tsarist governments of the nineteenth century. The assumption of a natural community of interests and values became more difficult to sustain under Vladimir Putin, Prime Minister from August 1999 and then Yeltsin's successor when the Russian President unexpectedly stood down at the end of the year. Putin owed something of his sudden popularity to his military assault on Chechen insurgents in the late summer of 1999, promising (in a notorious phrase) to 'wipe them out in the john', although he also owed something to the high price of oil on world markets. Increasingly, he asserted the authority of the federal government over a society in which it had often ceased to govern effectively: over the Russian regions, over the broadcast media and over the electoral process. The more power was centralized, the less it was exercised with the consent of elected institutions; but Putin was not (he explained) seeking a 'second edition' of the political systems of Britain or the United States,[6] rather a form of 'managed democracy' largely regulated by the central authorities. Within a system of this kind, the making of policy – and particularly of foreign and security policy – was once again a matter for the central authorities and particularly for a small group of associates around the Russian President.

FP – central auth + pt associates

★ once again, intimately linked to domestic objectives, personalities, etc

Putin → re–assertion of authority of federal government └ managed democracy

22

CONSOLIDATING THE PUTIN LEADERSHIP

'Who is Mr Putin?' demanded a journalist from the *Philadelphia Inquirer* at a press conference in Davos at the end of January 2000, shortly after Putin had assumed the responsibilities of acting President.[7] It was a question the new acting President himself did little to resolve, not least in the election of March 2000, in which he won a first-round victory with 53 per cent of the vote but without engaging in the customary exchanges with his leading competitors or providing an election manifesto of the conventional kind. Something of the nature of the new regime could, however, be inferred from the direction of its public policy. It was clear, first of all, that the authority of the federal government would be reasserted, not just in the continuing offensive against breakaway Chechnya, but also in relation to the other republics and regions. In May 2000, on Putin's initiative, seven new 'federal districts' were established, all but identical with the country's military districts. Each of them was headed by an envoy or 'plenipotentiary representative', centrally funded and responsible for ensuring that regional legislation conformed with that of the federation as a whole. Five of the new envoys had a background in the military or security services. Three months later, the position of regional governors was weakened more directly when they were deprived of their automatic representation in the upper house of parliament, the Federation Council.[8]

The first term saw related moves against the independent media, particularly television. In May 2000 armed police raided the offices of the Media Most conglomerate in Moscow, whose publications had taken a conspicuously independent line on the recent elections and the continuing conflict in Chechnya. The head of Media Most, Vladimir Gusinsky, was arrested in June on fraud charges, and shortly afterwards forced into exile after the assets of his company had been taken over by the state gas monopoly. There were further dramatic developments in April 2001, when Gusinsky's television channel, NTV, was taken over by the same company, to which it was heavily in debt; the staff of Gusinsky's weekly magazine, *Itogi*, were dismissed, and his liberal daily paper, *Segodnya*, was forced into liquidation. Not only did these moves ensure that all nationally broadcast television came under the effective control of the federal government; they also undermined the position of another of the corporate magnates or 'oligarchs' who had been able to establish a dominant position in the later Yeltsin years. An even more prominent oligarch, Boris Berezovsky, had been obliged to relinquish his controlling ownership of the first national television channel the previous year and to leave the country in what he described as a 'political emigration'. Nominally, these were commercial operations; but Putin had called for the 'liquidation of the oligarchs as a class',[9] and he appeared to have no particular attachment to the freedom of the press if it involved criticism of official policy and of those who were responsible for it.

A greater centralization of power reflected larger changes in the Russian political elite, and particularly the increasing influence of the *siloviki*, or 'force ministry people', with a career background in the military, the Federal Security Bureau (FSB) or one of the other agencies of law enforcement.[10] Just 4 per cent of those who held leadership positions in the Gorbachev years and 11 per cent under Boris Yeltsin, they had increased to 25 per cent by the first term of the Putin presidency, and a still higher percentage of the membership of the national government.[11] It was not, of course, surprising that Putin should promote people he already knew, and who had the same career background: he had joined the KGB himself on graduation from Leningrad University in 1975 and worked for it until 1991, returning as director between 1998 and 1999; there were 'no former chekists' (i.e. KGB staffers), he told a television audience in 2001.[12] Nor could it be assumed that the *siloviki* were a unitary group, still less one that was dedicated to the return of the Soviet system. But they appeared to share a commitment to the restoration of state authority, and took a hostile view of groups, individuals and organizations that could be seen as undermining national unity or weakening the position of the federal government; at least for some, their appointment was part of a 'conscious project to remake the Russian elite in the President's image'. Why would Putin give jobs of this kind to 'feminists and environmentalists', as one of the presidential envoys asked Western journalists, when the security of the country was at stake?[13]

Putin's second term, from his re-election in March 2004, appeared to mark an increasingly clear transition towards a firm or even authoritarian style of management. An important first step was the December 2003 Duma election, at which the strongly pro-Kremlin United Russia party (formed out of the pro-Kremlin Unity and at least nominally oppositional Fatherland–All Russia groupings that had contested the previous election at the end of 1999) emerged in a dominant position. United Russia defined itself as a party that was 'together with the President', and it enjoyed the considerable advantage of prominent and friendly treatment in the state-owned media. The international monitoring team from the OSCE certainly found that the media had 'failed to provide impartial or fair coverage of the election campaign', and that there had been an 'overwhelming tendency [in] the state media to exhibit a clear bias in favour of United Russia and against the CPRF [Communist Party of the Russian Federation]'. More generally, while the election had been 'generally well-administered', it had 'failed to meet a number of OSCE commitments for democratic elections, most notably those pertaining to unimpeded access to the media on

24

unfair advantage

a non-discriminatory basis, a clear separation between the state and political parties, and guarantees to enable political parties to compete on the basis of equal treatment'.[14]

The outcome was a decisive victory for United Russia, which for the first time gave the Kremlin a subservient, rather than at least occasionally rebellious, Duma. United Russia took 37.6 per cent of the party-list vote, well ahead of the Communists on 12.6 per cent and the Liberal Democrats on 11.5 per cent (a new left-patriotic party, Rodina (Motherland), took another 9 per cent, and no other parties reached the 5 per cent threshold). United Russia also performed strongly in the single-member constituencies that account for the other half of the seats in the Duma, taking an average of 23.5 per cent of the vote; this left it slightly behind independents, on 26.3 per cent, but well ahead of all the other parties. These results, taken together, gave United Russia 223 of the 450 seats that were in contention;[15] but by the time the Duma assembled for its first meeting at the end of December the United Russia fraction had increased to 300, as deputies from parties that had fallen short of the threshold and independents were persuaded to join the winning side.[16] This gave United Russia, and in effect the Kremlin, a commanding position in the new Duma, sufficient to adopt not just ordinary legislation but also constitutional laws, for which a two-thirds majority of the entire membership is necessary.

A victory on this scale had several further consequences. One of them was that United Russia was able to take over the chairmanship of the Duma, and its leader, Boris Gryzlov, duly became the new Speaker (the outgoing Duma had been headed by a Communist who had latterly become a Kremlin loyalist, Gennady Seleznev). It also took over the chairmanship of all the Duma's committees, including defence, the CIS and international affairs. A larger consequence of United Russia's dominant position was that the conduct of legislative business moved almost entirely out of the Duma itself, into the hands of the presidential administration and its subordinate bureaucracies – a relationship somewhat reminiscent of that of the late Soviet period, when the Communist Party had 'guided' the work of elected bodies at all levels. A strongly pro-Kremlin Duma, in turn, helped to shape the context for the presidential election, which was due to take place the following March. So predictable was the outcome that, for many Russians, there was no point in it – better to save money by installing Putin without a contest.[17] Another view was that Putin should be allowed to extend his presidential term to five or even seven years[18] – under the constitution, presidents are limited to a maximum of two consecutive four-year terms, and any modification would require a constitutional amendment.

Putin was obviously the favourite in the presidential contest, but he

pro Kremlin Duma – FP move to president/subordinate committees/bureaucrats.

avoided campaigning or taking part in discussions with the other candidates, explaining when the results were announced that he had 'deliberately chosen' not to do so because it was 'important to me to find out how people would react to my work, not to campaign stunts'.[19] He did, however, present an election manifesto, a lengthy and unremarkable address delivered to a carefully selected audience at Moscow University in mid-February 2004.[20] Shortly afterwards, on 24 February, he dismissed Prime Minister Mikhail Kas'yanov and his entire cabinet, although their performance, he acknowledged, had generally been 'satisfactory'.[21] The new Prime Minister, Mikhail Fradkov (b. 1950), had been Russian representative to the European Union, and before that a minister of trade, First Deputy Secretary of the Security Council and head of the federal tax police; a missing page in his official biography appeared to relate to a period of study at the KGB academy in the early 1970s, which was perhaps where he had learned his excellent English.[22] Newspaper commentaries certainly suggested that he could be seen as a protégé of Defence Minister Sergei Ivanov, and more broadly as another representative of the *siloviki* within the Russian leadership.[23] The new Foreign Minister was Sergei Lavrov (b. 1950), who had been Russian representative at the United Nations and was seen, like his predecessor Igor' Ivanov, as first and foremost a professional diplomat. This meant that the 'trend of the last several years, in which the most crucial foreign policy decisions [were] made not at the Foreign Ministry but in the Kremlin, [would] be continued'.[24]

The 2004 presidential election, in the event, was more of a coronation. Indeed for some time there was a possibility that Putin would face no opposition at all and that he would have to organize his own 'competition' to ensure that there was at least the appearance of a contest. The Communist Party, which had provided the most serious opposition in the past, fielded a regional governor, Nikolai Kharitonov, rather than the party leader, Gennady Zyuganov; the Liberal Democrats nominated a bodyguard, Oleg Malyshkin, rather than party leader Zhirinovsky; and the opposition party Yabloko, shaken by a poor showing in the Duma election, nominated no one at all. Of the others, both Irina Khakamada (formerly of the Union of Right Forces) and Sergei Glazev (one of the leaders of Rodina at the Duma election) stood as independents, without the support of their respective parties. None of the rival candidates expressed any expectation of defeating the incumbent president, and one of them, Speaker of the upper house Sergei Mironov, openly supported him. The outcome was such a foregone conclusion that there was serious concern at official levels that turnout would fall below 50 per cent, which would have invalidated the whole exercise.[25]

A provisional result was announced on 16 March, two days after polling, and a final result on 23 March 2004. Turnout, at just over 64 per cent, was down on the 69 per cent that had been recorded in 2000, and the vote 'against all candidates' almost doubled. Putin's margin of victory, however, was very much greater; he took 71 per cent, and a majority of the vote in every one of the country's 89 republics and regions. In four of the republics, Dagestan, Ingushetia, Mordovia and war-torn Chechnya, both turnout and the vote in favour of the President were over 90 per cent; in another republic, Bashkortostan, turnout was 89 per cent and the vote in favour of Putin was 92 per cent. These were Soviet margins of victory and they suggested the heavy use of 'administrative resource', or the powers of office. The contest itself, in the words of the OSCE monitoring mission, had once again 'failed to meet important commitments concerning treatment of candidates by the state-controlled media on a non-discriminatory basis, equal opportunities for all candidates and secrecy of the ballot';[26] the Council of Europe delegation found more elementary shortcomings, with the vote-counting process 'unsatisfactory or even very bad' in a quarter of the constituencies they visited.[27] But there was no doubt that Putin, in formal terms, had won a crushing victory.

Presidential authority was further consolidated some months later in the immediate aftermath of the dramatic hostage-taking crisis in Beslan in the northern Caucasus. The emergency began on 1 September 2004, the first day of the new school year and traditionally a time of celebration, when around 30 armed guerrillas seized a school in the town in North Ossetia and threatened to blow it up if they were attacked. Over 1,000 children, parents and teachers were held hostage for three days, in appalling conditions, in an apparent reprisal for the continuing war in Chechnya; the hostage-takers' demands included the complete withdrawal of Russian forces from the breakaway republic and the release of a group of militants who had been arrested on charges of attacking towns and villages in nearby Ingushetia.[28] A tense stand-off ended two days later when Russian special forces stormed the building after a series of explosions led to the collapse of the roof and an exchange of gunfire between the hostage-takers and those who surrounded them as children and adults tried to flee in the chaos. The Prosecutor General reported some days later that 326 had died and that more than 700 had been injured, but these totals were expected to increase considerably as investigations proceeded; the terrorists themselves had been 'completely wiped out'.[29]

Putin was widely thought to have reacted late and inadequately to previous crisis situations, especially the sinking of the *Kursk* submarine in August 2000. This time he interrupted his holiday to return to Moscow in order to take overall command. In a nationwide television broadcast on 4 September, just after the siege had been lifted, he spoke of a 'terrible tragedy' that had been a 'challenge to the whole of our people'. But rather than draw the lesson that a dialogue with moderate nationalists had become even more urgent, he defined the siege as an 'attack on our country' that had its origins in 'international terrorism'. His conclusion was accordingly that state security should be strengthened, and that a new and more effective 'crisis management system' should be developed.[30] The federal authorities were themselves discredited by the late, confused and inaccurate release of information, particularly in respect of the number that had been captured inside the building; by their clumsy handling of the emergency; and by their apparent inability to halt a series of related incidents, including the bombing of two passenger aeroplanes and a suicide attack outside a Moscow underground station the previous month.

Putin gave a more detailed response at a specially enlarged meeting of the government on 13 September. The system of executive government, he told his audience, had to be 'fundamentally restructured' in order to protect them against the terrorists who were trying to break up the country. National unity was the first essential; this meant a 'single system of authority', from the Kremlin downwards. This meant in turn that regional governors should be nominated by the President and then elected by regional assemblies, much as the federal government was formed in Moscow. Political parties should be strengthened, which would be facilitated if the Duma was elected entirely by the national party-list competition and no longer by individual constituencies. A 'public chamber' should be established, as a place in which 'broad-based dialogue' could take place. A new federal commission on the North Caucasus had already been approved, with responsibilities that included living standards (which lagged deplorably behind those of the rest of the country) as well as security; and the ministry responsible for regional and ethnic policy would be revived. Putin also referred, more vaguely, to a 'national security system' that would forestall and not simply respond to terrorist threats.[31]

This, some suggested, was a 'September revolution': at any rate, a sharp move towards the further concentration of power in the executive branch of a kind that had evidently been in preparation long before the outrage itself. An entirely new law, adopted in June 2004, had already introduced more burdensome procedures for the conduct of a referendum that made it 'practically impossible' for ordinary citizens to call one in the future.[32] Legislation to amend the existing law on regional government was enacted in December; from this point forward governors would no longer be directly elected but nominated by the President and then approved or otherwise by regional assemblies, which – like the Duma itself – could be dissolved if they rejected the President's choice three times in a row.[33] A law establishing a 'public chamber' became law in April 2005;[34] heavily packed with presidential nominees, it held its first meeting in January 2006. The new electoral law, abolishing single-member constituencies and raising the threshold to 7 per cent, was approved in May 2005.[35] The new law allowed political parties a monopoly on the right to nominate, giving the largest of them a number of advantages: in particular, those that secured party-list seats in a Duma election would not be obliged to collect signatures in support of a candidate in a subsequent presidential election. The law on political parties of 2001 was meanwhile amended so that a minimum of 50,000 rather than 10,000 members was required for registration;[36] the law had introduced a system of state funding for political parties, based on their electoral support, that similarly advantaged the largest and (generally) most obedient.

All of these were part of a series of broader changes that made it more difficult to advance alternative opinions, let alone a political opposition. The elimination of a substantial independent presence in the broadcast media had been an achievement of Putin's first term. His second term saw further action against Mikhail Khodorkovsky, the oil magnate who had been dramatically arrested in October 2003 on charges of tax evasion, but in practice (it appeared) for openly financing opposition parties and announcing political ambitions of his own. A lengthy trial concluded in May 2005, when Khodorkovsky and a close associate were sentenced to nine years' imprisonment and dispatched to a penal colony in a remote and environmentally hazardous region of Siberia.[37] A new law on non-governmental organizations, introduced in November 2005 and approved in January 2006, meanwhile closed off a further avenue of influence;[38] it gave the federal authorities much greater power than ever before to regulate the affairs, and particularly the finances, of bodies like Amnesty International and the Moscow Helsinki Committee, and was apparently intended to prevent NGOs playing anything like the kind of role they had assumed in the 'coloured revolutions' that had taken place elsewhere on former Soviet territory.

One important issue remained unresolved, the '2008 question': in other words, the situation that would arise in the spring of 2008 when Putin completed the second of his two consecutive terms of office, which was the maximum he was permitted under the Russian constitution. One option was to amend it, but this was a lengthy and difficult process (it could not simply be legislated), and Putin himself had repeatedly declared his opposition to any changes of this kind. Another option was to secure the nomination, and then with the backing of Kremlin-friendly media the election, of a reliable associate who would accept Putin's instructions and allow the former president to stand again in 2012; but there was a risk that an initially loyal subordinate might become attached to the powers with which he had been entrusted. A further suggestion was that Putin might become prime minister after he stood down, and that the prime minister, perhaps with the support of a majority party in the Duma, might become the dominant figure in the future, without necessarily amending the constitution.[39] Reforms of this kind, after all, had taken place in Ukraine as part of the contested transition from the Kuchma presidency to Viktor Yushchenko, and they were consistent with the discussions that had been taking place in Russia itself about a 'government of the parliamentary majority' that would bring executive and legislature into a closer and more balanced relationship.[40]

Western opinion became steadily more concerned about the fate of a Russian 'democracy' as the presidency strengthened its grip. Putin had made clear from the outset that Russia would not seek to reproduce the politics of Britain or the United States, where liberal values had 'deep historic traditions'; the state had always played a more prominent role in Russia, and a strong state was a 'source of order and main driving force of any change'.[41] Russia, Putin explained to Slovak interviewers in February 2005, had chosen democracy, but for its own reasons, and basic principles of democracy had to be 'adapted to the realities of contemporary Russian life, to our traditions and history'.[42] Official spokesmen presented this as 'managed democracy', a form of rule that was consistent with Russia's own circumstances and with the special difficulties of an enormous country that was conducting far-reaching changes within a relatively short period. Others were less sympathetic, not just Putin's domestic opponents but also his foreign counterparts. Western visitors to Moscow (for instance Angela Merkel, the German Chancellor, in January 2006) began to raise the issue of the continuing Chechen war more insistently. And the monitoring organization Freedom House, which had classified Russia as 'partly free' in the years of the Yeltsin presidency, moved it to the category of 'not free' at the end of 2004. It found the Putin leadership's 'anti-democratic tendencies … if anything, more pronounced in 2005'.[43]

FOREIGN POLICY DECISION-MAKING

Formal authority in matters of foreign policy, under the 1993 Russian constitution, is vested in the head of state – an office so powerful it has often been described as a 'super-presidency'.[44] It is the President, for a start, who determines the 'basic directions' of foreign as well as domestic policy, and who represents the country at home and abroad (art. 80). It is the President, again, who appoints and dismisses Russian diplomatic representatives, after 'consultations' with the appropriate parliamentary committees (art. 83). More generally, it is the President who provides 'leadership' in foreign policy, who conducts international negotiations and signs international treaties, and who

30

also carries out the ceremonial function of receiving the credentials of foreign diplomatic representatives (art. 86).

The executive arm of government in matters of this kind is the Ministry of Foreign Affairs, historically a professional service that has played a subordinate role in the policy process. At his first press conference in March 2004 the new Foreign Minister, Sergei Lavrov, reiterated the conventional position, which was that 'the President defines foreign policy, and the Ministry of Foreign Affairs conducts it';[45] the same formulation was offered when we pursued the matter in our own interviews with senior diplomats. In fact, at least three other bodies share some of the ministry's authority: the Security Council, which is chaired by the President himself;[46] the Ministry of Defence, headed by Sergei Ivanov; and the presidential administration, in particular its foreign policy directorate, headed by Sergei Prikhodko (b. 1957), a former diplomat who has served in communist and post-communist Czechoslovakia.[47] A further contribution is made by Sergei Yastrzhembsky (b. 1953), a former Foreign Ministry spokesman who has taken particular responsibility for advising the President on the development of relations with the European Union since he joined the administration in 2004. Yastrzhembsky worked in Prague for the journal *Problems of Peace and Socialism* during the 1980s, handled relations with social democratic parties within the central apparatus of the CPSU at the end of the decade, and was ambassador to Slovakia during the mid-1990s.[48]

Formally, however, it is the Ministry of Foreign Affairs that takes responsibility for the conduct of relations with other states, and it is through the ministry that the Russian government makes itself accountable to parliament in matters of this kind. A particularly important role in this connection devolves upon the committees through which the two houses of the Federal Assembly conduct much of their business. In the case of the upper house, the Federation Council, this means its Committees on Defence and Security, International Affairs, and the Commonwealth of Independent States.[49] In the case of the lower house, the State Duma, it means above all the Committee on International Affairs, chaired since the last election by Konstantin Kosachev (b. 1962), a career diplomat and then prime ministerial assistant before his election to the Duma in 1999, who has specialized in Russian relations with north-eastern Europe, particularly Sweden. Other Duma committees that play a part in the conduct of foreign relations include the Committees on Defence, on Security, and on the Commonwealth of Independent States and Compatriots in Other Countries.[50]

Committees meet 'not less often than twice a month', according to the Duma's standing orders (art. 24), and the official representatives of the President and government may take part in their proceedings as well as representatives of the ministries directly concerned, other deputies, the media, and academic experts (art. 26). Committees have the right to propose agenda items for inclusion in the Duma's order of business (art. 25) and can take initiatives of their own, such as calling parliamentary hearings on matters of public concern (art. 26); the Duma's standing orders make specific provision for hearings of this kind to be called to consider the adoption, suspension and abrogation of international treaties (art. 190). The appropriate Duma committees also take part in 'consultations' on the appointment or recall of Russian diplomatic representatives (art. 210); nominations are made by the Ministry of Foreign Affairs, have to be 'justified' and may be queried, but do not in the last resort have to be formally approved by the committee or by the Duma as a whole (art. 211).

The Duma is involved in the foreign policy-making process in other ways. For instance, it can adopt resolutions that set out its position on international issues, after they have been given preliminary consideration by the relevant committees. At the end of March 2004, for instance, the Duma adopted a resolution on NATO enlargement, prepared by the international affairs committee, that deplored the 'offensive character' of the Alliance's military doctrine and its predisposition for the resolution of international differences by force rather than through the mechanisms provided by the United Nations (the circumstances of its adoption were explained to us during our interview with a leading member of the Security Committee shortly before its publication).[51] The Duma has a role of particular importance in the consideration and adoption of international treaties. Treaties of this kind are presented for ratification by the President or the government and considered in the first instance by the Foreign Affairs or CIS Committee, or both of them, which then recommend an appropriate course of action to the Duma as a whole.[52] A number of these decisions have been controversial. The START-2 treaty, for instance, was signed in 1993 but not ratified until 2000, four years after the US Senate had approved it; the ratification of the Treaty of Strategic Offensive Reductions, signed by both countries in May 2002, was delayed until May 2003 because of the initiation of military action against Iraq earlier in the year; and the Kyoto Protocol of 1997 was finally ratified in 2004 after a 'stormy' debate, albeit by a large majority.[53]

The Duma can also interrogate leading officials in the 'government hour' that is a regular part of its proceedings. In May 2005, for instance, both Lavrov and FSB chief Nikolai Patrushev made presentations on Russia's role in a globalized world. Lavrov was the more upbeat, acknowledging difficulties in relations with Ukraine and Georgia, but showing little concern about the 'coloured revolutions' in the former Soviet republics. Patrushev was more cautious, warning that 'our opponents' were trying to weaken Russia's influence in what – in a Freudian slip – 'former CIS'. He drew particular attention to the use that was : governmental organizations and charities in this connection, in a law would be brought forward in the near future that woul their legal regulation.[54] Legislation of this kind had been foreshadowed in Putin's address to the Federal Assembly earlier in the year, and (as we have seen) it was signed into law in January 2006. Putin made clear in a speech the following month that the security services would use any means necessary to 'protect society from any attempts by foreign states to interfere in Russia's internal affairs'.[55]

The Federation Council is not obliged to consider all the legislation that reaches it from the lower house, but it is required by the constitution to do so in all cases that relate to the ratification of international treaties, state boundaries and questions of war and peace (art. 106). It must also approve the use of Russian troops in other countries (art. 102). The Federation Council has procedures that are analogous to those of the Duma for considering foreign and security issues, and for considering international treaties and the appointment and dismissal of diplomatic representatives. And both chambers have the usual arrangements for the exchange of delegations with parliaments in other countries and for relations with international parliamentary institutions. The Russian parliament is represented in several institutions that are specific to the post-Soviet region, including the parliament of the Union State with Belarus, the Interparliamentary Assembly of the Eurasian Economic Community, and the Interparliamentary Assembly of the member states of the Commonwealth of Independent States.

Nominally at least, this was a coherent system for the evaluation of international developments and for taking decisions that were carefully considered and consistent with Russian interests. There has, however, been constant criticism, particularly from those directly involved, that the variety of agencies that are engaged in Russian foreign policy-making are poorly coordinated and sometimes working at cross purposes. Kosachev himself, in published writings, has suggested that the various ministries and agencies have in fact been conducting their 'own' foreign policies, with the larger regions and energy monopolies doing much the same. When these various foreign policies diverged, he added, it was often the Foreign Ministry that had to play the role of intermediary. An example of this was the diversity of view that was expressed by a variety of domestic interests about ratification of the Kyoto Protocol, which had all kinds of implications – for relations with Europe and for the economy as well as for the environment. The same was true of international terrorism, and of the implications of EU and NATO enlargement, and of Russian policy in post-Soviet space.[56]

bureaucratic/agency/departmental problems/coordination/different issue FP's!

33

In particular, Kosachev suggested, it was far from clear how the presidential administration, the Security Council and the Foreign Ministry were to coordinate their positions so as to achieve a 'unified system' for the development and implementation of a national foreign affairs strategy. The Foreign Ministry had the intellectual resources to do so, but it 'acutely needed a new approach' on the part of the state, and its staff were overloaded with current business. This was partly a matter of money: 'However enthusiastic Russian diplomats are about their jobs, it's hard to expect heroic feats from people who spend all their time worrying about how they can meet the most elementary material needs of their families.' Those who could do so were leaving for private business, and the average age of the ministry's central staff was steadily increasing. Meanwhile, the Moscow State Institute of International Affairs, which traditionally provided a large part of the ministry's annual recruitment, was reorienting itself towards careers in commercial, political and information services of various kinds. Perhaps it would help, Kosachev suggested, if legislation on the state service identified diplomacy as a special category, and salaries were raised correspondingly?[57]

Kosachev was also concerned by the failure to present Russian policy in a positive way in other countries, and indeed at home, where sections of the media and self-interested politicians had their own reasons for writing Russian policy off as a series of capitulations. Better use could be made in this connection of the Russian diaspora in other countries, and of Russian transnational business. But there was also a need for 'powerful non-state analytical centres' of the kind that helped to underpin foreign policy in the United States, and had done so in the Soviet period; currently, too many of these contacts were 'unsystematic' and 'spontaneous'. Perhaps, he suggested, the Duma itself could play a larger role in this connection, as a representative institution that had close relations with the presidential administration, the Security Council and the Ministry of Foreign Affairs, and which had its own links with parliaments in other countries. The earlier they engaged in these discussions, Kosachev suggested, the more they would be able to influence them: it might, for instance, have been possible in the 1990s to persuade NATO to give a formal undertaking not to enlarge towards the east, and not to incorporate former Soviet republics. But it was impossible to influence global processes of this kind with a policy of 'total isolationism'.[58]

The intellectual shortcomings of Russian foreign policy have been given particular emphasis by some other public figures, among them Sergei Karaganov, deputy director of the Europe Institute of the Academy of Sciences and chairman of the influential Foreign and Defence Policy Council (SVOP). 'We know and understand less and less about the world', Karaganov complained, 'and in many respects we lack a system of foreign policy plan-ning and forecasting altogether'. In the Ukrainian presidential election of late 2004, for instance, they should have known better than to back the defeated candidate, Viktor Yanukovich; but 'amateurs' with 'commercial interests' had become involved (almost certainly a reference to Viktor Chernomyrdin, the Gazprom executive and former prime minister who had become Russian ambassador in the Ukrainian capital). Decisions of this kind, unfortunately, were 'very highly personalized'. 'Almost everything' was decided by the Presi-dent, with the Ministry of Foreign Affairs 'semi-removed from decision-making' and the Security Council 'nowhere to be seen'. As a result, even good decisions were never fully developed, and there was an increasing risk of serious misjudgments. This raised still larger questions about the political system as a whole – its over-centralization, reliance on individuals rather than institutions and lack of professionalism – and about the nature of polit-ical reform in general, which was increasingly reproducing an almost 'Soviet' system but without the Communist Party that had given it the capacity for effective action.[59]

Many of the same conclusions were drawn by a working group that met in early 2005 under Karaganov's chairmanship to prepare a 'situational anal-ysis' of Russian relations with the EU. There was general agreement that the Russian administrative apparatus, in its current form, '[did] not correspond to the scale of the tasks confronting Russian policy *vis-à-vis* Europe'. The bodies that conducted relations with the EU were too diverse and unco-ordinated, and had a 'manifestly insufficient number of qualified staff for productive work with the powerful Brussels bureaucracy'. Indeed different bodies conducted their 'own' EU policy and interacted directly with the corre-sponding sections of the European Commission, which ran totally counter to the practice of the EU itself (the EU, for its own part, found that the Foreign Ministry was 'not … an effective coordinator', and that the various Russian ministries promoted 'different agendas'[60]). More broadly, there was a great lack of understanding in the wider society, and even among the relevant deci-sion-makers, about the way in which the EU operated. Just 'dozens' had this kind of knowledge, and their number had not been increasing. The result was that the EU Commission was normally given responsibility for the prepara-tion of joint resolutions as Russian negotiators had 'neither the people nor the time' to prepare their own drafts.

Perhaps, in the longer term, only the establishment of a single agency with responsibility for the whole range of Russian relations with the EU offered a solution; it would, at least, make it more difficult for the EU nego-tiators to force through their own policies because of the lack of coordina-tion among their Russian counterparts. But there were other proposals from

So : rhetoric = cohesive, (BUT) → institution/bodies rel w. (EU) – (NOT) up to task, coordinated – contradictory agenda / goals, ineffective.

35

Karaganov and his colleagues – such as a 'broad public-consultative council on relations with the European Union' that could make timely suggestions for improving relations, and a special committee (or sub-committees) on relations with the EU within the Federal Assembly, as in many other countries. There should be a closer relationship with Russian business, which should be encouraged to make more comprehensive arrangements for its representation at EU headquarters. There should be a 'state programme for the study of the European Union', and perhaps a 'European college' based at the Moscow Institute of International Relations. In addition, every effort should be made to develop contacts at a societal level, between professions and other groups.[61] It was, of course, difficult to disguise the fact that proposals of this kind would involve a more prominent and better-rewarded role for those who put them forward; but they also reinforced a developing critique of a policy-making process that was personalized, opaque and often ineffective.

DEFENCE AND SECURITY POLICY DECISION-MAKING

Defence and security policy-making, in every country, has a number of distinctive characteristics. In formal terms, however, the procedures involved are very similar to those that relate to foreign policy. The constitutional responsibilities of the President are very extensive, including decision-making (as commander-in-chief), policy-making (as the person who authorizes the country's defence doctrine), and personnel (he appoints and dismisses the high command of the armed forces). It is the President who heads the Security Council and confirms the country's military doctrine (art. 83), and who acts as commander-in-chief and declares a state of war (art. 87). As with foreign policy, he is assisted by the staff of the presidential administration, in this case by Alexander Buturin (b. 1956), a graduate of the Frunze and General Staff academies, who takes particular responsibility for military-technical policy and the defence economy.[62] The apparatus of the Security Council is a part of the presidential administration, and may be seen as providing overall strategic leadership; so too are the seven presidential envoys, one of whom is the former Chief of the General Staff, Anatoly Kvashnin (b. 1946). In addition, General Gennady Troshev (b. 1947), who had been commander of Russian forces in Chechnya, takes particular responsibility for Cossack affairs, but is seen as 'not a heavyweight' by Kremlin insiders.[63]

Day-to-day management of the armed forces is the responsibility of the Minister of Defence, who is directly accountable to the President, although he is also a member of the federal government and takes part in its collective deliberations. Since 2001 the position has been held by Sergei Ivanov (b.

1953), who is generally regarded as Putin's closest associate. Their biographies, certainly, are closely connected: both attended Leningrad University and the KGB Academy, and became friendly when they were both assigned to the first department of the Leningrad KGB; in the late 1990s Ivanov was Putin's deputy in the FSB, and then succeeded him as Secretary of the Security Council when Putin moved on to the premiership. 'We worked together for about two years', Ivanov later told journalists; 'professional interests, the same age, roughly the same opinions'. Later on they 'didn't forget each other, sometimes spoke on the phone, although there were long gaps when we went abroad'.[64] Ivanov had enrolled in the interpreting department of the languages faculty of Leningrad University, specializing in English, and spent a short period at Ealing Technical College, near London; on graduation he was apparently 'able to make himself understood in five English dialects'.[65] In the view of Kremlin insiders, he is intelligent, affable and a very hard worker, but cautious in taking decisions;[66] he is also seen as 'moderately pro-Western', and is certainly a fan of the Beatles (he spent some time talking to Paul McCartney when the singer was in Moscow in 2003).[67]

The Defence Ministry itself is formally directed by the President, and exercises authority across the entire range of military activities as well as those for which it is directly responsible. In particular, it directs the work of four subordinate agencies or 'federal services': on military-technical cooperation, military procurement, technical and export control, and special construction. Under the 2004 legislation that defines its activity, the ministry is responsible for the development of defence policy and for the deployment of the armed forces themselves in appropriate circumstances, and also for the support of military servicemen and their families and for international cooperation. Day-to-day management is carried out by a small collegium, which 'decides the most important questions of the activity' of the ministry as a whole. It includes the minister (who takes the chair), his first deputies and deputies, the heads of the federal services for which the ministry is responsible, and the high command of the three services (army, air force and navy); decisions are taken by a majority, although in the event of disagreement the minister has the right to insist on his own opinion, provided he explains the circumstances to the President.[68]

Under the law on defence, as amended in 2004, the minister himself takes primary responsibility for operational matters.[69] In practice, however, they are devolved to the General Staff, in respect not only of the main services but also of military formations that do not come under the direct control of the ministry. These include Interior Ministry troops, the border troops that come under the auspices of the FSB, civil defence troops that belong to the Ministry of Emergency Situations, and railway troops.[70] The General

Staff is headed by a Chief, who automatically holds the rank of First Deputy Minister. At the time of Putin's accession this was Anatoly Kvashnin, but in 2004 he was replaced by Yury Baluevsky (b. 1947), seen by Kremlin insiders as a 'military functionary' who was opposed to NATO enlargement but who also wished to avoid public statements that might be a source of embarrassment, and who was less interested in bureaucratic infighting than his predecessor.[71] Kvashnin's dismissal was generally regarded as a success for the minister, who made clear that the former Chief of the General Staff had taken good care of the armed forces at a 'difficult stage in their existence' but that he had been less convincing in his plans for the future. Baluevsky's previous career had been spent at staff headquarters, which was consistent with the minister's apparent intention that the General Staff in the future should be 'primarily an analytical body, not a command-and-control structure'.[72]

The Defence Minister's responsibilities were extended further by the establishment, in March 2006, of a military-industrial commission attached to the Russian government, but chaired by the minister. In the view of some commentators, it was all but a 'parallel government'.[73] The commission, according to Putin's decree, is a standing body with responsibility for supervising the government bodies that are concerned with the design of military and security equipment and with ensuring the fulfilment of production agreements in such matters, including imports and exports; its staff form a part of the presidential administration.[74] The commission held its first meeting in early May 2006. According to its deputy chair, it was intended not to duplicate existing government ministries but rather to 'coordinate' their activity. Its powers were still greater than those of the corresponding bodies that had existed at earlier times, including, for instance, the ability of its chairman to suggest the adoption of decrees on military-industrial matters directly to the President; in addition, it has its own decision-making powers, which are binding on the ministries that are subordinate to it.[75]

Formally speaking, the Defence Minister is accountable to the Federal Assembly, and reports on his performance in the same way as the Minister of Foreign Affairs. In practice, the activities of the ministry are most closely considered by the specialized committees of each of the two chambers. In the Federation Council this means the Committee on Defence and Security, chaired by Viktor Ozerov (b. 1958), who represents the legislative assembly of Khabarovsk territory. Under the Federation Council's standing orders (art. 30), the Committee on Defence and Security deals with a comprehensive range of responsibilities: these include war and peace, foreign and domestic security, defence of the state borders, the national interests of the Russian Federation in territorial waters and on the high seas, the financing of the armed forces, international military cooperation, the status of servicemen, military-patriotic work, organized crime and terrorism, and civil and territorial defence. The deployment of Russian armed forces outside the national territory, under the constitution, is the exclusive prerogative of the Federation Council, and it must give its approval – at least formally – when the President declares a military situation in the event of an armed attack by another state, or a threat of an attack of this kind (arts 87.2, 102.1).

There is a more elaborate set of procedures to regulate these matters in the lower house, the State Duma. It has a Defence Committee, chaired by Viktor Zavarzin (b. 1948), who represents Kamchatka and has degrees from the Frunze Military Academy and from the Military Academy of the General Staff. It also has a Security Committee, chaired by Vladimir Vasilev (b. 1949), who represents the Tver' region and has a degree from the Academy of the Ministry of Internal Affairs. The Defence Committee is most directly concerned with the performance of the ministry itself: it deals accordingly with the legislation that defines the leadership and internal structure of the armed forces, and with the move from a conscript to a professional army. The Security Committee has somewhat broader responsibilities: it was the Security Committee, for instance, that was responsible for bringing forward the anti-terrorism legislation that was first presented in late 2004 and finally enacted in March 2006.[76] The new law gives the federal authorities new powers to tap telephones and control electronic communications; it allows air-defence troops to shoot down hijacked planes, and bans organizations whose purposes and actions include the propaganda, justification and support of terrorism. Actions of this kind are to be coordinated by a National Anti-Terrorism Committee, chaired by the director of the FSB, which was established by presidential decree in February 2006.[77]

As elsewhere, the Russian military are a publicly funded state agency and their funding is approved annually by the Duma as a part of the national budget. The pattern of spending since the mid-1990s is set out in Table 2.1. Since Putin's accession the share of the budget that is associated with defence has fallen slightly, but there were substantial increases after 2003 in both the budgetary totals that were approved by the Duma and the sums that were eventually spent (which were typically somewhat larger), and even more ambitious spending plans were set out in Putin's 2006 address to the Federal Assembly. Spending on law enforcement and security has increased more steadily, by about half since 2002. Independent estimates suggest a clearer upward pattern: expressed in constant prices and exchange rates, spending almost doubled between 1998 and 2004; expressed as a percentage of GDP, levels of spending rose from 3.1 per cent in 1998 to 4.3 per cent in 2003 – slightly more than the 4.1 per cent that had been recorded in 1995. These figures were greater than those for both the United States (3.8 per cent)

Table 2.1: Military and security spending, 1995–2006 (official figures)

	1995	2000	2001	2002	2003	2004	2005	2006
Defence expenditure								
% of total budget (plan)	20.9	20.7	18.0	14.6	14.7	15.5	17.4	16.0
% of total budget (out-turn)	20.6	18.6	18.7	14.4	15.1	15.9	9.7	–
As % of GDP	3.0	2.6	2.8	2.7	2.7	2.6	2.7	–
Law enforcement and security								
% of total budget (plan)	6.8	11.0	11.0	8.9	10.4	11.7	13.2	12.7
% of total budget (out-turn)	10.2	10.2	11.2	9.3	10.5	11.7	9.8	–
% of GDP	1.4	1.4	1.7	1.8	1.9	1.9	2.7	–

Sources: Derived from federal budgetary laws, various years, consulted at *www.minfin.ru* (for plan figures), and *Rossiiskii statisticheskii ezhegodnik* (Moscow: Goskomstat Rossii, 2004), various pages (out-turn and GDP figures).
* Proposed and subject to modification.

and the United Kingdom (2.8 per cent), although figures of this kind 'are not suitable for close comparison between individual countries and are more appropriately used for comparisons over time'.[78]

The armed forces, as these figures suggest, are unavoidably a participant in the political process. Formally, so far as members of the General Staff are concerned, they are 'outside politics'; in practice, research suggests, they have 'continued to show little interest in being a significant player in sovereign power issues', and were very reluctant to intervene in the showdown between President and parliament that took place in October 1993.[79] But they have every reason to press their funding concerns, and the kinds of problems they genuinely encounter in providing decent homes for officers and their families as well as new generations of hardware. The move from a conscript to a professional army has important implications for the entire society, and has been controversial. There has been even more public controversy about a series of cases of the maltreatment of servicemen, a problem of long standing. In a case to which President Putin himself drew attention, a 19-year-old private, Andrei Sychev, was reported to have been tied to a chair and beaten on his legs for three hours by drunken superiors on New Year's Eve 2005; but he received no medical attention for several days, by which time gangrene had set in, and his legs and genitals had to be amputated. According to the Soldiers' Mothers Committee, as many as 3,000 conscripts die from this kind of abuse (hazing) every year.[80]

The armed forces themselves have views on these matters, and some of them appear on the pages of the military journals. Decision-making in matters of security policy has, however, remained so centralized during the Putin presidency that we cannot readily assume that elite debates of this kind are a reliable indicator of the kinds of concerns that predominate in the smaller circles within which decisions are actually made. Putin, and others in the military leadership, may indeed be expressing concerns – about NATO enlargement, for instance, or the civil–military relationship[81] – that are widely shared by other elites and interests. But they may also have gone beyond the broad preferences of the political elite and chosen instead to promote a separate security agenda, relying on the President's prerogatives and a small circle of political loyalists. In this case Putin may be able to count on his continued popularity among the public at large, although we should not presume that Russian popular attitudes and preferences are reflected in specific security policy outputs or trajectories. Nevertheless, this may be the case at times, and it is certainly true that the *sustainability* of Russia's security policy over time is likely to be related to elite opinion and to broader public attitudes.

*weakly institut (perhaps intentional/allowed?) to validate P.
central read

THE PRESIDENTIAL BLACK BOX

In a weakly institutionalized system of this kind, it is the central leadership – as so often in Russian history – that matters most of all; and within the central leadership, a small group of the leader's closest associates. Positions of this kind are not defined by the constitution and are in constant flux, but something of their nature can be established from the patterns of interaction in which the President is most frequently engaged. We identified a number of these patterns in a related study, conducted with Russian colleagues and making use of high-level Kremlin informants.[82] Putin, on this evidence, likes most of all to work informally with small groups of leading officials, somewhat in the manner of the British Prime Minister and his 'sofa'. But there is an inner group of associates with whom he meets more often than with anyone else. To identify this inner core, we looked first of all at the composition of all the meetings in which the President directly participated. Within these, we looked at those that were conducted regularly, and then we identified an inner circle of officials who took part in virtually all of them.

P
State
= Jy

Putin, on this evidence, has three sets of regular engagements. On Mondays, there is a well-established and fairly public meeting with leading members of the government. On Saturdays, more quietly, Putin meets the other members of the leadership who are represented on the Security Council, although this is not a meeting of the Security Council as such. An established seating arrangement has come into existence at both of these meetings that helps to signal who is 'closer' than others to the ultimate source of authority, not unlike the way in which certain members of the Politburo sat in the front row on public occasions, with others in an implicit hierarchy behind them (these informal arrangements were changed somewhat in November 2005, when participants in the Monday meetings began to be seated on an alphabetical basis rather than in accordance with the long-established patterns of the past, although three of them remained in their usual places[83]). Apart from this, and even more discreetly, there is a third set of meetings with what our informants call the President's 'tea-drinking group'; they mostly come, like Putin, from Leningrad/St Petersburg, and many share his background in the security services.

There is quite a lot of overlap across the three groups, but two individuals figure prominently in all of them: Defence Minister and (since November 2005) Deputy Premier Sergei Ivanov, and Dmitry Medvedev, the former head of the presidential administration, who has also (since the same date) held the rank of First Deputy Premier. Ivanov can be seen as the leading figure in the group of leading officials with a force-ministry background that has become known as the siloviki; Medvedev is closer to the economic liberals, who form the other section of the ruling group. Putin appears to maintain an approximate balance between both of them, in order to avoid becoming unduly dependent on either. But their differences can also be exaggerated – it was, for instance, a leading 'liberal' within the presidential administration, Vyacheslav Surkov, who identified the political opposition as a 'fifth column' allied with outside interests that wanted to 'destroy Russia and fill its enormous geographic space with numerous unviable quasi-state entities'.[84] And it was Medvedev himself, in 2005, who warned that Russia could 'disappear as a state' unless its ruling group maintained their unity.[85] It is within this very small group of leading officials with direct access to the President himself that a foreign policy 'line' may be said to be determined; it is they, for instance, who are likely to have been more closely consulted than any others about the content of the President's annual address to the Federal Assembly, which in May 2006 began with a reference to Russia's 'closest neighbours' in the CIS and then Russia's 'constant dialogue' with the European Union before passing on to the United States, China, India and the Asia-Pacific region.[86]

A lack of institutional constraints is not, of course, the same as the absence of constraints of any kind. A Russian President is not accountable to elected institutions, his control of the electoral mechanism has become increasingly effective, and he need fear no challenge to his position from the courts of law. But there are constraints that stem from the international system: from Russia's diminished geopolitical weight (offset by the increased importance of oil and gas), and from the formal obligations to which the Russian state has become a party. And there are domestic constraints of an informal kind that stem from elite and public opinion. The views of other institutional actors must be accommodated, if covertly; the specialist advice of the Foreign

Ministry has a particular place in this connection, perhaps even the views of an individual ambassador.[87] Policies must be negotiated with elected institutions, in spite of the Kremlin's inbuilt majority, and cannot simply be imposed. Nor can the public be entirely disregarded. Putin has laid particular emphasis on his direct relationship with the Russian people – for instance, through his regular series of national interactive broadcasts. He also maintains an in-house survey facility that keeps him regularly updated, and has reacted irritably when surveys suggest his ratings are falling or that his policies are unsuccessful. The veteran pollster Yury Levada has even suggested that he may be a 'prisoner of his ratings' in that he is inhibited from undertaking actions that may be necessary because they are thought to be unpopular.[88]

Putin is not regarded as having had much success in improving public order, and least of all in regulating the Chechen conflict that brought him to power. But Russians take a much more positive view of the extent to which he has reasserted Russian authority in international affairs. In our 2005 survey, nearly two-thirds of Russians (65 per cent) thought Putin had been at least to some extent successful in restoring Russia's international position; but not much more than 40 per cent thought he had been successful in restoring public order, 35 per cent thought he had achieved some progress towards a settlement in Chechnya, and just 33 per cent thought there had been an improvement in living standards. Equally, nearly two-thirds of our respondents broadly approved of the conduct of Russian foreign policy (64 per cent, as compared with just 19 per cent who expressed some degree of dissatisfaction). Nor were these abstract propositions: more than a third of our respondents had at least one relative in another of the former Soviet republics (35 per cent), nearly half (46 per cent) had visited Ukraine, and more than a quarter (26 per cent) had visited Belarus. Whatever their formal status, the republics of the former Soviet Union – and particularly the Slavic republics and Kazakhstan – have remained a human community, and there are virtually no prominent politicians who do not favour a closer association.

In so far as he is influenced by informal constraints of this kind, Putin (or any conceivable successor) is likely to find that there is strong support for policies that at least appear to place Russia's own interests in the first place, without necessarily engaging in confrontation with other countries. The West, it is generally agreed, is interested in Russia's 'impoverishment and collapse' (66 per cent), and there is widespread support for the measures that have been taken against West-leaning oligarchs and non-governmental organizations.[89] At the same time there is overwhelming support for a closer relationship with the other former republics of the USSR, especially the Slavic ones, and for the defence of the interests of Russian speakers in other countries, especially in the Baltic. Putin, or any successor, will find substantial support if he proceeds 'as if' he shares these widely supported values (he appears to do so in any case, if his remarks about the demise of the USSR are any indication);[90] and although considerations of this kind are rarely central to electoral choices,[91] in the last resort every President has to obtain – and if necessary extend – his electoral mandate. The new Russian President who is elected in 2008 is likely to respect this constellation of interests and opinion, even though he will be much less obviously dependent upon them than his counterparts in the Western democracies.

3

Russian political engagement with the European Union

Margot Light

By the time the parliamentary and presidential elections took place in Russia in December 2003 and March 2004, the solidarity between Russia and the United States and Russia and the European Union that followed 9/11 had already been undermined. Russian opposition to the war against Iraq had soured relations with the US, and a number of contentious issues had arisen in Russia's relations with the EU as a result both of domestic developments in Russia and of the imminence of the enlargement of the EU, scheduled for 1 May 2004. Following the December 2003 parliamentary election, the Duma was dominated by the pro-presidential United Russia party, with little or no representation of those parties, Yabloko and the Union of Right Forces, that had previously been the most enthusiastic supporters of relations with the EU.

Did the views of Russia's foreign policy elites[1] reflect the changes that had occurred in the relationship with the EU? This chapter explores their attitudes at the beginning of Putin's second presidential term and examines whether they changed over the following five years. Is it still possible to distinguish between the three sets of attitudes that were evident at the beginning of Putin's first presidential term?[2] Do foreign policy elites identify Russia as a European state? How well disposed are they to the EU? What difficulties do they think enlargement will cause for Russia? What have been the main problems that have affected the relationship during Putin's second term?

To analyse the perceptions of the foreign policy elite, we use a combination of published sources and the opinions expressed during a set of interviews conducted in March–April 2004, on the eve of EU enlargement and before the tragic hostage crisis in Beslan and the Ukrainian presidential election, both of which caused tension between the EU and Russia. We interviewed 22 people drawn from the presidential administration, foreign policy-related committees of the State Duma, the business community, political parties, the Ministry of Foreign Affairs, state and private security structures, and non-governmental think-tanks. The interviews were semi-structured; we took detailed notes and, whenever we were allowed to do so, we recorded the interviews. We had conducted similar interviews in 1999 and 2000 in the course of an earlier research project, and this enabled us to evaluate how attitudes had changed over the intervening five years.

The interviews reveal the broad outlines of attitudes towards the EU and its impending enlargement. However, foreign policy elites are not, as a rule, well informed about the details of the relationship. They tend to have opinions about the dramatic highlights, rather than the minutiae of the Russia–EU relationship.[3] In fact, the relationship is highly institutionalized, with a dense network of regular political consultations and economic negotiations, frequently on highly detailed and technical questions. According to Russia's ambassador to the European Communities, 'the Russia–EU partnership is complex; it deals with a variety of important pragmatic tasks'.[4] In other words, 'low politics' predominates, although during Putin's presidency, concerns at the level of 'high politics' have increasingly hampered progress over issues of 'low politics'. The media, in Russia as elsewhere, prefer high politics (the security issues that are the subject matter of Chapters 4 and 5) to the practical details of low politics. For the purposes of this chapter, therefore, which investigates the low politics and the problems that have arisen in Russia's relationship with the EU, we need to turn to a specific section of the foreign policy elite: academics and analysts who focus specifically on the EU and whose publications appear in newspapers and in more specialized journals.

We begin by looking at the views that members of the foreign policy elite hold about Russia's identity, how they regard the EU and what they see as the main problems that Russia will face as a result of enlargement. We then turn to a more detailed exploration of the issues that have caused controversy in Russia–EU relations. We consider the border issues that have arisen between the EU and Russia: the imposition of the Schengen regime on the accession countries and the consequences for freedom of movement across borders between the EU and its new neighbours and for cross-border trade; the status of Kaliningrad; and the effectiveness of the Northern Dimension in alleviating some of these problems. Next, we examine the relationship between Russia and the EU in the field of Justice and Home Affairs (JHA) on issues related to soft security. General problems in Russia's relations with the EU are considered in the fourth section: in particular, the effect of the Chechen wars, the extension of the protocols of the Partnership and Cooperation Agreement (PCA) to the new members of the EU and the issue of energy security. We turn then to the question of Russia's future relationship with the EU to examine, in particular, whether Russian analysts and specialists consider it feasible that Russia might in the future join the EU. The chapter concludes with an evaluation of the state of Russia–EU relations, and offers an explanation as to why so many difficulties have arisen in the last few years.

RUSSIA, EUROPE AND THE EU

Between Mikhail Gorbachev's declaration that the Soviet Union was part of a 'common European home'[5] and President Vladimir Putin's claim in St Petersburg on the occasion of the city's 300th anniversary in 2003 that 'Russia is both historically and culturally an integral part of Europe',[6] there are countless examples of specialist, elite and official statements insisting on Russia's European identity.[7] Irrespective of their foreign policy views, Russian elites believe that Russia is part of Europe, but it is in the way in which they define Russia's identity that the differences between sets of attitudes are most evident. We found that, as in 1999–2000, we could distinguish three groups of attitudes: liberal westernizer, pragmatic nationalist and fundamentalist nationalist. Liberal westernizers tend to see Russia as indisputably part of Europe. 'We are in Europe … and always have been', one businessman told us firmly. For fundamentalist nationalists, by contrast, Russia's European characteristics are combined with its Eastern and Asian features to produce a distinctive Eurasian identity.[8] One interviewee who was very insistent on Russia's Eurasian identity claimed that the centre of civilization is not Europe but Russia. Another defined Russia as an 'East European–Eurasian Union'. For the more religiously inclined, Russia shares 'a Christian civilization' with Europe, but it has its own peculiarities, 'which stem from climatic differences and Russia's twentieth-century experiences'. Those with pragmatic nationalist views – the most numerous of our interviewees – are also certain that Russia is a European country, but they draw attention to its distinctive characteristics. Many of them share the fundamental nationalist conviction that Russia is Eurasian. According to a prominent deputy of the Duma, Russia is 'a unique part of Europe', while a senior Foreign Ministry official asserted that 'Russia is geographically and culturally European, but it has its own mentality'. According to the historian Aleksandr Chubaryan, champions of the idea of Russia's 'uniqueness' tend to distinguish 'Russian' Europeanism from 'classical' Europeanism, decrying the 'lack of spirituality' in the latter.[9]

One of our interlocutors insisted that although Russia is European, it is not Western. This reflects a general tendency among Russian intellectuals to differentiate between Europe and the West, and to include Russia in the former but not the latter. Vyacheslav Morozov argues that this is a continuation of a long-standing Russian tradition, inherited by the Soviet Union, of distinguishing between 'true' and 'false' Europe. During the Cold War, for example, NATO was perceived as the embodiment of 'false' Europe.[10] The distinction that many Russians tend to make between 'the good West of Europe/EU' and the 'bad West of America/NATO' appears to be a continuation of this tradition.[11]

Liberal westernizers and pragmatic nationalists are, by and large, well disposed towards the European Union. Indeed, among our interviewees, there was a consensus that the EU does not offer any threat to Russia. On the contrary, 'the EU opens opportunities for Russia to solve its internal as well as its external problems', one of our interviewees declared. On the other hand, the EU is often depicted in negative terms in the fundamentalist nationalist press. It is 'a difficult, petty and biased partner' in its relationship with Russia, and it is 'permeated through and through with hypocrisy and double standards'.[12]

Liberal westernizers either do not anticipate that enlargement will cause particular difficulties in Russia–EU relations, or believe that it is Russia's responsibility to resolve the problems that occur. They argue, for example, that market access will be easier because quotas will increase, and the problems that arise will not be caused by tariffs but because Russian goods are not competitive. As for the Schengen regime, 'it is a problem not for Russians but for the new members, because they are losing the Russian market'. Even one of our fundamentalist nationalist interviewees declared that 'it is a good thing that the EU is enlarging … it will make us develop, rethink'. More commonly, however, fundamentalist nationalists predict that Russia will suffer serious economic consequences as a result of enlargement, ranging from a decline in aluminium and agricultural exports to being deprived of its own energy resources.[13] While they are not opposed to enlargement, pragmatic nationalists are apprehensive about the consequences for Russia. One pragmatic nationalist gloomily predicted that 'even if tariffs are lower, it won't help. Russia has nothing apart from oil, gas, metals and wood to export to Europe'. Another argued that cross-border trade would be affected. One of our interviewees produced a list of future problems that would affect Russia's relations with the EU: the Schengen visa regime, Kaliningrad and tariffs. These were the issues that concerned many of the pragmatic and fundamentalist nationalists we interviewed.

Analysts and academics who focus specifically on the EU take for granted that Russia is historically, culturally and geographically an integral part of Europe. They see EU enlargement as 'a natural and objective process contributing to the enlargement of the zones of stability and economic prosperity on the European continent'.[14] They believe that the potential benefits to Russia of enlargement will outweigh the initial negative impact on Russian trade.

But like the pragmatic nationalists, they are anxious about the consequences of enlargement and about the impact on Russians of the imposition of the Schengen visa regime.

Given the extent to which Russian political elites identify themselves and Russia as European and their predominantly positive perceptions of the EU and of the benefits to Russia of good relations with the EU, it is surprising that the relationship between Russia and the EU has run into difficulties in the last few years. In order to understand why some Russian EU specialists argue that by mid-2004 Russia–EU relations were in 'deep crisis',[5] let us turn to some of the problems that have arisen in the relationship. For analytical convenience, we group them into border issues, soft security issues and general problems, although it will become clear that there is a great deal of overlap between these categories.

RECENT CONTROVERSIES IN RUSSIA–EU RELATIONS

The relationship between Russia and EU is complex and multifaceted, and a number of problematic issues have arisen before and during the Putin presidency. The issues examined in this section have been selected to cast light on the way in which, particularly during Putin's second term, areas that would seem to require the technical and functional problem-solving characteristic of low politics have turned into issues of high politics requiring top-level intervention. This has hindered progress in developing the kind of cooperative relations that both sides seemed to envisage when the PCA was first adopted.

Border issues

A number of contentious issues relating to borders have affected Russia–EU relations, including the demarcation of the borders between Russia and the Baltic states, but none has produced more anxiety among Russians than the introduction of a visa regime for travel between Russia and the few countries that Russians had been able to visit freely in the first ten years after the disintegration of the USSR. Indeed, as we shall see, the issue of visas has not only affected the role that Kaliningrad has played in EU–Russia relations and progress in implementing the goals of the Northern Dimension, it has also loomed large in EU–Russia cooperation in the field of JHA.

The Schengen regime and freedom of movement

The Schengen agreement – first signed by five EU member states in 1985 – replaced border and custom controls at internal borders with a unitary

49

system of rules for entry and exit at all external borders, a unified system of extradition and a Schengen Information System. It was designed to tighten external control of access into the EU so as to facilitate its internal integration by allowing the free movement of persons, goods, capital and services across the Union. By 1996, 13 out of 15 EU member states had joined the Schengen zone, and so had Iceland and Norway. The 1999 Amsterdam Treaty included the Schengen *acquis* in the legal system of the EU, a regime that candidate states had to adopt. This meant that they had to tighten their external border controls and implement the EU's common visa regime, although they would not formally have to join the Schengen zone immediately upon accession.[16] No opt-outs (such as the UK and Ireland have) would be permitted to candidate states because by the turn of the century the EU was rather less concerned with facilitating internal integration than with using Schengen to strengthen external border controls as a defence against the penetration of the EU by illegal immigrants and organized crime. EU officials and the governments of member states were unmoved by the argument put forward by many Western experts that visas are ineffective instruments in curbing either criminal activity or illegal immigration. Nor did they recognize the paradox that new members were expected to introduce 'hard' Schengen borders that could negatively affect their relations with non-EU neighbours, while the expected advantages of lifting border controls between old and new members, and the freedom to take up employment, would be delayed for several years after accession.[17]

The loss of the right to visa-free travel to the countries of Central and Eastern Europe has been an abiding concern of Russian policy-makers and foreign policy elites ever since the enlargement of the EU eastwards was first mooted. As we shall see, the implementation of a visa regime caused a particular problem for Kaliningrad, but there was also an issue with the border areas of Leningrad and Pskov oblasts and with informal cross-border economic and socio-cultural links more generally.

Russian concerns increased as the accession countries began to implement the Schengen system: in 2000, first the Czech Republic, then Slovakia, Estonia and Bulgaria introduced visa requirements for citizens of Russia. Russians were not persuaded by EU arguments that there were advantages to the Schengen system (for example, that one visa would give access to all Schengen countries), or that Russian business would gain from having identical customs rules and specifications for all EU member states. They complained that Schengen visas were valid for no more than three months and argued that the candidate countries were applying the Schengen conditions more strictly than existing EU members. There were long delays in receiving visas, stricter conditions, the number of people refused visas was increasing and the cost of visas was increasing.[18] It was particularly galling to Russians that whereas Russia was included in the list of 130 countries whose citizens require visas, 'citizens of the USA may enter the Schengen zone without visas if their visits are for less than three months'.[19]

When we interviewed foreign policy elites in 1999–2000, one of the main concerns they expressed about the consequences of EU enlargement was the loss of visa-free travel to Eastern Europe. In 2004 they appeared less concerned about the issue. Liberal westernizers asserted that the visa regime caused a problem for the new EU members, rather than for Russians, or that it was not just Russia's problem but also a problem for the EU, while pragmatic nationalists called the visa regimes 'inconvenient'. The only strong complaints we heard about visa requirements were from those interviewees we identified as fundamentalist nationalists. In the specialist literature, however, and in official statements about Russia–EU relations, the subject was very prominent. It is clear from these sources that the imposition of the Schengen visa regime by the accession states had turned into a serious political issue in the Russia–EU relationship, to the extent that it dominated the agenda and prevented progress on other issues.

To many, the imposition of the Schengen system symbolized the redivision of Europe. Foreign Ministry officials were particularly concerned about the consequences of the new visa regime. V. V. Kotenev, head of the Consular Department of the Ministry of Foreign Affairs, for example, argued in 2002 that there was a risk that the Schengen agreement would turn 'into a new dividing wall in Europe'.[20] A year later Deputy Foreign Minister Chizhov complained that 'an ever higher, difficult to traverse "Schengen wall"' had been constructed, which was 'becoming more inaccessible year by year'. It was 'already not far from being analogous to the Berlin wall'.[21] Igor Ivanov, then Foreign Minister, believed that 'Schengen contradicts one of the fundamental freedoms enunciated by the founding fathers of a united Europe – the freedom of movement'.[22]

The claim that Schengen visa requirements violate the fundamental freedom of Russians referred in particular to movement between Kaliningrad and Russia. It was a view that was prevalent across the political spectrum. Yabloko deputy Vladimir Lukin, then Deputy Speaker of the Duma, complained that simply 'because the EU has its rules', it was insisting that Russia removed its citizens' right to the freedom of movement from one part of its territory to another. Mikhail Margelov, chairman of the Federation Council International Relations Committee, wanted the issue to be discussed by the Parliamentary Assembly of the Council of Europe because of its responsibility for ensuring human rights and compliance with the norms of international law.[23] The fundamentalist nationalist press did not, on the whole, invoke the freedom of movement, not because it approved of Schengen, but because human rights are not, in general, part of the fundamentalist nationalist discourse. Instead they maintained that the Schengen requirements violated Russian sovereignty and pointed to the EU's double standards in 'being unable to "infringe" Lithuania's sovereignty, but demonstrably able to destroy Russian sovereignty'.[24]

Russian EU specialists were also concerned about the consequences of the implementation of the Schengen system. A usually very measured expert on the European Union, Yury Borko, pointed out that while the EU was sometimes right to criticize Russia for failing to observe human rights, it was itself preventing Russians from exercising one of the most fundamental of those rights – the right to the freedom of movement.[25] According to Nadezhda Arbatova, Russia and the EU 'ought to make a visa-free regime the priority concern of their activities'.[26]

Since the EU was insistent that the Schengen system could not be modified, in August 2002 President Putin proposed to the heads of EU member states the negotiation of an agreement to permit reciprocal Russia–EU visa-free travel. As we will see later in the chapter, the European Commission responded by linking progress on this issue to greater cooperation in combating illegal migration and crime. In particular, it was adamant that Russia would first have to conclude a Readmission Treaty with the EU that would enable the EU to return illegal immigrants who enter the EU from Russia. It also insisted that Russia should strengthen its passport control procedures, issue passports to all its citizens (universal 'passportization') and make its external borders more effective.[27] These seemingly elementary conditions are extremely difficult for Russia to fulfil. In effect, what the EU requires of Russia is very similar to what it imposed upon the new member states: in order to achieve visa-free movement between Russia and the EU, Russia would have to control external access to Russia from the Commonwealth of Independent States. Nevertheless, at the Russia–EU summit in St Petersburg in May 2003 the two sides agreed to study the possibility of visa-free travel. Little progress had been made by the time the Road Map for the Common Space of Freedom, Security and Justice was adopted at the May 2005 summit, however. Negotiations on a readmission agreement had not yet been completed and visa-free travel was envisaged only 'as a long-term perspective'.[28]

Kaliningrad

It was in relation to Kaliningrad that the visa issue became particularly acute, threatening to create an impasse in Russia–EU relations. Ceded to the Soviet Union at the Potsdam Conference in 1945, Kaliningrad was administratively part of the Russian Soviet Federative Socialist Republic, although it was physically separated from it by Belarus and Lithuania. When the Soviet Union disintegrated, Kaliningrad remained part of Russia, while Belarus and Lithuania became independent states. Travel by land between Kaliningrad and the rest of the Russian Federation now required the crossing of three borders, including those of Lithuania and Latvia, or of Lithuania and Belarus, or of Poland and Belarus. Poland and Lithuania granted visa-free travel to Kaliningrad residents, but other Russians from the mainland needed visas to travel through Lithuania. From the moment that the accession of Poland and Lithuania to the EU was mooted, it was clear that Kaliningrad would become a Russian exclave within the EU, and that people and goods would be able to move between it and the rest of the Russian Federation only by traversing EU territory. It was not until 2001, however, that the EU began to pay attention to the potential problems this would create.

Although the Commission recognized that Kaliningrad's economic development, environmental degradation, poor state of governance and absence of the rule of law were all matters that could impinge upon an enlarged EU, the most serious issues identified as arising from the enlargement process were the movement of goods and people to and from Kaliningrad, its energy supplies and fishing. The Commission did not think that special arrangements needed to be made for the movement of people apart from increasing the number of border crossing points between Kaliningrad and its neighbours and improving their physical infrastructure and information systems. In other words, the Commission believed that Kaliningrad's problems could be dealt with in a low politics problem-solving framework. There was absolutely no recognition that the freedom of Russians to travel to and from Kaliningrad was a highly sensitive subject for Russians.[29]

Russians were worried, too, that the already large socio-economic gap between Kaliningrad and its neighbours would grow. But the freedom of movement of Russians between Kaliningrad and the rest of the Russian Federation was considered an extremely serious issue of high politics, and it dominated the Russia–EU agenda in 2001 and 2002. By personally calling for visa-free travel for Kaliningrad residents and appointing Dmitry Rogozin, a fundamentalist nationalist, as his special envoy on Kaliningrad, President Putin politicized the issue and this made it harder for the two sides to reach agreement.[30] A compromise was finally reached in November 2002: from 1 July 2003 Russians could transit Lithuania to travel to and from Kaliningrad under a Facilitated Rail Transit Document (a single trip by rail) and Facilitated Transit Document (multiple trips by car) scheme which would be free of charge to all Russians. Lithuania agreed to accept Russian internal passports as a basis for issuing both types of FTD until 31 December 2004. Thereafter,

Russians would have to present an international passport to obtain an FTD or FRTD.[31] Poland introduced visas for all Russians on 1 October 2003, but they are free of charge for Kaliningrad residents.

Liberal westernizers and some pragmatic nationalists, as well as Russia–EU specialists, tended to criticize the politicization of the transit issue. In the words of one specialist, 'A steady stream of polemic from Moscow has branded the Kaliningrad transit visa requirements totally unacceptable, with politicians angrily declaring that the right of Russian citizens to move freely from one area of Russian territory to another cannot be made subject to decisions by EU bureaucrats'.[32] Another pointed out that the issue had 'torpedoed two EU–Russia summits ... and led to a sharpening of anti-European rhetoric in the Russian media and society'.[33] For fundamentalist nationalists the issue was cut and dried. The introduction of a visa regime for the Moscow–Kaliningrad route 'would inevitably lead to Kaliningrad being torn away from Russia'.[34] The government should have made it clear that 'any attempt to end, make difficult or seriously limit communications between [Kaliningrad] and Russia would be seen as an attack on our territorial integrity, to which we would respond by taking action on the basis of the right to self-defence provided by the UN Charter'.[35] Specialists, by contrast, tried to divert attention away from transit and visas to what they saw as the real Kaliningrad problem: the gap between the economic development of the region and its neighbours. This was bound to increase after Poland and Lithuania acceded to the EU, possibly to the point where the Kaliningrad region would destabilize both Russia and the EU.[36]

As for the November 2002 compromise, a diplomatic interpretation of the outcome saw it as a valuable compromise that 'removed one of the main obstacles to the rapid and multifaceted development of cooperation between the EU and Russia' and 'created the conditions for further work with the aim of achieving a visa-free movement for Russian and EU citizens throughout the European space'.[37] Many Western and Russian analysts took a different view, however. One Western analyst defines FTDs as 'visas by another name'; while to a Russian analyst the agreement represents 'a total loss for the Russian side', since Russians now have to obtain 'de-facto visas to move from one part of their country to another'. It simply demonstrated the incompetence of Russian negotiators.[38] It should be added that although the agreement produced a compromise solution for one of the problems afflicting Kaliningrad, none of its other problems – including the transit of cargo – were resolved. An interim agreement on cargo transit was reached on 27 April 2004 in the package of measures adopted when Russia finally agreed to extend the PCA to the ten accession countries.[39]

The Northern Dimension

The Northern Dimension was adopted by the EU in 1998 as part of its external relations. It aimed to promote economic development, stability and security in northern Europe, address cross-border issues, contribute to narrowing the disparities of living standards, prevent and ward off threats originating in the region and contribute to reducing environmental and nuclear threats. It envisaged cooperation between the EU and the north European countries in dealing with these problems, drawing on existing regional policies and financial instruments and specifically reinforcing 'positive interdependence between Russia and the Baltic Sea region and the European Union'.[40] Five priority areas of cooperation were identified: economic, infrastructure, human needs, environment, and soft security.

It is clear that apart from alleviating the many difficulties afflicting northern Russia since the collapse of the USSR, the Northern Dimension would have been an excellent means to deal with the economic, ecological and governance problems of Kaliningrad, including its impending status as an exclave of the Russian Federation located within the EU. The instruments that it envisaged were based on functionalist ideas about collaboration across borders as a method of resolving problems, leading to further cooperation.[41] However, despite the adoption of two action plans in 2000 (for the period 2002–03) and 2003 (for the period 2004–06), its potential to coordinate cross-border cooperation has never really been fulfilled.[42] Although it did create some links between Russian and EU border regions, 'there are very few independent, "made in the Northern Dimension" projects that have been worked out and agreed by all participants and … brought to the stage of implementation'.[43] According to Vladimir Ryzhkov, '[the Northern Dimension] has turned increasingly into a declaratory programme, and it is difficult to discern any concrete results'. Russian EU specialists tend to agree with this assessment.[44]

The revolving presidency of the EU is partly to blame – the Northern Dimension receives more attention when a north European member state holds the EU presidency and less when the presidency moves on after six months. In July 2006 Finland again took over the chair of the EU and it is likely to put forward a new political framework document for the Northern Dimension during its presidency. However, given the six-month rotation, it is doubtful that a new framework will make much of a mark.

It is generally agreed, however, that by far the greatest obstacle to the success of the Northern Dimension is lack of finance. It was intended to serve as an umbrella to ensure complementarity and coordination between existing regional initiatives, but it has never had its own budget. Yevgeny Gusarov, Russian Deputy Foreign Minister, identified the problem as early as 2000:

> If we reduce the matter to increased efficiency of the existing EU financing instruments, then a quite legitimate question would arise, namely, what is the specific role of the Northern Dimension? Is it supposed to serve only as a 'nice package' for projects that would have been implemented even if it didn't exist? Russia … believes that … its financial aspects could be elaborated in more detail.[45]

Deputy Prime Minister Viktor Khristenko used almost identical words a year later in criticizing the lack of finance, which he saw as 'the most acute unsolved problem within the Northern Dimension'.[46] It was anticipated that part of the funding would come from the other regional organizations and financial institutions, which would participate in and fund its activities (for example, the Council of the Baltic Sea States, the Nordic Council of Ministers), yet the EU has neither regularized channels of communication nor well-developed relationships with those regional actors.[47]

More important than the absence of funding, however, was the shift in EU attention. The new northern border was a salient issue for the EU after the 1995 enlargement. By the beginning of the new century, the EU's attention was focused on the broader range of problems – thematic as well as geographic – raised by the impending incorporation of ten new members and a concomitant shift in the EU's external borders. The EU would acquire not just new members but also new neighbours. Accession countries like Poland were more interested in developing an EU Eastern Dimension to incorporate Ukraine and Belarus as well as Russia than in the Northern Dimension.[48] Moreover, the eastern enlargement and the accompanying implementation of the Schengen regime, in particular, meant the abolition of more flexible visa arrangements required for the cross-border cooperation envisaged by the Northern Dimension.[49]

There were also serious obstacles on the Russian side that detracted from the effectiveness of the Northern Dimension. The adoption of the first action plan coincided with the election of Vladimir Putin to the Russian presidency and his campaign to reduce regional autonomy within Russia and to strengthen the federal centre. The regional interdependence and cross-border cooperation explicitly fostered by the aims of the Northern Dimension are not compatible with strengthening the 'power vertical'. Moreover, the cross-border cooperation and regionalization that are the core of the Northern Dimension challenge Russia's traditional concept of national sovereignty. Still further, the geopolitical realism that predominates in Russian thinking about security and the preference that Putin has shown for conducting the Russia–EU relationship at the level of high politics do not easily incorporate the soft security concerns that are the prime focus of the Northern Dimension. Finally, on a practical level, there is very little reciprocal funding on the Russian side. Indeed, according to some Russian analysts, there is a tendency in Russia to see the Northern Dimension either as a means of extracting further funds from the EU to develop Russian infrastructure, or as an additional opportunity for diplomatic manoeuvring.[50]

Clearly, the Northern Dimension has not been sufficiently effective to mitigate the problems of Kaliningrad or to deal with other cross-border soft security concerns in the region. Have other attempts to foster Russia–EU soft security cooperation been any more successful?

JHA and 'soft' security issues

Ever since the disintegration of the USSR, the EU has been apprehensive that 'soft' security threats to its wellbeing would emanate from the former Soviet Union. Although early fears of massive westward migration of Soviet citizens proved to be groundless, the danger that the porous borders of the newly independent states would enable illegal immigrants from the rest of the world to penetrate the EU remained a serious concern. In effect, the EU has 'embedded internal security objectives into foreign policy agreements' with Russia.[51] Article 6 of the PCA establishes a regular political dialogue in the hope of bringing about 'an increasing convergence of positions on issues of mutual concern, thus increasing security and stability'. The PCA also contains a section on Cooperation on Prevention of Illegal Activities, including illegal immigration, and it identifies the environment as a priority issue in Russia–EU relations.[52] The TACIS programme committed approximately €300 million to nuclear safety projects in Russia in the period 1991–2001.[53] Soft security issues figure prominently in both the EU's Common Strategy on Russia and the Russian response, the Medium-Term Strategy for the Development of Relations between the Russian Federation and the EU. The Country Strategy Paper for the Russian Federation adopted by the European Commission on 27 December 2001 defines the 'soft' security threats from Russia as nuclear safety issues and environmental pollution, the fight against crime, including drug trafficking and illegal immigration, and the spread of diseases.[54]

Within the European Commission, soft security issues fall within the domain of Justice and Home Affairs, which expanded from a small task force set up in 1992 to a full directorate-general in October 1999 'as a "compensatory measure" for the safeguarding of internal security after the abolition of internal border controls in the Union'.[55] It soon acquired an external dimension which was formally adopted at the Feira

European Council in 2000 and includes effective control of the EU's external borders and the signing of readmission agreements with countries from which migratory flows originate; the fight against financial crime, money laundering, corruption and trading in human beings; the fight against drug trafficking; the strengthening of non-military aspects of crisis management and security through police cooperation in crisis regions.[56]

Since April 2001 there have been regular JHA ministerial troikas with Russia involving the Ministers of Justice and of the Interior of the country holding the EU presidency, the country representing the next presidency, and the EU Commissioner on JHA on the one hand, and the Russian Ministers of Justice and of the Interior on the other. There was also was a full (15+1) JHA Ministerial in Luxembourg on 25 April 2002. In May 2003 the EU–Russia Cooperation Council was turned into a Permanent Partnership Council (PPC), which, it was planned, would meet more frequently and in a variety of formats, including the format of JHA to deal with soft security cooperation between Russia and the EU. The European Commission, the EU presidency and the Russian presidential administration (which can coordinate all relevant Russian ministries) all participate in ministerial meetings under the new PPC. The first meeting of the PPC in the JHA format took place on 26 October 2004. At the May 2003 EU–Russia summit it was also agreed 'to intensify cooperation, with a view to creating in the long-term a Common Space of Freedom, Security and Justice', and to construct a road map setting out a number of agreed objectives and four areas for cooperation in order to achieve this goal.[57] The road map was adopted at the EU–Russia summit in May 2005. At the same time, environmental issues were transferred to the road map for the Common Economic Space.

'Soft' security cooperation has been most successful in the field of combating organized crime, although, as one Russian analyst points out, 'police cooperation between Russia and the EU lags behind criminal cooperation'.[58] A joint EU–Russia Action Plan on Combating Organized Crime was adopted in April 2000. Since then issues related to organized crime have been discussed at all EU–Russia summits. In November 2003 a strategic cooperation agreement was signed between Russian law enforcement authorities and Europol. The TACIS programme allocated €10 million in 2001, €11.5 million in 2002 and €12 in 2003 to assistance programmes related to soft security issues, including combating organized crime. Russia and the EU also both participate in the Baltic Sea Task Force on Organized Crime, which was established in 1996 and consists of the personal representatives of the Heads of State and Government in the Baltic Sea region, including

Russia, as well as representatives of the European Commission and the EU presidency. In general, however, progress in cooperating to combat organized crime has been slow, in part because of the lack of reform in Russian law enforcement.[59] According to one Russian observer who is very critical of the failure of the Russian government to take advantage of the opportunities offered by JHA cooperation, 'modernization of the law enforcement agencies, perhaps the most overdue reform, is not even on the political agenda'.[60]

Other areas of EU–Russia JHA cooperation include action to combat money laundering, reform of the Russian legal and judicial system, action to prevent illegal migration, including trafficking in women, cooperation between police liaison officers at a bilateral level between Russia and individual EU member countries, and border management and control (including customs control) at border crossings between Russia and EU member states, as well as between Russia and third countries.[61] In fulfilment of these aims, Russia's Committee for Financial Monitoring and the EU launched a programme in April 2003 to bring its information system up to EU standards.[62] Russian officials have also expressed interest in pooling efforts with the EU to combat the cross-border narcotics traffic and proposed a 'joint European legal space' and the establishment of a Russia–EU Domestic Security Council.[63] The EU and Russia also cooperate in the struggle against international terrorism, but since much of this cooperation overlaps with issues related to external security, this aspect of JHA is dealt with in Chapter 4.

It is thus clear that there is a great deal of overlap between cooperation in JHA and the border and visa issues discussed in the previous section. Minimizing cross-border security threats requires viable border and visa regimes, for example, which, in turn, require legally binding border agreements between Russia and its neighbours. Russia concluded a border treaty and a readmission agreement with Lithuania in May 2003. But although a border treaty was concluded with Estonia in May 2005, Russia rescinded its signature when the Estonian parliament, in its law of ratification, referred to the 1920 Tartu treaty, thereby, in the Russian view, making possible future territorial claims on Russia.[64] Despite expectations that a Russian–Latvian border treaty would also be signed in May 2005, negotiations stalled after Latvia's parliament issued a declaration saying that the border should return to its pre-Second World War position.[65] Although the delay in concluding these border treaties is a source of irritation, the EU's chief concern is Russia's porous southern borders. These are the borders that are the main stumbling block preventing the conclusion of the Russia–EU readmission treaty, which is a prerequisite for visa-free travel.

The Russian leadership recognizes the problem. Foreign Minister Lavrov, for example, admits that a 'readmission [treaty] is impossible till Russia solves border problems with its neighbours' and that this requires negotiating readmission treaties with Russia's southern neighbours, since Russia does not want to have to 'admit people extradited from the EU who are not Russian citizens, but citizens of our southern and eastern neighbours'.[66] Russian analysts who believe that Russia is not itself doing enough to make Russia–EU visa-free travel possible argue that this formulation is an attempt to shift responsibility to third countries.[67] Nevertheless, Russian officials appear optimistic that they can resolve the problem of porous southern borders and that the abolition of visas for travel between Russia and the EU could become a reality by 2010. There is a considerable gap between this expectation and repeated EU statements that a visa-free regime is envisaged 'in the long-term perspective'.[68]

Russian specialists on the EU are generally favourably disposed towards cooperation in the field of JHA, since it is clear that with regard to cross-border threats, Russia and the EU have common interests and goals.[69] They point to the many instances of successful practical cooperation in the Baltic region to ameliorate acute cross-border soft security problems.[70] They argue that jointly addressing shared soft security problems could 'solidify a win-win foundation to the relationship' which would 'spill over positively into other, more difficult areas between Russia and the EU'.[71] However, here, as in so many other spheres of Russia–EU cooperation, they complain that JHA 'measures … are more discussed than realized'.[72] They also point out that Russians resent being considered the source of all non-military threats facing the EU. For example, they see themselves as victims of drug trafficking, rather than the source, since most of the drugs in Russia come from Afghanistan and are destined for consumption in Western Europe.[73] In fact, however, the real obstacle to more effective JHA cooperation is the lack of reform in the Russian law enforcement and judicial systems. Moreover, once the decision was made to create a Common Space on Freedom, Security and Justice, Russian attention became fixated on the freedom of movement that this implied and the momentum in other forms of JHA cooperation became dissipated. An article on Russia–EU relations by Vladimir Chizhov demonstrates this very clearly. In discussing the agreement to create four common spaces, he maintains that 'the common space of freedom, security and justice is based on a well-defined spectrum … of cooperation, with "freedom" being a priority area here in so far as it includes the removal of barriers to the free movement of people … and a gradual transition to visa-free travel'. He barely mentions other aspects of JHA cooperation.[74]

With regard to Russia–EU cooperation on soft security issues, therefore, as in relation to the other issues discussed above, there is a great deal of potential for cooperation, but 'most of the action remains planned rather than imp mented'.[76] One might conclude that Russia–EU relations suffer from a degree of stagnation, but some Russian analysts go further than this to argue that by mid-2004 Russia–EU relations were in deep crisis. What other problems have occurred in the relationship that might lead them to this conclusion?

Stagnation or *crisis*

General problems

Three separate problems are examined in this section. The Russian government would argue that the first, the war in Chechnya, does not concern Russia–EU relations. In fact, however, given the conditionality that governs the EU's relations with third states (the Maastricht Treaty makes the provision of development cooperation conditional on the rule of law and respect for human rights and fundamental freedoms), the war in Chechnya has been a background factor impinging on Russia–EU relations since 1994 and it will continue to affect the relationship. The other two problems, the extension of the PCA to the new EU members and energy security and the Russian–Ukrainian gas dispute, were unexpected; both present further examples of the way in which high politics increasingly tends to intrude on low political issues in Russia's relations with the EU.

high/low

The war in Chechnya

The Russian government has always maintained that the situation in Chechnya is an entirely domestic matter. EU officials and the governments of member states, on the other hand, believe that the way in which the wars in Chechnya have been prosecuted infringes both the letter and the spirit of the principles that Russia has endorsed by signing up to the PCA and to other international agreements. As a result, the wars in Chechnya have acted as an indirect brake on Russia–EU relations. As we have seen in Chapter 1, the outbreak of the first war in 1994 delayed ratification and implementation of the PCA until 1997, and when Russia launched the second war in 1999, the EU responded by temporarily suspending TACIS funding for all programmes except for specific priority areas including human rights, the rule of law, support for the development of a civil society and nuclear safety. The European Parliament has debated Chechnya a number of times and has adopted several resolutions condemning Russian policy in Chechnya and urging the Russian government to negotiate a political settlement to the conflict. The topic of Chechnya was raised regularly at the six-monthly EU–Russia summits in 2000 and 2001 and the Council of the EU has made a number of critical statements about Russia's conduct of the war. The Russians claimed that EU criticism was caused by 'a deficit of information',[76] but in

general they appeared to be prepared to tolerate the criticism. In May 2001, however, the Foreign Minister, Igor Ivanov, remarked that the EU had wasted a year and a half on discussions about Chechnya.[77]

Ever since the beginning of the second war in 1999, President Putin has consistently asserted that Russia is fighting international terrorism in Chechnya (a claim that contradicts his adamant insistence that Chechnya is Russia's domestic concern). It was not until the terrorist attacks on the United States on 11 September 2001, however, that the international community, including the EU, appeared to give some credence to his assertion. The EU moderated its criticism of Russian conduct and Chechnya was not mentioned in either of the joint Russia–EU statements made at the two summits in 2002, although the EU High Commissioner for External Relations, Chris Patten, assured the European Parliament that the subject was discussed during the meetings.[78] Paradoxically, however, Chechnya became an even more contentious issue in Russia–EU relations after the EU had ceased to raise the issue publicly. The venue for the tenth Russia–EU summit was moved from Copenhagen to Brussels, for example, when President Putin refused to travel to Denmark because the Danish authorities declined to ban a meeting of the World Chechen Congress in Copenhagen at the end of October 2002. The Moscow Dubrovka theatre siege occurred shortly before the Congress met and Valery Loshchinin, Deputy Foreign Minister, accused the Danish authorities of conniving with Chechen terrorists. He alleged that Akhmed Zakaev, President Maskhadov's envoy who organized the Congress, was responsible for planning the siege.[79] The Russian government accused the EU of double standards in refusing to label Chechens as international terrorists. They were particularly incensed when the Danish and British courts refused to extradite Zakaev to Russia and when the British courts granted him political asylum in November 2003.[80] In a report for the EU Council and Parliament on relations with Russia, the EU Commission, in turn, appeared to question Russia's commitment to core universal and European values and the pursuit of democratic reforms.[81]

Russian criticism of the EU's response to Chechen terrorism became far sharper in September 2004, after the Beslan siege (see Chapter 2), when a tactlessly phrased request for information about the siege from the Dutch Foreign Minister (the Netherlands held the presidency of the EU at the time) caused outrage in Russia. The Russian Foreign Minister, Sergei Lavrov, called the remarks 'profane'.[82] The diplomatic row was rapidly smoothed over and the Russian government agreed to an EU proposal to establish regular consultations on human rights, the first of which took place on 1 March 2005.[83] Nevertheless, there was considerable resentment at what was perceived to be an attempt to interfere in Russia's domestic affairs, and Russian objections to European 'double standards' continued. On the EU side, the political measures that President Putin introduced in Russia in response to the Beslan siege aroused concern, while the European Parliament continued to criticize Russian policy in Chechnya.[84]

Apart from the six-month suspension of economic aid, the wars in Chechnya and Russia's methods of dealing with terrorism have not had a direct impact on Russia–EU relations. Nevertheless, they do not provide a positive environment for a thriving and developing relationship. As one Russian analyst argues, 'Moscow and Brussels are bogged down in debates on vexed questions' as a result of which 'whenever the partners proceed from long-term goals and projects to urgent tasks requiring immediate decisions, their embraces give way to a standoff'.[85]

The extension of the PCA to the accession states

In the months preceding EU enlargement, Russia's extension of the PCA to the ten accession states was the cause of further tension between Russia and the EU. From early on in the enlargement process, Russian EU specialists had been warning of the negative economic consequences of enlargement. They also recognized that there would be countervailing economic advantages, and in their analyses they attempted to present an objective balance sheet of the gains and losses. They were alarmed, however, at how little the Russian government was doing to negotiate with the EU to ameliorate the negative consequences.[86] Despite their warnings, and the bland mutual assurances which were proclaimed after successive EU–Russia summits that both Russia and the EU desired 'to address questions that arise in … [the enlargement] context', little progress was made in negotiating about the particular issues that would affect the Russian economy.[87] It was only at the beginning of 2004, when the question arose about the status of the PCA after enlargement, that the economic consequences of enlargement became the focus of Russia–EU relations.

EU officials maintained that the gains to Russia from the lowering of customs duties on Russian goods in the new member states from 9 per cent to 4 per cent on average would more than compensate for any losses enlargement might entail. The Russian government, for its part, argued that Russia would suffer significant economic losses. Although EU tariffs were lower in general than those of the accession states, the reverse was true for some products that represented a considerable proportion of Russia's trade with the Central and East European countries, particularly aluminium, mineral fertilizers, other chemical products, fuel elements for nuclear power stations, wood and agricultural produce. Moreover, following enlargement, Russian exporters would have to pay anti-dumping charges on some goods, charges

more than action

RU eco loss bc of EU enlargement.

that they did not have to pay before the accession countries joined the EU. The export of Russian goods to Central and East European markets would also be adversely affected when the accession states implemented the EU's high technical standards and rigid sanitary and environmental protection regulations. The Russian government was also concerned that the cost of moving cargo between Russia and Kaliningrad would rise precipitously if goods traded between them were to be subject to the same procedures and charges associated with international trade. The anticipated losses to the Russian economy as a result of enlargement were estimated at anywhere between €150 million and €300 million per year.[88]

The EU apparently expected that Russia would automatically extend the PCA to all ten new members prior to the enlargement on 1 May 2004. On 30 January 2004, however, the ambassadors of the EU member states were invited to the Ministry of Foreign Affairs, where Chizhov handed them a document listing Russian concerns, insisting that 'the issue of extending the PCA is not merely a technical procedure that can be implemented automatically'. Most of the fourteen points in the Russian list concerned trade and tariff issues (for example, the consequences for Russian agricultural exports once the Central and East European countries adopted the EU's tougher hygiene standards), but access to Kaliningrad and concerns about the status of ethnic Russians in Latvia and Estonia were also included. The EU's response was brusque: to avoid a serious impact on EU–Russia relations 'the PCA has to be applied to the EU-25 without precondition or distinction by 1 May 2004'.[89] There was a furious reaction in Russia. Chizhov declared that Russia expected to participate in European affairs as an equal partner, Mikhail Margelov accused the EU of using 'the language of sanctions', while Dmitry Rogozin retorted that 'Russia is not about to act on orders from Brussels'. Since the Council meeting which issued the EU's response was attended by representatives of the accession states, Russians were convinced that their fears that the former socialist states would turn the EU against Russia had been realized.[90]

Despite the harsh rhetoric, both sides seemed to recognize, if rather belatedly, that compromise was essential. On 27 April, virtually on the eve of enlargement, Russia signed a protocol extending the PCA to the new members. Attached to it was a joint statement listing 'outstanding issues' that both sides undertook to address[91] In effect, the joint statement was a compromise; it dealt with some of Russia's concerns (including the transit of goods between Kaliningrad and Russia) and gave a transitional period during which the terms of some existing bilateral agreements would continue to operate. Nevertheless, there are other outstanding issues that continue to produce discord.

64

Energy security

Unexpectedly, a new problem arose in Russia–EU relations in 2006: energy security, and, more specifically, the issue of gas. The energy crises in 1973 and 1979 and the First Gulf War had put energy security on the agenda worldwide. On the initiative of the European Commission, an Energy Charter was established in 1991, to promote East–West energy cooperation. In 1994 the Charter was developed into an Energy Charter Treaty, a legally binding multilateral instrument dealing with intergovernmental cooperation in the energy sector.[92] Although Russia signed the treaty, it has not yet ratified it.

The EU imports more than 80 per cent of the energy it consumes, a large proportion of it from Russia. As a result of both EU enlargement and increasing consumption, the proportion of Russian energy in the EU's total energy imports rose from 24 per cent in 2001 to 27.5 per cent in 2005, of which gas imports increased from 41 to 50 per cent.[93] Since its existing pipelines primarily traverse Russia from east to west, Russia is as dependent on the European market as the EU is on Russian supplies; although there are potentially huge markets in the Far East, it will take a number of years to construct pipelines from Russia to China or the Pacific coast.

In recognition of the EU–Russia 'mutual dependency',[94] an Energy Dialogue was established at the sixth Russia–EU summit in 2000, which was designed to

> provide an opportunity to raise all the questions of common interest relating to the sector, including the introduction of cooperation on energy saving, rationalization of production and transport infrastructures, European investment possibilities, and relations between producer and consumer countries.[95]

There are regular meetings under the dialogue, and a number of reports have been produced, the most recent in November 2004. This cooperation at intergovernmental level was supplemented during the UK's presidency of the EU in October 2005 by the establishment of a Russia–EU Energy Forum designed to serve as 'an industry-wide platform for the business community to discuss the future of energy cooperation between Russia and EU, its challenges and prospects'.[96] There has, therefore, long been recognition on both sides that energy security is an important issue, and there are a number of ways in which potential problems could be resolved.

The prelude to the dispute that arose in 2006 was the increase in state ownership of Russia's energy resources following the arrest of Mikhail Khodorkovsky, head of Yukos, in 2003 and the subsequent acquisition by the state-owned oil firm Rosneft of Yuganskneftegaz, the largest Yukos asset, in 2004 and of Roman Abramovich's Sibneft by Gazprom in 2005. This consolidated Gazprom's position as a global energy giant and provoked anxiety in Europe and the United States that the Russian government would attempt to use energy as a political lever. Their fears appeared justified when, without any transition period, Gazprom raised the highly subsidized price at which it sold gas to Ukraine to the world price level, thus effectively quadrupling Ukraine's costs. Although there were sound market reasons for the price increase, the timing (mid-winter and at the start of the Ukrainian parliamentary election campaign) and the politicization of the dispute (Putin himself became involved) suggest that the more pro-Western foreign policy pursued by President Yushchenko after the 'Orange Revolution', which included a publicly announced determination to join NATO and the EU, played an important role. When the negotiations with Ukraine broke down, Gazprom cut off Ukraine's gas supply. The pipelines through Ukraine carry 80 per cent of the EU's supplies from Russia to Europe, and during the dispute supply to the EU was briefly disrupted, according to Gazprom, because Ukraine was siphoning off gas.[97] The EU Gas Coordination Group held an emergency meeting to discuss not only security of supplies but also diversification of energy carriers, while both the EU and the US administration called on Russia and Ukraine to resolve the dispute. The European media, by and large, accused Russia of launching a gas war, while remaining silent about Ukraine's role in the dispute.[98]

The implication that Russia was an unreliable supplier provoked a bitter response in Moscow. Prime Minister Mikhail Fradkov sent a message to the EU Council that

> the Ukrainian side, pursuing its selfish ends, deliberately decided to … shift responsibility … to the Russian side … Under the present situation, Russia deems it necessary to confirm its readiness to fulfil undeviatingly all the agreements and contracts with our partners in the European Union … in the interests of strengthening energy security of the continent.[99]

Paradoxically, the Russia–Ukraine gas dispute occurred immediately after a major new project had been agreed between Russia and Germany to build a 1,200 km-long North European Gas Pipeline linking Vyborg in Russia and Greifswald in Germany via the Baltic Sea. Although the pipeline will significantly reduce Russia's dependency for gas transit on Poland and Ukraine, it will increase the EU's dependence on Russian gas, despite the EU's policy debate about the need to diversify EU energy supplies.[100]

The 2006 Russian–Ukrainian gas dispute highlighted what had already become clear when the North European Gas Pipeline deal was announced: on questions of energy, EU member states retain national control and they tend to follow their national interests, even when their national interests conflict with the interests of the EU as a whole or with the interests of other member states. It also demonstrated the fragility of the Russia–EU strategic partnership and the rapidity with which both sides resort during a crisis to rhetoric reminiscent of the Cold War. However, it is a mark of the complexity and multifaceted nature of that relationship that the tensions caused by events in the North Caucasus, the PCA extension issue and the Russian–Ukrainian gas dispute did not prevent progress being made on other fronts. Thus, despite these major difficulties, work continued on formulating the road maps that would lead to the creation of the four common spaces planned at the Russia–EU summit in St Petersburg in May 2003.

4 common space ?

Russian membership of the EU?

Whereas in the course of the 1990s Russian officials, politicians and academic analysts sometimes suggested the possibility in principle of Russia joining the EU, few have seen this as a realistic option in recent years, at least in the foreseeable future. For some, it is simply a question of size: Russia 'will always be too large for Europe'. For others, size *is* a problem, since 'Russia is too huge a country to be able to avoid dominating the European Union if and when it becomes a member'.[101] But a greater problem is the socio-political backwardness of Russia and its low living standards. Were it to apply for membership, it would be rejected and the fear is that, having applied, it would share Turkey's fate of being an 'eternal candidate'.[102] For still others, apart from the fact that Russia cannot meet the Copenhagen criteria, there is the problem that Russian elites would not willingly subordinate themselves to a supranational organization.[103]

Many of the analysts who do not think Russian membership of the EU is feasible argue that Russia should, nevertheless, adopt the EU's norms, rules and principles because this will facilitate its modernization. Moreover, modernization will enable future integration to take place. According to one commentator, 'The integration process will serve as the instrument of Russia's modernization and, at the same time, the success of this stage of modernization will enable Russia to progress further towards integration.'[104] However, it is precisely the expectation that Russia should adopt EU rules and standards that some see as the stumbling block to future relations. The partial loss of sovereignty is difficult for any country, but it is deemed by some experts to be peculiarly difficult for Russia because of its historical traditions and perception of the world.[105] In any case, in the last four years, a new Russia has emerged, which 'does not conform with the existing Europeanization concept, according to which Moscow should gradually adopt the principles suggested by the EU as regards a nation's domestic and foreign policy'.[106] Since Russia is not willing to adjust its policies to EU requirements, the relationship can proceed only if it 'turns into a street with two-way traffic', that is, on the basis of 'norms and rules that have been worked out together'.[107] Because Russia is a great power, it will never 'have its course exclusively set on the European Union … Russia's foreign policy will always be reflective of the global dimension'. Thus, unlike the countries included in the European Neighbourhood Policy (ENP), an initiative first launched in 2003, Russia will never be able to accept the EU's offer of 'all but institutions', nor will the Norwegian or the Swiss models of relations with the EU suit it.[108]

Despite the general agreement that EU membership is impossible in the medium term, a number of analysts and academics believe that it is feasible in the long term, providing Russian democracy continues to develop. Perhaps surprisingly, they include not just those whom we would classify as liberal westernizers, but also some whose views more generally appear closer to pragmatic nationalism.[109]

Whatever their views about Russia's potential membership of the EU, few analysts are satisfied with the PCA, and most argue that when it expires in 2007, it should be replaced by an agreement that reflects Russia's particular status and its unique relationship with the EU, for 'an "advanced partnership" requires the formalization of a full-fledged, legally binding treaty, as opposed to political accords and joint statements regularly issued at Russia–EU summits'.[110] For some, the new agreement should aim at transforming Russia through gradual and consistent integration into the EU. It might be named an Agreement on Special or Advanced Association between Russia and the EU. The word 'special' would signal that this agreement was unlike other association agreements and would indicate due consideration of Russia's importance and status, as well as its role in the termination of the Cold War and in the anti-terrorist coalition.[111] For others, the relationship should be restricted to selective cooperation, enshrined in bilateral treaties and ad hoc agreements in particular sectors, or in the form of a long-term treaty that would provide for close economic and political relations between two mutually independent economic and political actors on the world stage.[112]

Russian officials and politicians are clear that 'Russia has no aim to join the European Union either as a full-fledged or associate member in the near future'.[113] They rarely criticize Russia's current relationship with the EU in public, and neither do they discuss what changes Russia should seek in its relations with the EU when the PCA expires in 2007.

CONCLUSION

Russia has more agreements with the EU than with any other multilateral organization, and the frequency, regularity and intensity of the interactions between the two parties are greater than the contact that Russia has with any other organization. Yet, as we have seen, there is considerable dissatisfaction on both sides with the relationship. A sense of disappointment is reflected in the report on relations with Russia drawn up by the Commission in 2004, which was requested by the European Council because 'relations have ... come under increasing strain with divergence between EU and Russian positions on a number of issues'.[114] Some Russian analysts diagnose the problem as far more severe than strain. The relationship is experiencing 'a systemic crisis'; there is a contradiction between the 'serious divergences in the political sphere and harsh economic competition' and the 'programme of cooperation aimed at the acceptance by Russia of European rules and norms'.[115] The issues that have been discussed in this chapter provide part of the explanation for the deterioration in the relationship since 2000, but there are other, broader factors that undermine the relationship. Some are structural; others derive from the conflicting principles on which the EU and the Russian state operate.

The complexity and inflexibility of the Brussels bureaucracy, on the one hand, combine with the absence in Russia of suitably qualified administrative support or coordinating mechanisms to deal with the EU, on the other, to complicate Russia–EU relations. It is conventional wisdom for EU members themselves, as well as non-members, to complain about the Brussels bureaucracy or the Eurocracy. Russians find fault with 'the rather woolly decision-making procedure that takes place in Brussels'.[116] They cannot understand the inflexibility of the EU and its reluctance to compromise (the insistence that the Schengen system cannot be modified is a case in point). The EU Commission, in turn, finds fault with the inadequacies of the Russian bureaucracy and the lack of coordination within the Russian government. Russian analysts have the same complaint. When they began to analyse what the economic consequences of enlargement would be, for example, they pointed out that there were simply too few experienced negotiators in the Ministry of Trade.[117] Two years later Russian specialists on the EU maintained that '[Russian] policy towards the EU suffers ... from a weakness of bureaucratic support', insisting that 'official bodies engaged in routine interaction with the EU need seriously to improve their work'. They proposed that either an existing institution should be assigned the role of coordinating Russian policy, or a special agency should be established to 'coordinate efforts to work out and advance a single Russian position on all aspects of relations with the European Union'.[118] One reason offered by a Russian specialist on the EU for supporting a simple extension of the PCA in 2007, for example, is that 'the catastrophic shortage of qualified experts, in addition to the marked disunity among government agencies, makes it very difficult to form an efficient task force' to negotiate a new agreement.[119] Two consequences follow from this lack of capacity: first, the Russian government usually confines itself to responding to policy proposals emanating from Brussels and rarely puts forward its own initiatives, which in itself gives rise to complaints about being treated as the 'junior partner'. A second problem is that increasingly during Putin's presidency progress on anything substantive has depended on agreements at very high levels – mini-summits – and these have been infrequent and liable to be hijacked by broader problems in the Russia–EU relationship – that is, by issues of high politics.

Quite apart from not really understanding how the EU works and the shortage of qualified personnel, the marked preference in Russia for bilateral rather than multilateral relations also hampers the Russia–EU relationship as a whole. This preference is compounded by the personal relationships President Putin has established with individual European leaders (for example, Chancellor Gerhard Schröder, President Jacques Chirac and Prime Ministers Tony Blair and Silvio Berlusconi) and by attempts to use these relationships to exploit differences of opinion between member states. Russian experts admit that these relationships have been useful in the past, but warn that they are becoming less and less effective.[120] Schröder and Berlusconi have already lost power, and both Chirac and Blair are at the end of their tenure. In short, Putin has already lost key allies in his bilateral diplomacy, so even if he continues to favour bilateralism, his hand is far weaker than it was a few years ago. But the blame is not entirely on the Russian side. European leaders themselves cultivate these personal relationships 'to take up with Russia bilaterally issues that the union as a whole could or should address', and in the process they sometimes undermine EU policy.[121] The 1999 Common Strategy was intended to ensure harmony between EU and member-state policy towards Russia; recognition that it had not achieved this goal was one reason for undertaking a review of EU policy in 2004. The problem, according to one Western analyst, is that several member states consider Russia to be too important a global player to let the EU lead in relations with it.[122]

A further impediment to deepening relations is the growing hostility on the part of Russia to the intrusive nature of EU policy and to the imposition of Western values and norms. This has been most evident in Russia's resentment of the EU's reaction to Russian policy in Chechnya and the way in which it deals with terrorism, and the belief that the EU and some of its member states have double standards with regard to international terrorism and the status of those whom Russians regard as terrorists. More recently, it has been reflected in the dismissal of European anxiety about the political reforms introduced in the wake of the Beslan siege. The realist-geopolitical school of thought that currently predominates in Russia is increasingly resistant to the EU's attempts to Europeanize Russia through a 'constant striving to enforce its own legislation and standards ... as a condition for cooperation'.[123]

Closely related to the resentment that this engenders is anger, on the Russian side, that the EU is reluctant to treat Russia as a special case, and, conversely, weariness on the part of the EU that Russians expect special treatment. Policies that do not distinguish between Russia and other EU neighbours are particularly offensive to Russians. They were upset, for example, that the EU's Wider Europe–New Neighbourhood initiative in 2003 appeared to put Russia in the same category not only as Belarus and Moldova, but also as the states of North Africa.[124] Chizhov, for example, stated categorically that 'Russia does not regard itself either as an object or a subject of this policy. Our relations with the EU are built on principles of strategic partnership'. In the event, Russia was not included in the European Neighbourhood Policy; instead, Russia and the EU decided to create the four common spaces (see above).[125]

In a review of Russian policy towards the EU conducted by a group of Russian experts and policy-makers in 2004, 'the absence of a strategic vision concerning its place in the pan-European context' was identified as the main problem in Russia–EU relations, and, as a result, 'practical issues (cargo transit, visas, etc.) turn into insurmountable obstacles bordering on crises'.[126] Moreover, Russia frequently attempts to link problems that are not directly connected, which means that 'even relatively simple questions remain unresolved and the potential for escalation rises accordingly'.[127] The absence on both sides of a clear vision of their future relationship is compounded by a shared tendency to adopt broad programmatic schemes, which then have to be filled with content. This is not conducive to a steady incremental growth in the relationship. The Northern Dimension was an early example; the road maps to the four common spaces are the most recent. This leads to what one analyst has called a 'virtualization of cooperation', in other words, 'concealing a lack of substantive content ... under increasingly rich layers of dialogue and cooperation'.[128]

Given the commitment of both sides to maintain the relationship, and the recognition by both of the importance of the other, it is, perhaps, too dramatic to argue that Russia–EU relations are experiencing a 'systemic crisis'. However, the problems discussed in this chapter make it clear that a concerted effort will be required to regain momentum in the relationship.

4

Russian security engagement with the European Union

Roy Allison

As Chapter 3 shows, the Russian leadership has found it difficult to develop a policy of committed engagement with the EU during Putin's presidency and has been involved in testy negotiations with Brussels on a variety of questions. Among these, some progress has been registered in developing common policies that address the soft security concerns of EU states.[1] But this field of cooperation will require long-term efforts and will remain controversial as long as Russia feels the EU should view it as a victim of challenges rather than a source of non-traditional security threats. The difference in approach of the two parties also reflects the instinct and tendency among Russian policy-makers to focus on 'high politics', or geopolitics, and in security terms this means issues that include a military dimension or the projection of power by the state. This chapter assesses the elite debate and dialogue over Russia–EU security engagement at this level as well as the record of and potential for related policy initiatives.

For our analysis several important questions should be kept in mind. Do foreign policy elites and policy-makers in Moscow view Russia–EU interaction over 'high politics' as a channel to draw Russia more broadly into the European mainstream, or at least to overcome politico-security 'dividing lines' in the enlarged Europe? How is this influenced by Russian interpretations of the EU–NATO relationship? If some kind of Russia–EU security partnership were to develop, might this ameliorate the difficulties encountered by the parties over functional low politics issues? Or are there core geopolitical and security policy differences between Russia and the EU, which aggravate the difficulties of low politics and the dissonance of the two sides over norms and values? Why has Russian security engagement with the EU ultimately achieved so little?

The chapter initially assesses the debate in the Russian foreign policy elite over security relations and 'high politics' with the EU as well as Russian interpretations of the difficulties that have frustrated greater cooperation in this field. As with the previous chapter, we rely on published sources and interview materials for this purpose. There follows an analysis of actual policy achievements and future options for the Russia–EU security dialogue, including the Russian responses to the European Security and Defence Policy (ESDP). The chapter then considers the consequences of the formation of the EU's new security neighbourhood to the east after the 2004 enlargement and questions whether a dynamic of geopolitical rivalry is beginning to displace efforts at cooperation in Russia–EU relations. The conclusion identifies a number of serious constraints on the development of a Russia–EU security partnership, which are unlikely to be overcome during Putin's second presidential term.

RUSSIAN ELITE DEBATE

The debate in the Russian foreign policy elite about the EU as a potential security partner has been fluid and based on aspirations and illusions as much as on pragmatic policy. It has been poorly informed and determined by broad preconceptions about the potential and preferences of the EU rather than by any deeper understanding of the nature of the European project. It shows an attraction to 'high politics' and geopolitical categories, even if the Russian leadership and political elite ultimately recognize that the EU is primarily an economic/trade rather than a security actor. For this reason the debate is quite revealing about Russian thinking on options for overcoming 'exclusion' from Europe and deserves the separate attention it receives in this chapter. But few practical proposals for the Russia–EU security dialogue have followed – it often appears to have a virtual character – and it is undoubtedly true that the stuff and substance of practical interaction between Moscow and Brussels is in the area of 'low politics'. Moreover, the Russian foreign policy elite remains sceptical about the defence potential of the ESDP in the period of Putin's presidency, just as it had been sceptical of the Western European Union in the 1990s.[2]

Perspectives on EU–NATO interaction

A key aspect in this Russian debate has been the interpretation of the EU–NATO relationship. Views on the security dimension of the EU have not divided Russian political opinion as distinctly as views on NATO. Indeed, to the extent that greater EU autonomy could be perceived as detracting from the effectiveness of NATO, even fervent Russian nationalists may favour the former. A key link here is the common view in Moscow of the EU as a partner in Russia's long-standing project of developing a pan-European collective security system of some kind. The result is that for much of the Russian political elite, including the upper echelons of the Russian military, 'the degree of the ESDP's autonomy from NATO remains the foremost criterion according to which the compatibility of the ESDP with Russian interests is to be assessed'. The less influence the US (including through NATO) has over the ESDP, the better it is viewed for Russia.[3]

On this issue two broad political trends may be identified from the late 1990s to around 2002. 'Euro-enthusiasts' expected Europe to develop a political and military potential somewhat independent from the US and NATO and argued that Russian interaction with the emerging EU military structures would hopefully push NATO into the background. But other 'alarmists' viewed this outcome with scepticism, or would make Russian cooperation with these structures conditional on the ESDP's radical break with NATO, to prevent the EU's security potential becoming 'an appendix to NATO's military machine'. Another perspective is associated with those who approve of Russia prioritizing its relations with NATO and the US, and oppose Russia's cooperation with the ESDP because this is seen as being against NATO and the US. Paradoxically, therefore, this brings strongly anti-NATO Russians and pro-NATO activists into the same camp.[4]

Given that the membership of neither the EU nor NATO has been static, Russian elites could also understand the EU (previously in the form of the WEU) as the incarnation of an alternative project in Europe to that of NATO enlargement. This is expressed in a 'European' rather than a 'transatlantic' definition of military interactions within the continent. This could give rise to an exaggerated image of a future 'united Europe' with a fully-fledged military structure or 'European army', since many Russian commentators were unaware that in essence ESDP meant creating crisis management instruments rather than shifting from national to 'European' means of ensuring military security. On the other hand, Russian debates could also result in an alternative approach, with implicit warnings on the eventual implications of the 'militarization of the EU'.[5] This could shade into the fear that an independent European military capacity would represent an existential threat to Russia's interests.

However, much of this debate appeared increasingly surreal or dated during Putin's first term as President and into the second term. It is premised on the assumption that Russia has a realistic option of promoting its relations with the EU at the expense of NATO's role in Europe, and that the EU faces a choice between Russia and the US/NATO. But the belief that Russia can play to any significant extent on transatlantic contradictions rests on a distorted assessment of NATO and the strength of transatlantic ties. It has become even less realistic or relevant with Putin's gradual rapprochement with NATO and strategic focus on the US, which wins cautious approval from many Russian pragmatic nationalists. At the same time Putin's pro-European official position, as a parallel track, has had a disorienting effect on political loyalists in Moscow. Nonetheless, in this period of flux, several contrasting positions can be identified in Russian debate on the security dimension of the EU.

Liberal Westernizers

The belief that Russia should adopt a long-term strategy of joining the EU, including an appropriate security partnership, comes naturally to those liberal Westernizers who do not see Russia as facing a choice between the EU and the US/NATO. Convergence with the West is to be grounded on Western norms and integration with Euro-Atlantic institutions, resulting in a Euro-Atlantic security community, including a Russia-within-Europe, perhaps institutionalized at a high level by an EU–Russia Council.[6] From this perspective transatlantic differences over strategic culture and international order, highlighted by the Iraq war, are not considered to be fundamental. But this extent of association with Western values, and even the suggestion that a Russian–Western security community could develop eventually, is definitely a minority perspective in Russian elite thinking under Putin.

Liberals are prone to identify a wide field of potential military interaction for Russia–EU relations.[7] One proposal is that the EU should create a new organizational structure devoted to the threat of 'super-terrorism', under which ESDP could be developed and EU rapid reaction forces adapted to the new threats. This structure should then have close diplomatic contacts with the US and Russia. At the same time it is accepted that the Russian armed forces are not ready to cooperate effectively with European forces in counter-terrorist operations,[8] although this is no reason to retard Russia–EU security ties more broadly. Alexei Arbatov, then deputy chairman of the Duma Defence Committee, argued in 2003 that Russia will be unable to undertake a deep military reform in the long term without the EU, which is necessary for defending the security and territorial integrity of the country in the south and east. The EU, in turn, he argues, will be unable to become an independent military superpower in the long term without Russia.[9]

A Euro-Atlantic orientation, liberals understand, is inconsistent with CIS-focused Eurasianism. Many in Russian political, business and intellectual circles consider that for better or worse a policy of integration with other CIS states is incompatible with one of integration with the EU in the four 'common spaces', including close coordination in foreign policy and security activities.[10] But some liberals have become sceptical over the aim of integration with the EU. The views of 'liberal westernizers' shade into more 'realist' perspectives on potential Russian cooperation with the EU, downplaying normative convergence while still favouring a high level of strategic partnership between Russia and the EU. Those Russians who favour this outcome have been disconcerted, however, by the EU's 'wider Europe' and 'European Neighbourhood Policy' approach to countries east of the enlarged EU zone. They criticize this approach for downgrading Russia as a specific object of EU attention in favour of a broad approach to stability among EU neighbour states and as a result weakening the case of the pro-EU lobby in Moscow.

Pragmatic nationalists

Pragmatic nationalists include those in the elite who follow Putin's lead, and favour the practical, military-technical approach of cooperation with Western states through the NATO–Russia Council (NRC) over the ambivalence and potentially unwelcome conditionality of the ESDP. Like Putin they still accept the importance of overall cooperation with the EU, to the extent possible on Russian terms, and in this sense have a pro-European orientation. But they reject any partnership with the EU based on normative convergence as an infringement of Russian sovereignty and expect a clear strategy to protect Russian interests on matters ranging from Kaliningrad to Chechnya.

At the same time Russia's geopolitical interest in limiting the consolidation of the US as a 'unilateral power' is viewed as a compelling reason for Russia to work alongside an EU 'that acts as a more powerful and efficient partner [than before] in foreign and security policy areas'. Some analysts argue that, notwithstanding the tight links between the EU and NATO, the formation of an independent European crisis management capacity will result in another centre of political influence in the world, and this is seen as desirable since it contributes to the Russian goal of multipolarity.[11]

But such multipolarity is not a synonym for crude international wedge-driving. Russia is considered to benefit from working with an EU that has growing security capabilities, irrespective of whether Russian official policy is one of 'Europe first' (the formal position for much of Putin's first presidential term) or of 'America first' (the traditional Russian position that had reasserted itself by Putin's second presidential term). Russian interests, it is argued, require cooperation rather than a deepening of disagreements in the transatlantic relationship, because of the need to work in common, including with Russia, against new threats. Against this background, it is suggested, an EU–Russia Security Council should be formed that would be located within the framework of a broader security alliance based on the G-8. This body could coordinate policies on weapons of mass destruction (WMD), terrorism and various soft security challenges.[12]

These elite figures are mostly doubtful, however, that security interaction with the EU will actually address Russia's wider security challenges or even be particularly helpful in combating terrorism. But they favour developing a dialogue in this field for a modicum of geopolitical balancing, and if this assists the technocratic goal of the modernization of Russia and offers some assistance with soft security challenges, then so much the better.

One prominent analyst, for example, doubts that in the foreseeable future the EU will be able to develop armed forces comparable with those of the US. But the central dilemma is that 'Russia is a European country, but not a contemporary European country'. For this reason he views it as necessary 'to modernize Russia through Europeanization in all spheres, including military reform'.[13] The deputy chairman of the Security Committee of the Duma, for his part, favours an agreement with Europol against organized crime. But he urges cooperation with the EU in this field to be set in the broader context of cooperation with other regional structures such as the CIS and its subsidiary Collective Security Treaty Organization.[14]

If not much positive is expected from the security aspect of the EU, from this centrist elite position, not much negative is feared either. Duma deputies from both the United Russia Party and the Communist Party do not consider the ESDP to be a threat or to present problems for Russia. The only worry of one member of the CPRF fraction with a security background was that 'if the EU engages in peacekeeping it should be even-handed', for example between the Serbs and Albanians in Kosovo.[15] This reflects broader worries (see below) about the possible future use of EU rapid reaction forces.

Fundamentalist nationalists

More alarmist perceptions of security engagement with the EU still exist, however, within the Russian political elite. Some still fear that the ESDP will be an appendix of, or directly controlled by, NATO. This is a natural response for those who still believe it is impossible to separate the EU and NATO, since 'they are two sides of the same thing', with all the negative consequences of EU enlargement that this implies.[16] Alternatively, there is anxiety that an independent European military potential would be an existential challenge to Russian interests. Moreover, for 'Eurasianists' or proponents of a Russian CIS-focused policy, warnings are heard that the ESDP might interfere in what they would define as Russia's exclusive zone of interest and influence.[17] Many senior Russian military officers share this outlook.

Nevertheless, the initial response of some trenchantly nationalist Russian generals to the EU decision in 1999 to develop a rapid reaction force of 60,000 troops was one of cautious interest. Russia could consider cooperation with the EU force, it was emphasized, only if this force is created with a goal of reducing and not augmenting NATO's role in Europe.[18] Hopes rose among some Russian officers that the ESDP might advance the goal of an all-European collective security system at the expense of transatlantic ties. In early 2001 the Russian Ministry of Defence proposed joint conceptual work, joint operations and military-industrial cooperation with the EU. This moment of opportunity passed, since the EU stalled on this dialogue when new post-9/11 imperatives came to the fore.

More recently Russian military views have displayed a basic lack of knowledge about what the ESDP has to offer, traditional institutional conservatism and fear of pressures for greater transparency. Officers are aware that Russia would have to carry out a radical reform of its armed forces before meaningful cooperation with the EU over crisis management could happen.[19] The chairman of the Defence Committee of the Duma tried to turn the tables on the EU in December 2004, accusing most EU countries of being 'apprehensive of the military and political rapprochement with Russia'. He complained of conditions and restrictions placed on Russia in EU initiatives that excluded Russia from taking part in the process of 'European military construction ... on an equal footing' and 'prevented the rate of cooperation with the EU exceeding that with NATO'.[20] To explain how Russian officials have reached this rather pessimistic view, we need to assess the nature of the Russia–EU security dialogue and also the extent of progress on the agenda for security cooperation since 2001.

POLICY ACHIEVEMENTS AND FUTURE POTENTIAL

The Russia–EU security dialogue

Sceptics of EU procedures could view the Russia–EU security dialogue as over-institutionalized, as heavy on process and light on substance. The potential benefits of habituation from meetings that are more frequent than EU interaction with any other third party should not be dismissed. But there is no evidence that this in itself can help create a common security culture or foster a sense of security community between two such different actors, even in the long term. Indeed, the tangible policy achievements of this dialogue during the period of Putin's presidency are rather meagre. This suggests that regular Russia–EU institutional interaction may help sustain an illusion of activity.

In addition to semi-annual summits, the two sides hold consultations on security and defence matters between the EU Political and Security

Committee – the COPS troika, the principal EU body vested with security decision-making – and the Russian ambassador in Brussels. This includes a monthly meeting with COPS officials, which appears to have worked comparatively well. Expert-level discussions on issues of disarmament and arms control also occur. Since May 2002 meetings have been held between the EU Military Committee chairman and officers from the Russian Ministry of Defence, and Russia has a liaison officer attached to the EU Military Staff.

The formation of a Permanent Partnership Council (PPC) in May 2003 (replacing the Cooperation Council) was intended to reinforce official interactions, but this did not meet for a year and still does not seem effective. Significantly, the EU has rejected Russian suggestions for the formation of an EU–Russia Council that would mirror the NRC. After the decision to establish EU–COPS monthly meetings Putin anticipated that it would be 'a prototype for the setting up of a permanently operating body to deal with the security issues … of the world, not least Russia and a united Europe'.[21] But the EU has been unwilling to offer Russia regular and institutionalized influence on the ESDP project.[22] In essence, it believes that decisions on ESDP are to be taken by the member states and not by external partners, irrespective of their geographic scope or 'great power' self-perception. This is fundamental to understanding the tentative nature of the security dialogue and helps explain why so little has been accomplished since Russia first proposed in May 2002 the creation of a 'Russia–EU Action Plan' in the field of ESDP.

It is true that the broad goal of such security policy interaction is now agreed: a common Space of Cooperation in the field of External Security. This would cover strengthened dialogue on the international scene; combating terrorism; cooperation on the non-proliferation of WMD; cooperation in crisis management; and cooperation over civil protection. The plan was mandated by the May 2003 EU–Russia summit in St Petersburg, at which Brussels agreed to the Russian objective of working towards the creation of four common spaces to achieve a united Europe. A 'road map' of actions to achieve objectives under the common space of external security was proclaimed at the May 2005 EU–Russia summit in Moscow.[23] But so far not much has been done to implement this aspiration.

The various dimensions of the security dialogue can be summarized as follows.[24]

Foreign policy coordination

The attempts of Russia and the EU to coordinate broad foreign policy positions, in particular on the Balkans and the Middle East, have included various security questions. During the Putin presidency the EU has taken the lead on developing joint statements on the Balkans, while cooperation over the Middle East has been greater and more even-handed.[25] However, Russia–EU discussions on political means to resolve the Iraq crisis early in 2003 had little effect.[26] Iran has been discussed, for example in the PPC meeting in April 2005, but EU and Russian positions have diverged on how far to press Tehran over its nuclear programme. The EU is likely to continue to seek to influence Russian policy towards the conflicts in Moldova and the South Caucasus, but this has achieved meagre results so far and may become entangled with efforts to advance the EU New Neighbourhood Policy (see below).

Russia–EU statements on conflicts further afield, such as the India–Pakistan conflict, have been made but have not so far resulted in any cooperative efforts. In the future, however, to the extent that the EU seeks to develop a more active global role, efforts may be made to coordinate policies with Russia in Asia, since Russia is not only a European but also an Asian power. Potentially this could become a core element in bonding the EU and Russia. If Russia's proximity to China as a rising power causes increasing uneasiness in Moscow from a geopolitical point of view, then such anxiety could be reduced in the next few years through deeper structural cooperation with the EU and a more profound security-political orientation to the western part of the Eurasian landmass. But as of 2006 this outcome remains open to conjecture.

EU conflict prevention and crisis management operations

Despite its importance, little progress has been registered in this field. In October 2001, Russia and the EU agreed to set up an 'urgent interaction channel' to handle crises.[27] The two sides subsequently exchanged documents on concepts of conflict prevention and crisis management. In early 2002 the Russian Ministry of Defence offered the EU detailed proposals for joint work on crisis management, with an emphasis on joint planning and possible multinational peace support units. In June 2002, the EU in turn elaborated the modalities for Russian forces to participate in EU crisis management operations. Provision is made for consultations with Russia, but Russian participation is envisaged as no more than an input to an operation that is designed and led by the EU.[28] Russia will not have a place in the initial decision-making forum. This deflated Russian expectations of equal decision-making in the planning and implementation of operations. Instead, the EU Military Staff, in charge of operational guidance, offers some military coordination for crisis management with Russia, particularly in the field of joint planning and civil emergency operations.

Russia agreed to only a nominal involvement in the EU Police Mission in Bosnia and Herzegovina which commenced in January 2003 (the EU's role in the Balkans was enhanced by the handover of peacekeeping forces to the EU in Macedonia in March 2003 and in Bosnia in December 2004, and by progress to realize its Headline Goal of forming a 60,000-strong EU rapid reaction corps by 2007). The minimalist Russian role in this mission was much publicized, but it remains a unique case of such cooperation. Moscow has declined the EU invitation to take part in several other peacekeeping and policing operations and warned that 'our response to subsequent proposals will be the same unless we agree on an acceptable format'.[29] Further east beyond the Balkans in CIS regions, Russia expects a format that allows it to retain a dominant position; it has conceded no more than a possible EU input into Russian-led operations in the CIS regions (see below).

Apart from the impasse over the format of Russian involvement in EU crisis management operations, it is difficult to conceive of Russia having more than a peripheral role in future operations of this kind without a major overhaul of the Russian military system – a challenge that applies equally to peacekeeping operations under the NRC. It is fair to conclude that 'in its present form and quality, this system allows for very limited and often mutually frustrating cooperation'.[30]

Another area for potential cooperation is civilian crisis management. In 2003 the Russian Ministry of Emergency Situations offered the EU a concept for this. But the EU has failed to develop such concepts of its own to feed into a possible joint conceptual framework. The momentum of this process has now fallen behind the parallel NATO–Russia dialogue in the NRC. A Russian proposal for the establishment of a Pan-European Centre for Disaster Management, formally proposed in April 2003, is similarly being eclipsed by dialogue in the NRC on the 'consequence management' of major incidents.[31] However, the Russian Ministry of Emergency Situations, which has acquired considerable experience, could offer a role beyond the proposal for a disaster management centre. The EU envisages a broad approach to conflict management, employing 'soft' instruments beyond purely political-military means. But political and conceptual problems arise again if the trajectory of Russian domestic development does not suggest Russia–EU convergence in relevant laws and regulations.

Combating terrorism

Common interests provide the basis for practical cooperation in combating terrorism. By 2004 Russia presented this as a cornerstone of Russia–EU cooperation in creating the 'common spaces' for external and internal security.[32] Since October 2001 Russia and the EU have been committed to exchange information on terrorist activities and networks; not to allow such groups on their territories; and to block the financial sources for terrorism.[33] An agreement between EUROPOL and Russia is intended to provide for the exchange of technical and strategic information. An offshoot of these activities is Russia–EU cooperation against organized crime, which could build on a joint action plan in 2000 to combat organized crime in the Russian Federation. However, so far progress on the ground against such crime has been limited and Russia still complains that the two sides lack legal provisions on the methods and conditions of cooperation over anti-terrorism.[34]

A significant difficulty arises from the EU's rejection of Russia's definition of its role in the Chechnya conflict simply as counter-terrorism. Chechnya is particularly controversial, since it intersects Russian national security strategy and the normative dimension in Russia–EU relations. For the EU, especially the European Parliament, Chechnya is not just an 'internal affair' to Russia, since violations of human rights are viewed as threats to international security. An impasse on this core issue has soured dialogue more broadly, as shown by Putin's reaction in autumn 2004 to the Beslan siege and acrimonious Russian attacks against the initial EU response to that crisis. Russia demanded that the EU should adopt 'an unconditional application of uniform standards in the struggle against terrorism'.[35] This dispute in the first place constrains Russia–EU coordination against transnational terrorism. But it also confirms that Russia is most unlikely during Putin's second presidential term to be willing to involve the EU and other European organizations in sponsoring a political settlement and post-conflict reconstruction in Chechnya.

At the same time the possible horizontal escalation of instability among republics and regions in the North Caucasus increases the gravity of a variety of non-traditional security risks and their potential impact on the enlarged EU zone. The EU cannot address such spillover effects without fully engaging Russia. Indeed, the stability of Russia itself has to be a basic goal built into EU interaction with Russia, and this should be clearly understood on the Russian side, contrary to the conspiracy theories of some Russian politicians.

Nuclear and other WMD risks

The EU, like NATO, has to counteract new security risks over the coming decade, which requires an agenda of cooperation with Russia, even if this is undertaken outside the established ESDP framework. WMD proliferation, and the potential links between this and 'hyper-terrorism', have emerged as a key American national security priority and are at least a significant security concern for the EU. This brings new urgency to a cooperation framework in the spheres of nuclear safety and disarmament agreed between Russia and the EU, as well as to the implementation of the Chemical Weapons Convention (CWC).

EU funding has also supported a Cooperation Programme for Non-Proliferation and Disarmament in the Russian Federation since 1999. Its focus on enhancing nuclear safeguards in Russia (especially safe storage of highly enriched uranium) has been quite successful. It has also explored options for the disposal of nuclear materials, especially plutonium, and dealing with decaying Russian nuclear submarines. Progress here has been slow because of a lack of will (partly since, for the EU, these are more local matters and less likely to be connected to terrorism) and funding shortages.[36] Since June 2002, EU programmes for securing Russian WMD materials and infrastructure have been part of the G-8-led Global Partnership Against the Spread of Weapons and Material of Mass Destruction. This includes an agreement signed in May 2003, though tellingly only after five years of negotiation, establishing a multilateral legal framework for nuclear-related projects carried out by Western countries in north-west Russia.[37]

Military-technical cooperation

Already in 2000 Russian leaders hoped to take part in equipping European forces with hardware such as artillery systems and helicopters as well as in joint scientific and research projects.[38] Limited progress in this field has frustrated Russian military industries hoping for contracts to revive their fortunes.[39] Russia, as well as Ukraine, has offered to remedy the EU deficit in strategic airlift, and Russia–EU joint statements ritually refer to the exploration of cooperation over long-haul air transport. However, the European decision to create an independent European capability in the form of the A-400M aircraft has effectively shelved the Russian offer. The EU has also shown limited interest in using Russian military-relevant satellite imaging for ESDP purposes, despite Moscow's proposals to complement Russian and EU assets in this field.

ESDP as a challenge for Russia?[40]

The Russian leadership regards the European Security and Defence Policy with scepticism and some apprehension. This response reflects a variety of concerns. Ideally, Russia views ESDP as a channel to strengthen its standing and capabilities as a front-rank security actor in Europe. But Russia seeks clarity about the geographical scope and nature of the operations that could be advanced under ESDP and hopes for assurances that such operations would be mandated by the UN and OSCE, where a Russian veto could be wielded on undesirable options for the use of force. These constraints are not acceptable to an EU that is in a phase of seeking to broaden its scope for independent action on peace support and crisis management. Consequently, the NATO–Russia Council, with its Russian membership and equality on decision-making in various areas, as outlined previously, can outbid EU security structures for Russian attention.

Indeed, even after the EU has developed its rapid reaction corps and has arrived at a unified decision, it will always be up to the NATO allies to approve the use of these means for EU-initiated actions. Hence it is reasonable for Russia to conclude, given progress in the NRC, that the options for EU–Russia security and defence cooperation are better explored in a general context of Russia–NATO relations and rapprochement. Moscow might gain some influence in an EU operation through the NRC. Russia could even consider the idea of trilateral NATO–EU–Russia cooperation in crisis management, although the modalities of this have not been discussed on an official level. Anyway, the apparent failure of the Berlin–Paris axis (and Russia's flirtation with this axis) to stop the US and its coalition partners from waging war in Iraq could suggest the inherent weakness of the Europeans to the Russian leadership and further discourage Moscow from taking ESDP seriously.[41] This is implied by Putin's reinforced focus on the US as the primary strategic actor, certainly on issues of military security, since at least summer 2003. It confirms the general point argued by Western analysts of the ESDP, that 'although Putin might be a European at heart, his head seems to be Atlanticist'.[42]

At core Russia and the EU are divided in their interpretation of the remit and objectives of ESDP. For Moscow ESDP should provide 'a model of European security that ensures Moscow an equal voice on all European security issues and more broadly serves as an instrument to create a greater Europe', the common European security space. But for the EU the ESDP is simply a limited instrument of EU foreign policy. In considering its involvement in ESDP operations, Russia seeks optimally to obtain equality with EU members states at every level of decision-making. But the EU cannot countenance this objective.[43] This creates an impasse that may well prevent the two sides from reaching an agreement on a joint conceptual framework for peace support.

Given these differences, despite the EU's military weakness relative to the US and NATO, Russia is concerned that even without a UN mandate EU rapid reaction forces could be projected some 4,000 km around Europe. This would enable them to reach areas of direct Russian interest, such as Transdniestria or Abkhazia, or further afield in the South Caucasus and Central Asia. After discussions with Russia in April 2004, EU Commission President Romano Prodi noted that 'the EU is interested in more active cooperation with Russia in order to reach a lasting settlement to the smouldering conflicts of the Dniester region and the North Caucasus'.[44] Putin himself has described Chechnya as 'a smouldering conflict with constant casualties'.[45] In this context, despite the present EU focus on peacekeeping in the Balkans, Moscow is wary that EU crisis management in the future could focus on Russian 'internal affairs' or on the territory of Ukraine and Belarus, as well as long-standing frozen conflicts in CIS states.

Moscow may calculate that the dissension between major EU states revealed by the Iraq war and continuing weaknesses in the capability of the ESDP make these scenarios of EU intervention in CIS states less probable. But Russian officials understand that deficiencies in ESDP military means could be offset by the ability of the EU in principle to borrow NATO assets and capabilities for crisis management, as agreed between the two institutions at the end of 2002.[46] So Russia is likely to hold firm in its opposition to the concept of humanitarian intervention, which it portrays as Eurocentric and as an illegitimate justification for NATO's previous Kosovo operation in 1999, and to work to de-link it from dialogue with the EU on crisis management. Apart from this, Russian responses to ESDP are likely to continue to reflect a defensive attitude towards the growing EU interest in its new security neighbourhood to the east.

THE EUROPEAN UNION'S NEW SECURITY NEIGHBOURHOOD

Russian suspicions over the geographic remit of ESDP crisis management relate to broader questions about Russian interest in ensuring stability in the 'wider Europe', what some in Europe have termed a new 'grey zone' or the 'new Eastern Europe' formed of Ukraine, Belarus and Moldova. The enlarged EU has acquired new borders with Russia, Belarus and Ukraine; following the accession of Romania and Bulgaria in 2007, EU borders will extend to Moldova and the Black Sea. EU enlargement, therefore, brings the EU new border management problems, a new proximity, including a new security neighbourhood, which overlaps with Russia's security neighbourhood, in part of what Moscow has traditionally viewed as the 'CIS space'. Russia is not prepared to accept this placidly as a new stage in European development, defined by EU thinking on 'fuzzy' states and multi-level interactions, played out through regional and sub-regional linkages as well as action plans with the EU. Rather, it is viewed as the basis of an alarming competition between zones or spheres of influence, where the EU and Russia represent different poles of attraction and offer different integration processes.

Such traditional Russian security thinking has little common ground with official efforts by the EU to formulate its policy towards non-accession countries to the east. The European Security Strategy, adopted in December 2003, proposes that the EU should try to form a belt of well-governed countries on its periphery.[47] This reflects an approach of 'preventive engagement' beyond the borders of the enlarged EU and is conceptually related to the EU's 'Wider Europe–Neighbourhood' framework. The latter represented the first attempt by the EU to develop a policy towards its new eastern neighbourhood (and included the possibility of EU engagement in crisis management and even 'internal security arrangements' in the new neighbours).[48] It was presented in March 2003, modified into the European Neighbourhood Policy (ENP) and approved by the EU Council in June 2004. The overarching aim of ENP is to foster closer relations with a broad group of regional countries – Russia, Ukraine, Belarus, Moldova, as well as states of the South Caucasus and the southern Mediterranean – to support their stability and development through national action plans.

This approach, however, which has mainly been driven by the EU Commission, spreads EU policy thin across a diverse range of countries and many functional issues, and its premises appear inconsistent with those of a Russia–EU strategic partnership between equals. It is also unclear how the ENP is expected to relate geographically to the Common Space of External Security signed up to by Russia and the EU.

Crucially, Moscow has been dismissive of the Wider Europe concept and has rejected participation in the ENP. Russian Deputy Foreign Minister Vladimir Chizhov observed that 'one can well understand the desire of the EU to set up around its border a "near abroad" that is amicably disposed and maximally oriented towards its own, that is EU, standards'. But he compared this to Soviet aims after the Second World War and advised the EU to avoid a repetition of past mistakes. The main Russian worry appears to be the EU's potential to act as a revisionist force in its 'new neighbourhood' at the expense of Russia, including through greater involvement in conflict resolution. Although Chizhov accepted the need for 'joint' Russia–EU actions to safeguard security in Europe, he referred pointedly to the persistence of long-standing conflicts 'in Transdniestria and Northern Ireland, Transcaucasia and the Basque Country'.[49] The wish to intervene in the often 'tortuous processes' of resolving such conflicts, he claimed, 'can only increase the risk of their aggravation'. Russian policy, he noted, assumes also that the ENP does not contravene 'integration processes in the CIS'.[50]

Moldova/Transdniestria and the South Caucasus

Chizhov's warnings were for the EU to mind its own affairs rather than those of the Russian backyard. However, the EU feels compelled to remain proactive over unresolved conflicts in its new security neighbourhood to mitigate their effects on the EU zone. In particular, the unrecognized republic of

Transdniestria, which borders Ukraine and Moldova proper, is viewed as a deeply criminalized territory and source of festering soft security challenges on the future EU perimeter.[51] Clashing Russian and EU concepts for the settlement of the Moldova/Transdniestria frozen conflict came to a head at the OSCE meeting in Maastricht in December 2003. Russia accused the EU of intervening to sink its own settlement plan associated with Putin's envoy Dmitry Kozak (which would effectively have transformed Moldova into a confederation). The disenchantment this left on both sides diminished the likelihood of a common position being forged in the OSCE over this conflict during Putin's second presidential term.[52]

In December 2004 the EU Commission revealed a proposed ENP Action Plan for Moldova, which is framed in terms of a 'strategic partnership' and presents support for a viable solution to the Transdniestria problem as a key objective.[53] The following April, after a visit to Moldova by the EU's newly appointed Special Representative for the country, hopes rose among EU states that the EU–Russia summit in May could advance the process of conflict resolution, particularly in Transdniestria.[54] But the issue resulted in dissension rather than bridge-building. The road map for the Common Space for External Security formalized at the summit papered over the dispute. It agreed rather vaguely on the need for enhanced 'dialogue and cooperation in the settlement of regional conflicts, inter alia in regions adjacent to EU and Russian borders'.[55] But the testy relations of the two sides on this issue were reflected in the assertion of Konstantin Kosachev, the chairman of the Duma Committee on International Affairs, that Moscow had 'rejected all attempts by the EU to change the settlement formats of the so-called "frozen conflicts" on post-Soviet territory'.[56]

Russian officials seem reluctantly ready to accept some role for the EU as a mediator in the Transdniestria problem and more willing for the EU to assume the principal responsibility for post-conflict reconstruction here.[57] But they still cannot countenance an EU peacekeeping operation on the ground in the region, or in Abkhazia, the other breakaway republic and unresolved conflict on the western periphery of the 'CIS space' (on the Georgian Black Sea coast).[58] The same applies to the Nagorno-Karabakh frozen conflict.

As an alternative, Russian officials have suggested the possibility of an EU contribution (possibly in civilian personnel or as a civil-police mission) to a Russia-led operation in the CIS. This would preserve Russia's assumed role as the security manager among CIS states, while offering the EU a limited peace support or post-conflict stabilization role. But even this would require an agreement on the modalities of such a combined operation – with all the problems noted above that this entails.[59] The mainstream Russian view remains firmly that Moscow's regional interests, role and influence endow it with the main responsibility for peacekeeping in the post-Soviet area, while the EU should take the lead position in peacekeeping in the Balkans. Such a division, a specialist argues, 'could increase the interest of the actors in cooperating and compel them to avoid "prohibited zones" for developing partnership'.[60]

This zonal approach is wholly inconsistent with the assumptions of the ENP and the changing political dynamics of the EU enlargement process. It is true that in practice the EU has been reluctant to become directly involved in conflict resolution in the South Caucasus, not least because this could serve to displace the OSCE and UN role in the region. However, Russia's growing criticism of the OSCE as a security provider may eventually force a reassessment of this restraint and result in proposals to triangulate the roles of the EU, Russia and international organizations. A specialist discussion on the need for the EU to adopt a long-term political approach to affect the climate and conditions of conflict settlement talks for the South Caucasus has already begun.[61]

Nevertheless, the continued caution of the EU was reflected in its response to an appeal by the Georgian Foreign Minister in March 2005 for the EU to replace the suspended OSCE monitoring mission on the Georgian–Russian border with a NATO or EU monitoring mission. The Russian Foreign Ministry flatly rejected this proposal, describing it as an effort 'to act as a sort of barrier between Georgia and Russia'.[62] After the EU–Russia summit in May, Javier Solana, the EU High Representative for the Common Foreign and Security Policy, confirmed that 'we are not planning, not even discussing, the possibility of sending our soldiers to any country'. In fact the EU offered only to help train Georgian police security forces and border guards 'so that they can adequately stand up to the threat of terrorism'.[63] Since Georgia has been concerned about potential Russian 'preventive strikes', this EU role could still draw the EU into Russian–Georgian border tensions. More optimistically, however, the EU decision indicates the potential for EU–Russia cooperation on common soft security threats in their shared neighbourhood. Definitions of terrorism in the Caucasus could make this a controversial field for joint work. But common ground should be possible, for example, over combating illegal drug trafficking or managing migration.

An 'Eastern Dimension' for EU policy

EU policy towards its new security neighbourhood is significantly influenced by the political dynamics of enlargement. As with NATO enlargement, EU enlargement has brought into the fold new members, the Baltic states and Poland in particular, which believe that a resurgence of the Russian threat is possible and that this would have an immediate impact on them. These seek to influence the general EU perception of Russia and may be attempti to divert the EU both from a priority and specific strategy for Russia and from the concept of Russia–EU strategic partnership.

Poland especially has had an active role in seeking to develop an 'Eastern Dimension' for the Common Foreign and Security Policy, loosely modelled on the latter's Northern Dimension (see previous chapter) and intended to promote stability, security and prosperity in four states: Ukraine, Belarus, Moldova and Russia.[64] Poland has been committed to a networking conception of regional cooperation. At the same time, it seeks to maintain some kind of dividing line between Europe and 'non-Europe' with clear geopolitical and hard security connotations.[65] In this context Warsaw questions the solidity of Russia's European credentials and aims at 'democratizing' and 'Europeanizing' the post-Soviet lands located between Russia and the EU's eastern borders. This approach has two key prongs: bringing Ukraine closer to the EU and promoting regime change in Belarus. The Polish interest in this policy is likely to be reinforced under the nationalist Polish leadership elected in parliamentary and presidential polls during September and October 2005.

Hard security issues per se are not part of the Polish initiative for an EU 'Eastern Dimension' and Russia is unprepared to develop an action plan with the EU under the ENP. However, the longer-term impact of the existence of a bloc of EU countries sceptical about privileging cooperation with Russia is not clear. Russian specialists scorn their likely efforts in the EU to gain dividends 'due to their status of "pseudo-frontline" territories', but predict that, to Russia's discontent, they 'may attempt to act as the "lawyers" of the CIS countries in Wider Europe'.[66] In point of fact, the impact of this kind of activism by Poland or the Baltic states in the EU's eastern neighbourhood will be limited if it is not rooted in some kind of EU common strategy for the region, and this has yet to emerge.

Russian evaluations of the emerging East European geopolitical landscape tend to be sweeping and gloomy. By 2004 some Russian analysts argued bluntly that for many in Europe 'the dividing line between integrable and unintegrable spaces lies along Russia's western border', which explains the EU's readiness to develop a project in the western part of the CIS to decrease Russia's influence in Belarus, Moldova and Ukraine. This is consistent, it is claimed, with discussions initiated by the EU 'about the demarcation of the Ukrainian–Russian border and the establishment of a tougher border regime there'.[67] Moscow has criticized Ukraine for devoting too much attention to fortifying its borders with Russia and Belarus. In spring 2006 Russian officials also openly opposed the enforcement of a border and customs regime agreed between Ukraine and Moldova, with strong EU plies to the Transdniester sector of the border between [68] Any comparisons between the Ukrainian–Russian and l European border regimes are bound to be controver- to read grand geopolitical designs into practical issues of nt. Indeed, many in Russia believe that Ukraine's strategy and its interest in the 'Eastern Dimension' initiative, are linked to a policy of maintaining closer relations to those countries that are more critical of Russia. As a result, Ukraine is viewed as an instrument in the strategic weakening of Russia and its distancing from the EU.

In practice, for more than ten years Ukraine has been developing security relationships with its western neighbours and this is reflected in the stability of their joint border. This does not mean that Ukraine can escape the security procedures associated with the extension of the Schengen *acquis* to the external border of the EU.[69] However, the election of Viktor Yushchenko as President of Ukraine in December 2004 has generated political pressure on the EU to go beyond the ENP and find ways of engaging Ukraine and providing more substance to the EU post-enlargement regional policy.

Kiev has also upgraded its diplomatic campaign to persuade the EU to accept that Ukraine would be eligible for EU membership once it has met the Copenhagen criteria. This makes Russian leaders uneasy, since it indicates that Ukraine is distancing itself from Moscow's preferred policy of 'Russia and Ukraine together to Europe' and that Ukraine's EU choice clearly has priority over the Russian-promoted Single Economic Space. The latter attempt to draw Russia, Ukraine, Belarus and Kazakhstan into a common association is considered by Kiev to be geopolitically as much as economically motivated. President Putin has affirmed that 'if Ukraine wants to join the EU, if it is admitted to the EU, we could only rejoice'.[70] But he knows that this is a distant prospect, if feasible at all, predicting that 'it will not even be on the agenda' for the next 15–25 years.[71]

More uncertain is the Russian reaction if Ukraine under Yushchenko were to bid to establish significantly closer links with the ESDP, especially if Russia's own security engagement with the EU were to stagnate.[72] It would be easy for Moscow to perceive this in geopolitical terms even if Ukraine's interest were to be primarily in cooperation over a range of soft security issues, not least because Russia is sensitive to Ukraine's parallel relationship with NATO. Responding to speculation about overtures between NATO and Ukraine under a Yushchenko presidency, Russian Foreign Minister Sergei Lavrov warned against the idea of building 'a new wall between the eastern border of Ukraine, so to say, and what lies on the other side of that wall in the east'. He described this as a 'relapse into Cold War thinking'.[73] Given Ukraine's growing affiliation with NATO, Russia's evolving policy could confirm Ukraine as an object of competition between Russia and Western institutions, which could frustrate further progress in Russia's security dialogue with NATO and the EU.

CONCLUSION

Little substantive Russia–EU cooperation has resulted from dialogue over high politics and military/security issues. Frustrated initiatives, unrealistic expectations and disillusionment have characterized efforts in this field at a succession of high-level meetings. Since the 2004 EU enlargement this has been accompanied by a harder edge of mutual criticism and subdued rivalry.

In one respect this outcome has reflected difficulties with the process of dialogue and the expectations of the two parties. The Russian leadership and political elite have been dissatisfied with the fitful progress in negotiations with the EU over a variety of sensitive but non-security disputes of low politics, as discussed in the previous chapter. Moscow has viewed some border issues and the vexed question of Kaliningrad as more serious because of their impact on Russian sovereignty and they have become issues of dissension at the level of high politics; Moscow has made clear that solutions are only achievable in top-down negotiations. It can be argued that the overall relationship should have been built from the bottom up, and that the top-down approach favoured by the Russian leadership has caused the process of dialogue to stall or become mired in practical obstacles. This outcome has also reflected EU disillusionment over the prospects for Russian domestic reforms, which has contributed to the failure of the EU to project a consistent, coherent policy on how to engage Russia or to develop an EU-wide strategy for relations with Russia.

The EU has only begun to configure policies on security issues with a significant military dimension and this has discouraged serious Russian attention to such policies as a basis for Russia–EU cooperation. More recent efforts by the EU to provide substance to the ESDP have been received sceptically and even defensively in Moscow by officials concerned about the possibility of an 'Eastern Dimension' in EU policy and about the influence of new EU member states on this policy. 'Brussels has found itself in a situation of a permanent conflict of interests' over the EU–Russia relationship, one influential Russian politician argues, since 'the "large" states want stability while the "small" states are doing their best to keep Russia outside Europe'.[74] The EU has not adopted an 'Eastern Dimension' that diminishes the priority of Russia–EU partnership and may never do so. But Moscow is pessimistic about security rapprochement with the EU, as it expects that the enlarged EU will be significantly less friendly to Russia, more sensitive to human rights, and at the same time more insistent on EU engagement in the former Soviet Union.

The controversy around the Ukrainian presidential election in winter 2004–5 stoked up suspicions and an atmosphere of recrimination between Moscow and Brussels. Poland came under sharp Russian criticism, despite the fact that Warsaw sought to involve the EU in the Ukraine crisis in a way that would engage Russia and not antagonize it. During Putin's second presidential term the Russian leadership has interpreted EU and broader Western approval for democratic transformation in CIS states as a geopolitical challenge, as discussed further in the final chapter of this volume. This reinforces Moscow's determination not to accept interaction with the EU on security matters on terms that make Russia an object of EU policy rather than an 'equal' partner, whether this applies to soft security issues or, for example, Russian involvement in EU crisis management operations. Despite the difficulties, however, the two parties will need to find common approaches to manage joint and increasingly overlapping interests in the EU's new eastern security neighbourhood.

This is impeded by the basic structural differences that separate the two sides. The EU does not function as an effective geopolitical counterpart to the unitary and increasingly centralized Russian state. Putin, for his part, has been reluctant to consider the EU a serious partner; he has tended to view it as a form of Brussels bureaucracy that can be pressured by bilateral treaties with major European states on security as on other areas of policy. These states have often reciprocated this emphasis on bilateralism.[75] Putin has also promoted a series of trilateral meetings with Germany and France.[76] This reflects a traditional Russian fixation on power and nation-states in international politics, especially with respect to harder security issues, which shows no indication of diminishing during Putin's leadership, even if relationships with individual EU leaders depend on their continued success in elections. To the extent that Putin favours multilateralism, his preference is to project Russian policy through some kind of concert of great powers in which Russia has full membership rights (such as the UN Security Council or the G-8) rather than through EU-style bureaucratic institutional processes.

Efforts to develop a Russia–EU security partnership also face another systemic challenge, arising from the effects of 9/11 and in particular the Iraq war. These have placed Russia in the unwelcome position of trying to avoid the need to choose in its security policy between the United States and much of Europe in the definition of threat perceptions and the role of military means in counteracting them (in this respect NATO has acted as a rather convenient hybrid for Russian dialogue with Western states since 2003).[77] Moscow is loath to accept a US-defined international order and still declares its attraction to joint approaches to security challenges through multilateral institutions. But this position clashes with Russia's continued orientation to traditional hard security and geopolitics, for example over the issue of military 'pre-emption', which places it in better company with the US than the EU. With challenges around its periphery, it seems unlikely that Russia will accept the EU model of security through interdependence, let alone EU 'post-modern' approaches to the use of force, when Russian sovereignty is perceived to be at stake. This reinforces the temptation to fall back on familiar bilateral relationships rather than rely on an amorphous security relationship with the EU.[78] It also helps explain why Moscow has been more attracted to the explicitly interest-based and US-influenced security dialogue on practical policy issues that it has developed with NATO.

5

Russian security engagement with NATO

Roy Allison

The previous chapter confirms that the Russian leadership and foreign policy elite remain wary and sceptical of the European Union's potential as a security actor. This reflects concerns about the EU's role in the shared neighbourhood as well as the hesitant and rather limited Russia–EU security relationship to date and the amorphous nature of the 'common space' on external security. Neither party can feel confident that their interaction will provide a channel for deeper Russian engagement in European security affairs or avert new security policy divisions on the margins of the enlarged Europe. Nor can they rely on the OSCE to fulfil such tasks, despite Russian proposals in the 1990s that this all-European body should expand its remit. Might then NATO, especially the NATO–Russia Council (NRC), provide the institutional setting for these important tasks?

In security policy terms NATO overshadows the EU in Europe. To be sure, NATO's European role has become more ambiguous in recent years. But it still derives authority from its military prowess, its traditional role in locking US interests into Europe, its growing European membership, and its focus since 2002 on a new security agenda in common with Russia. Could this provide the basis for a substantive and inclusive security policy engagement of Russia with the enlarged Europe? Or will traditional Russian suspicions of NATO and hostility to the process of NATO enlargement strictly limit the potential for NATO as an agent to deepen Russian inclusion in Europe?

In response to these questions this chapter first analyses differences of view in Russian elite debate, mostly below the level of official discourse. Secondly, it examines the priorities, achievements and future potential of Russian state policy towards NATO. The agenda for cooperation under the NRC is shown to coexist with Moscow's traditional distaste for NATO enlargement. Thirdly, the chapter assesses options for and constraints on deeper Russia–NATO collaboration. Popular Russian attitudes towards NATO, perceptions of threat and other security issues are explored separately in Chapter 6, using survey data and the results of focus groups.

NATO OR THE EU AS RUSSIA'S PRINCIPAL SECURITY PARTNER IN EUROPE?

The question whether Russian engagement with NATO might overcome security divisions in Europe requires us to return to Moscow's fluctuating assessment of the relative merits of partnership with NATO and the EU.[1] A core consideration is Putin's recognition of NATO as the primary security actor on the European continent (although when the choice presents itself Moscow favours bilateral channels and agreements with major European states, and the United States, to negotiations in multilateral formats). The way in which NATO and the EU can complement one another in efforts to draw Russia into the European mainstream will depend on the nature of the security concerns at issue, the further evolution of these institutions in the post-9/11 environment, and Russia's own fractured domestic political development.

As previously described, from Russia's perspective the EU has represented no serious security policy challenge and since it lacks real military capabilities it has sought to focus on 'soft security' concerns. The enlarged EU's interest in its new eastern neighbourhood certainly makes Russia nervous – increasingly so. However, for Moscow it is NATO that still represents a clear and present challenge to Russia, if officially no longer a threat. NATO also has the means, through engaging American power, to influence high-priority security issues and so is a serious negotiating party.

At the same time, traditionally the Russian preference has been for NATO to become more 'European' and less 'American', to develop its political functions and downgrade itself as a military organization. Through resulting closer Russia–NATO cooperation, it could be argued, this could offer Russia a 'back door' to Europe, while the 'front door', the EU with its various conditions for close relations, let alone membership, remains only partly ajar, if not shut. However, in reality by 2006 Russia was developing some form of partnership with a NATO that was less militarily cohesive but if anything more US-driven than at the beginning of the decade. Moreover, this is a NATO in which European states are divided on significant issues and which increasingly defines its tasks in extra-European terms.

As a result, it is difficult for Russia to retain a meaningful option of promoting its relations with the EU at the expense of NATO's role, and Moscow denies that its policy reflects this traditional objective. Suspicions that Russia is seeking 'to play on the contradictions between these two organizations or "drive a wedge between old and new Europe"', Russian officials insist, 'are nothing but an echo of the mentality of the era of dividing lines'. Their position is that 'we have no need to choose between the European Union's ESDP, NATO or somebody else'.[2] Indeed, if Russia were to revive hopes of playing on transatlantic differences, despite their seriousness since 2003, this would misunderstand the character of transatlantic relations. And there is little evidence that Russia has tried to capitalize on disputes between the US and its key allies in this period.

Russian policy choices would be simplified if the traditional 'anti-NATO' approach of Russia's European engagement and anti-NATO currents in the Russian elite were gradually to subside. This could deliver an overall rapprochement between Russia and the West.[3] But it has been difficult to achieve as the political dynamic between the sides has soured and NATO enlargement has aroused new Russian anxieties. Nevertheless, the NATO–Russia Council, formed in May 2002, has escaped broader Russian censure of NATO activities and has become established as a channel for security dialogue. The format of this new body helps explain this outcome. The NRC, like the G-8, functions as a purely intergovernmental organization, where Russia can be included as an equal partner by consent of the existing member states. Such an arrangement would be extremely difficult for the EU to match, even with the requisite political will on all sides, because of the EU's emerging 'supranational' character on key issues of concern to Russian interests.

For Russia, NATO now represents a security partner (in the form of the NRC) that does not appear intrusively concerned about Russian domestic affairs and that speaks a similar language of hard security. To be sure, this partner encroaches on Russia geographically, carries an uneasy psychological legacy and has recently absorbed new members that are often critical of Russia. But for Moscow the dialogue with NATO has become easier than with the EU. The latter is perceived as high-handed and as the purveyor of a Europeanness in security as in other fields, which makes demands of Russia for collaboration that are linked to a much wider agenda of domestic transformation and that run counter to Russia's current illiberal domestic political trajectory.

RUSSIAN ENGAGEMENT WITH NATO

Since at least May 2002 and in contrast to the 1990s, Russia and NATO have actively been trying to identify areas for cooperation in the framework of a new international security agenda. In principle this effort could result in policy convergence on a spectrum of issues that could mesh Russia into the mainstream of European security concerns and provide a sense of inclusion in NATO deliberations on security, without actual membership of the alliance. However, even as this effort has been under way, Russia's political interest in exploring options for developing a substantial security relationship with NATO appears to have waned, as the Alliance has become hostage to fissures in the transatlantic relationship.

This apparent decline in Russia's commitment to a process of extensive collaborative engagement with NATO (even if the security dialogue with the EU has fared worse) reflects several judgments among policy-makers in Moscow: first, that NATO no longer represents a coherent entity with clear purposes and a firm decision-making capacity; second, that it has lost its momentum despite the accession of new member states through a far-reaching process of enlargement and despite agreements on out-of-area functions and deployments. Indeed, some in the Russian elite turn this round and consider NATO to be fading into irrelevance just because of enlargement. They associate the American preference for coalitions of the willing with the 'unwieldy' size and diversity of strategic outlook of the Alliance. This then leads to the further Russian judgement that the United States under the Bush administrations has been developing the strategic lines of its policy without much regard for NATO, while NATO has been struggling to adjust to this dissociation of its key member.

Russian decision-makers continue to assess how far the 'coalition of the willing' concept, expressed most clearly in the formation of the Iraq war coalition, has displaced the core concept of alliance underpinning NATO's role in Europe. How, they can reasonably ask, will this impact on NATO's integrity, its military utility and its capacity to develop common security relationships with states outside the core article 5 zone formed by the Alliance? Indeed, some reflect, could the 'coalition' approach provide an opportunity for Russia to supplant European Allies as a partner of choice for the US? For those thinking in this way it is believed that Russia missed an opportunity during the Iraq crisis. However, according to another line of thinking Russian policy should itself be built on temporary coalitions, which can be formed whenever common interests arise.

If the US is ready to engage in collective military action without involving NATO, a further question arises: how far will NATO's traditional 'hard' security function atrophy and be displaced by 'softer' functions? Such functions have traditionally been regarded with less respect and priority in Moscow than military security, but they might provide an easier base line for cooperation with Russia. Indeed, if NATO's collective defence function is diluted and its political profile enhanced, this may allow for greater interaction with Russia in some kind of collective security framework. In particular, this could provide the basis for a grand bonding exercise between Russia and NATO, as well as Russia and the US, in combating terrorism. This could even transform the NATO acronym effectively into the 'New Anti-Terrorist Organization'.

The Russian leadership appears interested in defining partnership with NATO on the basis of this outcome, but is still sceptical about its progress.[4] Combating terrorism is presented as a new paradigm for Russia–NATO relations, especially through the NRC. But this new definition remains very much a work in progress, despite some useful achievements since 1992 as surveyed in this chapter. Moreover, Russia remains inclined to adopt a differentiated approach in its policy towards NATO countries. In January 2005 Defence Minister Sergei Ivanov specified that Moscow was particularly interested in cooperation with those NATO member states that share its approaches to the fight against terrorism and with those that have armed forces matériel more comparable to that of Russia.[5]

Despite NATO's interest in partnership with Russia or some kind of 'partnership plus', the Russian political leadership continues to be ambivalent about the quality of the relationship. It would be optimistic to accept the claim by an aide to Putin that the 'political and military establishment of Russia on the whole has overcome the NATO syndrome inside it'.[6] The Russian leadership currently perceives NATO as neither friend nor enemy. Sergei Ivanov spelt this out (glossing over more conservative views by some Russian generals) in October 2004: 'Any NATO country is, of course, not an ally of ours, but not an adversary either. There are no strategic conflicts between Russia and NATO. Our common threats come from the south'.[7] Russia has opted to wait to see, first, how NATO proceeds to rearrange itself in response to American strategic priorities and, second, whether the Alliance is significantly affected by the absorption of new member states that are historically suspicious of Russia and are close by or adjoining Russian borders.

Despite the concerns of the new NATO members, Moscow is aware that the purely European component of NATO policy is declining as it is influenced by American global policy concerns.[8] Paradoxically, however, the reawakening of Russia's interest in NATO as a security actor in Europe may depend on whether and how NATO finally becomes a global player, seeking to use its newly formed 17,500-strong Response Force beyond its Afghanistan commitments, perhaps in Central Asia or Moldova. This would compel a Russian response and test the overall quality of the Russia–NATO relationship. Some Russian analysts believe an 'Asianization' of NATO could benefit Russia by compelling Washington to take Moscow seriously again.[9] As previously noted, others hope that Moscow would gain from a dilution of the collective defence function of the Alliance. Such views form part of a broader elite debate on what kind of relationship Russia should form with NATO.

RUSSIAN ELITE DEBATE ON NATO SINCE 2000

Elite debate on NATO in Russia has been strongly influenced by Putin's move towards rapprochement with the Alliance after the 9/11 attacks, and even before that his decision to unfreeze Russia–NATO relations by welcoming NATO Secretary-General Lord Robertson to Moscow in February 2000. Putin's response to a BBC interviewer in March 2000 that he did not see why Russia would not join NATO, naturally under certain conditions, challenged the dominant Russian antipathy to NATO and helped to reset the parameters of elite discussion. From early in his first presidential term, Putin sought to form a consensus favouring a balanced foreign policy, based on a rational analysis of Russia's real needs, of national interests and their defence – a form of pragmatic nationalism.

However, Putin's security policy outlook has been pragmatic in so far as it supports cooperation with major Western states and institutions to advance Russian interests. In this sense it is West-focused, but at root it is a form of great-power realism and not based on a pro-Western ideological orientation. Indeed, Putin has reflected and then reinforced a new dominant policy outlook, a sort of operational code, of a new Russian elite group, especially since late 2003, which seeks to assert Russian great-power interests and tends to be illiberal in domestic affairs. It may be technocratic, but in essence it is neither pro-Western nor supportive of Western political or civic values. It is an approach that finds it easier to privilege NATO than alternative multilateral institutions as Russia's Western security partner.[10]

This tendency can be contrasted in Russian debate to the beleaguered minority frame of thinking of liberal Westernism, which has existed only on the fringes of Russian political debate since the eclipse of liberal politicians in the State Duma at the end of 2003. During Putin's presidency liberal Westernizers appear less idealistic about the West than in the early 1990s. But, as before, such liberals do not dissociate Western institutions from the values that underpin them. In the Putin period they have not viewed NATO, with its strong security profile, as necessarily the best or preferred institutional channel for the desired goal of integration with the West.

By contrast, those attracted to fundamentalist nationalism within the Russian elite find rapprochement with Western structures difficult to accept, especially institutions under strong American influence, and they respond to NATO with ingrained suspicion if not open hostility. Putin's NATO policy has had to contend with this significant domestic political current of opposition to his policy to the West, which combines Communist Party (CPRF) supporters and nationalists unreconciled to the aftermath of the Cold War.

Overall, it appears that Putin can muster a significant body of at least lukewarm support among the Russian elite for his policies on NATO, but these policies remain controversial.[11] Moreover, Russian elite interest in NATO has declined since the Prague NATO summit and the accession of new members, including the Baltic states, to the Alliance in April 2004. As noted previously, this partly reflects a new uncertainty about NATO's internal cohesion and effectiveness.

Pragmatic nationalists

Pragmatic nationalist support for partnership with NATO has developed on the basis of various expectations and strains of thinking. For some in the Russian military and security establishment NATO could act as the gateway to a balance-of-power system, a new Concert of Powers, each with its sphere of influence. A variation of this great-power type of thinking is the view of Russia acting with NATO as a club of world rulers – rather in the way Moscow has perceived its role in the G-8. Others perceive association with NATO as a means of containment of Muslim or Chinese pressures; NATO here enters the perennial Russian debate over its civilizational identity and is used in opposition to those who characterize Russia as a multi-ethnic Eurasian community. Finally, some have resurrected beliefs from the early 1990s that entering Western arms markets with Russia's military products via NATO, if this is possible, would help rescue Russian high-tech industries.[12] This hope has been encouraged to some extent by Russian accession to the NATO Standardization Agreement.

Pragmatic nationalists generally deplore NATO enlargement but view the NATO–Russia Council as a positive mechanism. This is clearly articulated in the views of Mikhail Margelov, the chairman of the Russian Federation Council's International Affairs Committee, who appears as a quasi-official foreign policy spokesman. On one hand, he warns that NATO's 'mechanical expansion' serves to incite isolationist sentiments in Russia and that the anti-Russian bias of the new Baltic members of NATO may influence the Alliance. This enlargement ousts Russia 'to the continent's east so as to undermine its beneficial position in the Eurasian centre'. Yet at the same time he anticipates that 'Russian military-oriented government contracts' will grow with NATO expansion.[13] He also views the NRC as an effective forum for political consultation and for various joint military-technical programmes, and even suggests that it should act as 'an instrument to help resolve conflicts that may arise, both between its members and with neighbours cooperating with Russia in the common interest'.[14] A specialist in the Russian presidential administration similarly laments Russia's loss of its buffer zone in Europe through NATO enlargement, but rates the NRC highly as a channel to resolve disputes. At the same time she notes that NATO's efforts to settle extra-European problems, such as Iraq and Muslim extremism, could result in a cooling of relations with Russia.[15]

Another prominent pragmatic nationalist, Dmitry Rogozin, who chaired the State Duma International Affairs Committee until December 2003, is notable for his nationalistic rhetoric, including over NATO enlargement. However, at the inception of the NRC he viewed it as a chance to transform Russia–NATO relations by focusing on specific pilot projects. He felt that the NRC format should allow for 'the institutionalized possibility of evolution in the field of Russian integration into NATO political structures'.[16] Surprisingly, even the Liberal Democratic Party chairman, a fundamentalist nationalist on other issues, waxed lyrical on the formation of the NRC in May 2002. He described it as 'more important than the October [1917] revolution' and suggested that in the future we may mark 'the creation of a new community of free European and American nations'.[17]

Some prominent Russian specialists have offered lukewarm support for Putin's position towards NATO, but have remained sceptical about NATO's future. For example, after the formation of the NRC Sergei Markov, director of the Institute of Political Studies, argued strongly for tight cooperation with the Alliance.[18] By 2004, however, he characterized NATO as an empty and dying organization that had failed to transform itself to meet new security challenges – this goal required the formation of a new organization, NATO-2.[19] Early in Putin's term Sergei Karaganov criticized NATO's efforts to find a new role through a doctrine of humanitarian intervention, and for acting as an instrument of the US in European security.[20] In 2003, after the creation of the NRC and the invasion of Iraq, he remained sceptical that NATO would find a role for itself, except perhaps 'if a serious conflict arises between the North and the South'.[21] Since then, however, he has speculated on NATO's evolution into an extra-European macro-institution and approved Russian rapprochement with NATO to address specific security problems, 'especially as NATO still has the potential to become a global military and political union, indeed even the UN's "mailed fist"'.[22]

Some Russian officers have come to favour Russia–NATO cooperation in the hope that it will be accompanied by a dilution of the collective defence profile of NATO. One prominent military scholar pointed to article 5 of the Washington agreement, which covers the collective defence function of NATO, as well as to the principle of consensus associated with it, as 'the major obstacle to further transformation of NATO'. But he suggested that this could be counteracted by the expansion of NATO's functions to a broad area of security issues, beyond collective defence.[23] Similarly, parts of the Russian Ministry of Defence have presented the idea of Russia–NATO cooperation leading to 'a full-scale collective security system'. This also reflects hopes for commercially advantageous military-technical cooperation and arms modernization programmes.[24]

Interviews in spring 2004 reveal that some State Duma deputies who are members of the Communist Party fraction as well as of the United Russia fraction accept the pro-Putin position on NATO. NATO and Russia are described as potential rivals but no longer enemies. A deputy of the CPRF fraction with a security service background noted that Russia should examine NATO's strategic doctrine and 'adapt ours accordingly'; that if NATO is not hostile, then enlargement cannot harm Russia and the accession of the Baltic states is not dangerous. But a Russian specialist observed in this context that 'the new members are unpredictable', that 'NATO will need reorganization and consensus will be hard to achieve'. Worries that the Baltic states do not fall under conventional arms treaty limits, and that NATO could use these states' military infrastructure, were also expressed in the Duma. However, the NRC was viewed positively as a forum for consultations. A member of the *siloviki* and CPRF fraction even supported 'constant cooperation' between Russia and NATO and maintained that 'we would prefer to be NATO's "partner of choice" but new members have their own views [on this] and this is natural'.[25]

Liberal westernizers

Russian elite support for liberal Westernist positions on NATO declined steadily in the 1990s and suffered grievously from the NATO campaign against Serbia, when many liberals became vocal critics of NATO policy; they remain quite sceptical of NATO interventions and intentions. Boris Nemtsov, the then leader of Russia's Union of Right Forces, is unusual in having declared his unequivocal support for the idea of Russia's accession to the Alliance. However, this occurred after Putin himself had observed that he was relaxed about this idea and soon after the post-9/11 shift in Russian security policy.[26] In contrast, the co-leader of the Union of Right Forces, Anatoly Chubais, has moved rather far from Nemtsov's line to a more nationalist stance. In 2003 he argued that 'Russia should set aside the task of joining NATO', since 'there is nothing for us to do there, we are not part of it in either geographic or political terms'.[27]

Indeed very few leading members of the Russian elite have accepted that NATO represents a security community of shared values and political cohesion rather than a pooling of military assets and defence commitments. Grigory Yavlinsky, leader of Yabloko, is exceptional in his emphasis that 'NATO needs to be a united alliance with a strong set of values', that 'it is bad for Russia when there are divisions'.[28] But liberal Westernism is more easily distinguished by the conviction that NATO enlargement represents no threat to Russia, and some politicians from the Union of Right Forces (URF) also adopt this position.

Such liberals may even accept the view that, looking ahead, 'the policy of fanning domestic contradictions forces the post-Soviet states to seek NATO membership' and 'Russia's closest neighbours look at their potential NATO membership as a stabilization factor'.[29] A URF deputy affirmed in this context that Russians are not overly worried by NATO extending enlargement to territories that have never been part of Russia, even to the Baltic states. But he accepted that a NATO presence in Tbilisi or Tashkent would be seen differently by Russians and would be used by politicians as a way to increase political tensions.[30] The same could be true of debate about Ukraine's potential accession to NATO; liberals could be divided on this issue.

Fundamentalist nationalists

Fundamentalist nationalism is expressed in a quite different image of NATO, which for some Russian politicians is used for populist politics. The attacks of the Communist Party leader Gennady Zyuganov on Putin's 'liberal fascism', and the dark warnings of the most nationalist of the newspapers about NATO preparations 'to invade Russia',[31] tap a powerful current of scepticism in the Russian elite about rapprochement with NATO. An adviser to Putin in the presidential administration has pointed out that during the parliamentary election campaign in December 2003 the political parties that proposed a harsh policy towards NATO received a great deal of support. NATO enlargement is opposed in his view by the 'political class' in Russia in general.[32]

This was reflected in a strongly critical statement by the State Duma in March 2004 on the accession of seven new states to NATO. It characterized NATO military doctrine as 'offensive' and spoke of the creation of a 'grey zone' in Europe, since the Baltic states are not covered by the arms restrictions of the Conventional Forces in Europe (CFE) Treaty.[33] Dmitry Rogozin, leader of the Rodina faction, proposed that Russia should strengthen its military group in Kaliningrad Province.[34] A draft resolution of the Communist group in the Duma described NATO expansion as the most serious threat to

Russia since the Great Patriotic War. Prominent deputies still think in terms of geopolitical conspiracies. One argues that the incorporation of the Baltic states into NATO is part of an American geostrategic plan to take away the areas that make Russia a great power – that is, access to the Baltic and Black Seas. Others view NATO enlargement more generally as producing a new line of division in Europe and as a channel for the geographic extension of US influence. Even politicians from the opposition Liberal Party argue that 'NATO has no role in the war against terrorism'.[35]

Such views are supported by many disillusioned senior Russian military officers, whose careers collapsed while Russian military capabilities declined and NATO enlarged. Russian military opinions on NATO vary but the majority of officers are influenced by a realization that a clear enemy provides the justification for rises in the military budget and that partnership with NATO will increase pressure for unwanted forms of military reform and clearer civilian control over the military. Diehard nationalist views on NATO are found among leading retired Russian officers who have gone into politics.

Colonel-General Valery Manilov, the first deputy head of the Defence and Security Committee of the Federation Council, for example, views NATO enlargement close to Russian borders as creating 'a threat to Europe and the world', with the potential for 'confrontation and re-militarization'.[36] Army General Igor Rodionov, chairman of the People's Patriotic Party of Russia, scornfully observes that, given the flying time from the Baltic states' border to Moscow, 'Russia's leadership will be constantly aware of our nation's vulnerability to an external threat – and ... will be more obedient'.[37] Colonel-General Leonid Ivashov, who has specialized in geopolitical diatribes, argues that the Alliance is 'compressing the space around Russia from the west and the south' and that the military infrastructure of the new NATO members is being turned against Russia.[38] He even claims, with more than a tinge of paranoia, that a status of forces agreement with NATO will provide it with the chance to intervene in Russia, to establish foreign control over 'Russia's nuclear weapons, its remaining combat-ready units and ships, ... and other infrastructure'.[39]

Serving officers in other parts of the Russian security establishment also commonly harbour deep suspicion of NATO. For example, some officers of the Ministry of the Interior, who characterize NATO as 'a relic of the East–West axis', question 'why Russia won't become the object of NATO's policy in future, as Yugoslavia became in the past'. The NRC is considered to be only consultative and with little impact.[40] An official of the Federal Security Service bluntly rejected the possibility of a rapprochement between Russia and NATO, arguing that both NATO and the EU are Russia's main geopolitical adversaries in a struggle for territorial control.[41]

Among specialists, other Russian critics of NATO muster more reasoned arguments. They maintain that the new NATO members are seeking a military and nuclear umbrella 'against the possibility of change in Russia', and that the traditional purpose, 'to keep the US in Europe and Russia out of Europe and to limit Germany's influence', still prevails. For them enlargement 'shows Russians that NATO is not an alliance of democratic countries but an alliance of anti-Russian countries' and 'a threat to Russian–European relations'.[42] Moreover, some Russian business circles, which realize that they cannot compete with Western companies, oppose closer relations with the West and NATO. Those who are dependent on the Russian defence sector and military enterprises also may expect an improvement in their fortunes from a deterioration in Russia–NATO relations.

POLICY ACHIEVEMENTS AND FUTURE POTENTIAL

This survey of Russian elite debate indicates that there exists a significant undercurrent of opposition to Putin's instrumental and pragmatic policy towards NATO. This policy has firmly criticized NATO enlargement but has developed a framework for cooperation with the Alliance, which creates at least a potential for an expedient partnership. In turn, this may ameliorate the core challenge of 'dividing lines' and the risk of Russian exclusion from the rest of Europe. The NATO–Russia Council has been the key structure in developing the new agenda for cooperation.

The NRC as a new forum for cooperation

The creation of the NATO–Russia Council in May 2002 was intended as a measure to move beyond the frustrations of the NATO–Russia Permanent Joint Council (PJC). Russia had expected the PJC would enshrine its special relations with the Alliance. But it found itself having to contend with consolidated positions formed by the 19 NATO member states acting in unison – whereas at the beginning of the 1990s Russia could speak to countries of the North Atlantic Cooperation Council (NACC) on an individual basis. The 'at 20' format of the NRC pleased Moscow, since it requires joint decision-making through consensus, assisted by a high-level preparatory committee. At the same time, just because a topic is on the NRC agenda does not preclude the Allies from discussing it among themselves. There exists an informal principle of 'retrievability', whereby any NATO member can withdraw an item from the NRC agenda; but apparently this has rarely been used. Putin has expressed satisfaction that Russia 'has as much right to vote as all other NATO members on a number of issues that interest us'.[43]

He must be aware that NATO had no such practice with any other non-member country.

Despite some Russian suspicions that the NRC had been devised simply to mitigate the impact of the second wave of NATO enlargement, Putin has used it to shift the focus of Russian attention from the enlargement controversy to the exploration of some form of partnership with NATO.[44] Most optimistically, the NRC holds out the hope of an enduring partnership and genuine collaboration based on deep and meaningful consultations on an expanding agenda of issues, including some regional political issues. Such consultations could build on NRC procedures that envisage ministerial meetings to discuss current conflicts.[45] For example, an NRC session in June 2004 on the margins of the Istanbul NATO summit focused on Afghanistan, Iraq and peacekeeping issues.

At present the NRC is convened twice a year at the level of foreign ministers and defence ministers and not less than once a month at the level of ambassadors to working groups specializing in specific sectors. NRC Chiefs of Defence and General Staff also have meetings. Already by the end of 2003 some 20 Russian ministries and departments were enlisted in overall cooperation with NATO, and from 2005 it was planned that these could receive targeted funding from NATO for joint projects – such as joint training exercises and visits by experts. Against this background it is possible too that Russia may reconsider its previously negative attitude to using the potential for NATO's Partnership for Peace (PfP) programme, for which funds are also allocated.[46]

If deeper collaboration becomes possible in the future, this could evolve into an informal 'alliance with the Alliance' or Russian 'associate membership' in NATO. This implies that Russia would gradually become a real player in significant areas of NATO decision-making and activities, albeit outside the collective defence commitment of NATO membership.[47] For Russia the key issue is the capacity of the NRC to act as a genuine mechanism of joint decision-making. This depends on the absence of voting in the Council and the use of the principle of consensus to the extent that consensus can be reached on particular issues, with the assistance of the preparatory committee, and on focusing on issues where there are common concerns and approaches.[48]

Russia has not achieved and is unlikely to achieve the maximalist goal described by the Russian General Staff in spring 2002 to 'become an equal partner of NATO in matters concerning the formation of a new European security system'.[49] But by the end of 2003 the Russian Foreign Ministry characterized the NRC as 'an effective mechanism of constant political consultations, of elaboration and adoption of joint decisions and of implementing joint actions'.[50] A year later the Russian objective was described as a 'union' with NATO, 'a special form of partnership and cooperation whereby Russia, while participating in NATO political activities, collective decision-making and joint operations with the Alliance … would preserve its full sovereignty and strategic independence'.[51] This positive vision contrasts markedly with Russia's sparing appreciation of the effectiveness and potential of Russia–EU consultation mechanisms. A key issue for Russia is that the NRC, unlike the EU, does not discuss the domestic affairs or political values of its partners. Moscow seeks pragmatic, instrumental cooperation with NATO and has no interest in a form of integration with NATO structures that could constrain its internal policies or ability to develop its own strategic goals.

Russia and NATO have been fleshing out a range of fields for security policy collaboration in the framework of the NRC. Many of these potentially address European security concerns, even if they are characterized as part of a wider transnational agenda of security management. Some are driven by the post 9/11 imperatives of global anti-terrorism. Others respond, rather, to the traditional unfinished business of the post-Cold War European security environment, while still others appear to be what we might term 'goodwill initiatives', motivated primarily by the pragmatic effort to identify and kick-start common projects to foster cooperative mindsets and the political will that might allow more ambitious forms of collaboration to follow.[52]

The first category of issues has the potential to bond Russia and NATO around high-priority security concerns, but equally it could drive them apart if differences in interpretation over the nature of and responses to the 'war on terrorism' become entrenched and politically charged. The second category involves the substance behind former dividing lines in European security, where progress cannot be rapid and may be more effectively addressed outside the new and still fragile channels for Russia–NATO dialogue. But the agreement of the NRC on a joint statement on the Ukraine crisis in December 2004 suggests it has some potential in responding to major 'East–West' controversies in Europe. This is also implied in Putin's comment to the Russian Security Council the following month that Russia and NATO 'as partners … are able to hold frank discussions and work out solutions for settling crisis situations'.[53]

The third set of issues is based implicitly on the assumption that 'spillover' is possible from agreement on more peripheral security concerns to agreement over more challenging fields. But this remains no more than a worthy aspiration and is clearly dependent on the overall state of the Russian relationship with leading NATO countries. Inevitably many of the NRC initiatives that are publicized serve the function of the 'public diplomacy of partnership' and are as much about changing the psychological climate between Russia and NATO as about concrete achievements in combating terrorism or other fields, and this in turn will reflect political dynamics.

Let us now review the progress achieved with the NRC agenda in various fields in order to assess their potential to foster partnership and avert new divisions between Russia and the enlarged Europe.

Combating terrorism: the new security paradigm

The campaign against terrorism is viewed both in Russia and in NATO as an overarching task because of the multifaceted threat they now perceive it to represent. This requires a comprehensive response at different levels, from (1) threat assessment (for the prevention of attacks), through to (2) protection and anti-terrorism (to act against terrorist activities before they occur) and counter-terrorism (active measures to respond immediately to terrorist attacks), to (3) consequence management (after such attacks). On each level the NRC has been developing cooperative projects so as to coordinate the efforts of Russia, European NATO states and the US.[54] The agenda for cooperation is set out in the NATO–Russia Action Plan on Terrorism proclaimed in December 2004.[55]

The first level – threat assessment – requires the sharing of intelligence between Russia and NATO states, which in practice has been not been easy. This happens better in bilateral channels as nations are not keen to share intelligence in multilateral formats and the NRC is no exception to this. On a bilateral basis, Russia has been exchanging intelligence with NATO countries that have strong intelligence services 'on various regions of the world where cells of international terrorist structures are operating'.[56] But at a meeting of NRC defence ministers in October 2004 Russian Defence Minister Sergei Ivanov bluntly observed that exchanging intelligence with NATO states would be done in different degrees depending on the 'sincerity' of the countries concerned.[57] Despite the much-vaunted provision of Russian intelligence on Afghanistan to the coalition forces that ousted the Taliban in 2001, intelligence-sharing has not done much to boost Russian confidence in NATO or vice versa.

Nonetheless, the two sides have reportedly created an algorithm for exchanging intelligence reports over terrorism. Joint threat evaluation is proceeding. Four NRC joint intelligence assessments of the different aspects of the terrorist threat have been agreed, and five more are under development. Terrorist and related WMD threats are understood to include those to freight and passenger transport; chemical, biological, radiological and nuclear threats; and threats to airspace management, which requires the coordination of systems and sharing of data. NATO and Russia have already prepared documents on the joint assessment of threats to military contingents in the Balkans, to land infrastructure from civilian aircraft attacks and vice versa, and to civilian aircraft from land-based strikes.

The second level, anti-terrorism, is represented at one end of the spectrum by exploring options for cooperation in the destruction of stockpiles of munitions, small arms and light weapons to keep them out of terrorist hands, as well as in developing effective control over transfers of man-portable air defence systems. At the other end of the spectrum of violence, in March 2004 a command post exercise played out a scenario under an NRC working group involving the use of ballistic missiles by a 'rogue' state or terrorist group. A proposal also exists for the joint planning and conduct of anti-terrorist information and psychological operations.

A core issue is the relationship between combating terrorism and military power. Three high-level Russia–NATO conferences have been held on the role of the military in combating terrorism; these have formulated concrete recommendations for follow-on work in such areas as armaments development. Russian companies seem willing to cooperate with NATO on developing anti-terrorism technologies. Both Russian and NATO military forces have special capabilities that could contribute in the fields of chemical, biological, radiological and nuclear weapons defence. Similarly, their militaries could share airborne early warning information to protect against the threat of rogue aircraft; also, they could assist early detection of terrorist attacks from the air, on the ground and at sea, in cooperation with civilian authorities.

However, outside these specific fields the broader contribution of Russian military forces for defence against terrorism is much more problematic. Russian traditions on the use of military forces and its unreformed military sector do not combine well with the demands for effective intelligence, policing and security service work in countering terrorism that are prioritized in particular by European NATO states. On the NATO side, it is argued that military forces should have a clear definition of the tasks they may have to undertake in response to terrorism. NATO has agreed on its own concept, and the NRC is considering the development of political-military guidance to provide a framework for its own cooperation in this field. As part of this, Russia has contributed a draft conceptual document on the role of the military in the war on terrorism, which the NRC is studying. But any agreement that emerges may need to be at rather a high level of generality, which will limit its value.

Some specific fields for cooperation appear more promising. In October 2004 Russia announced that vessels from its Black Sea Fleet would be ready to take part in Operation Active Endeavour – maritime cooperation to deter, defend and protect against terrorism in the Mediterranean Sea.[58] This promises to result in an expanded Russian participation in NATO's anti-terrorist naval patrols in the Mediterranean from summer 2006. Joint tasks have been assumed to prevent the delivery and transport of weapons of mass destruction and their components. Such naval cooperation may not have the same visibility as joint military actions on land, but it still assists the public diplomacy of partnership. According to Defence Minister Ivanov, it allows for Russian participation in 'actions as part of the NATO operation'; indeed it represents the first time that the armed forces of the two parties operate together in a collective defence operation. Ivanov has even predicted that it will 'help our country to integrate into the European community'.[59] But Russian sensitivity to such cooperation closer to Russian shores is shown by its opposition to extending the naval operation to the Black Sea – a position shared by Turkey, despite US support for the idea.

More generally, exercises have been held to improve NATO–Russia interoperability in combating terrorist threats. In 2004 nearly 60 joint events were scheduled. But these were agreed only after a rather public dispute over the programme between the Russian Ministry of Defence and General Staff and so far they have been mostly rather small-scale. More recently Russia has anticipated greater compatibility between the two sides' special forces. Real progress on interoperability has depended, however, on Russian readiness to accede to the NATO Partnership for Peace Status of Forces Agreement (PfP SOFA), which regulates the legal status of both sides' armed forces on each other's territory. Russia finally signed this agreement in April 2005. The longer-term goal to enable a breakthrough in cooperation is an actual joint NATO–Russia operation. But the mutual confidence for this step has not yet been achieved.

The third level of response to terrorism is consequence management. Russia and NATO have explored options for practical cooperation on managing the consequences of terrorist attacks. A civil emergency planning and response exercise hosted by Russia in Noginsk in September 2002 focused on chemical terrorism. Another – Kaliningrad 2004, in June 2004 (focused on counteracting the environmental damage of terrorist action against an oil platform in the Baltic Sea) – is part of an effort to develop a standing NRC civil emergency response capability.[60] Since at least summer 2003 there have been plans to create a reaction force for dealing with possible consequences of terrorist attacks on chemical and nuclear installations.[61]

The succession of serious terrorist incidents that Russia suffered in summer and autumn 2004 must have sharpened Russian concerns about the risk of an attack aimed at further mass casualties – a risk that takes advantage of the often weak security of Russia's dispersed infrastructure. Russia appears to be particularly vulnerable to low-tech but potentially devastating attacks, as well as to the ultimate concern of attacks with weapons of mass destruction. The director of the Russian Federal Security Service, Nikolai Patrushev, has accepted there is a possibility that international terrorists 'may use weapons of mass destruction'.[62] This offers a window for more significant NRC cooperation, but progress will depend on whether Moscow lifts some of its security sensitivity with respect to its territory. Some encouragement was offered by a visit arranged in August 2004 for NATO emissaries to an installation on the Kola Peninsula that is used to store strategic missile warheads and tactical nuclear weapons. A Russian exercise to demonstrate the security of its nuclear facilities was showcased for NATO.[63]

Finally, recent proposals have been floated on assistance in resolving hostage crises. This idea has resonance after the siege of the school in the North Caucasus town of Beslan in September 2004, which concluded in chaos and hundreds of deaths and also revealed multi-level weaknesses in the response of Russian security services. NATO offered a strong statement of sympathy for Russian losses and of uncompromising opposition to terrorist acts. But the domestic security measures announced by Putin in the aftermath of this attack do little to address the NRC agenda on combating terrorism, especially as regards specialized training and force development. The related issue of Chechnya has been a controversial subject for the NRC (though less so than for EU forums). So long as Moscow characterizes the Chechnya conflict overall simply as a terrorist challenge, yet insists that it should be resolved exclusively by Russian efforts, it cannot offer a basis for developing NRC partnership or consolidating a common Russian and Euro-Atlantic security platform.

Other fields for collaboration

The focus on terrorism should not obscure possibilities for Russia–NATO cooperation in other fields related to European security, which could build bridges across the continent at large.[64]

Crisis management and peacekeeping is perhaps the most prominent among these. In this respect Russian efforts have been focused so far on equal, full participation in planning peacekeeping operations in the Balkans, on summing up the Balkans experience in crisis management and on mapping out joint plans for further cooperation in a broader context and coordinating efforts with the UN, the OSCE and other international organizations.

Russian participation in the KFOR peacekeeping operation (which followed its participation in the multinational peacekeeping missions in Bosnia and Herzegovina – IFOR and SFOR) was a mixed experience. At the operational level, issues of control in planning and coordination between

Russia and other NATO participants arose periodically, although tactical-level cooperation appeared to be excellent, at least between Russian and US forces.[65] NATO and Russian troops took part in joint training, joint patrolling, and joint de-mining tasks. Liaison functions developed on the tactical and strategic levels. However, in January 2003 Moscow announced the withdrawal of its peacekeeping contingents from the Balkans, involving about 1,000 troops, and this was completed during June–July 2003. Russia thereby lost the opportunity for day-to-day cooperation with NATO.[66] Russian leaders may have concluded that the political functions and value of these units were no longer worth the cost of retaining them in the Balkans.

Russia has insisted that its military forces will no longer join 'NATO-led' operations. New joint NATO–Russia peacekeeping operations, however, are conceivable. Russian spokesmen note that in principle the option of Russia's conducting joint operations with NATO, even outside the Alliance's traditional area of responsibility, cannot be ruled out, despite the difficulty in thinking of locations for such an operation where the interests of the parties would coincide. The main Russian concern has been described as 'to coordinate political approaches to a particular situation requiring joint action and to ensure that such action has a proper, international legal basis'.[67] Already in September 2002 the NRC approved a document on 'Political Aspects of a Generic Concept for Joint Russia–NATO Peacekeeping Operations'.[68] The Russian Foreign Ministry describes this as 'built upon truly equitable partnership' inasmuch as it concerns 'political control and strategic governance of possible joint peacekeeping'.[69] The document sets out a framework for consultation, planning and decision-making during crises.

An NRC working group on peacekeeping operations is trying to address political-military, military and operational aspects of such joint operations. This is the objective of the first Russia–NATO military-political exercises, so-called 'procedural exercises'. The two sides are also studying the prospects for interaction on logistical support for peacekeeping operations. Work for the operational compatibility between special purpose forces began as part of the cooperation plan for 2005, which included some 50 operational compatibility exercises. Larger-scale exercises were planned for 2006. This activity is part of a long-term Interoperability Framework Programme.[70] Sergei Ivanov notes that in 2007–8 Russia and NATO plan a complex exercise involving airlift and the deployment of a joint contingent in a 'crisis area'.[71] This optimistic goal offers one benchmark for NRC cooperation.

In the meantime the Russian Defence Ministry has shown interest in a NATO multinational combined arms support and technical support centre, and is studying the possibilities for Russian representatives to take part in its activities. Russia–NATO cooperation in military transport aviation, including its employment in peacekeeping operations, is under consideration. Russia has announced the formation of its first professional peacekeeping brigade, the 15th Detached Peacekeeping Motorized Rifle Brigade, comprising just over 2,000 troops. It is based near Samara, and servicemen will take part in the Russia–NATO programme for operational compatibility, although this will be used for missions in the CIS as well as for any potential joint Russia–NATO operations under a UN mandate.[72] By early 2006 it was claimed to be combat-ready and deployable to any region of the world.

On one level all these plans are threatened by the weakening of the cohesion of NATO over the Iraq war. However, to the extent that the high end of NATO military operations is hived off to 'coalitions of the willing', then crisis management and peacekeeping emerge more as core future NATO activity and offer channels for engagement with Russia.

The catch is that within Europe the geographic location of an NRC peacekeeping deployment is most uncertain. The Balkans look set to become a target for future ESDP, rather than NATO, crisis management tasks, with the EU assumption of peacekeeping responsibilities in Bosnia, and Russia may need to choose between the EU and NATO in assisting the stabilization of this region. On the other hand, a Russia–NATO peacekeeping operation on the margins of Europe in the CIS region is likely to be rejected out of hand by the Russian leadership in the next few years. This is not on the NRC agenda, but is not inconceivable. In principle the option of NRC peacekeeping could assist the resolution of 'frozen conflicts' in CIS states where one side trusts NATO and the other trusts Russia.[73] This could be accompanied by intensified efforts to use the NRC as a political channel for dialogue with Russia in resolving these conflicts. A senior Russian officer, perhaps anticipating new zones of tension, has also raised the idea of developing a mechanism of joint response and crisis control, including possible military measures, in response to a further destabilization of conditions in Central Asia and the South Caucasus.[74] Potential Russian participation in the NATO Response Force in a wider geographic context is not inconceivable in the medium term, but would depend on a much deeper partnership between Russia and the Alliance.[75]

Arms control and confidence-building measures have become a contentious area of NATO–Russia interaction, focused as it is on ratification of the Agreement on Adaptation of the CFE Treaty by all signatories and its entry into force. NATO and the US are only ready to ratify this agreement, which would be accompanied by the Baltic states and Slovenia joining it, if Russia complies with pledges it made at the 1999 Istanbul OSCE summit on withdrawing its military facilities from Georgia and Moldova. Moscow insists that the issue of these bases is a bilateral matter unrelated to the CFE Treaty, and the State Duma ratified the adapted version of the treaty in June 2004.[76] In essence the NATO Allies and Russia have different interpretations of what constitutes 'full implementation' of the CFE-related commitments that Russia undertook at the Istanbul summit. Although the NATO position is correct in legal terms, the complexity of the issue has made it a difficult issue for public diplomacy.

Against the background of this dispute, Russia has threatened to abandon the CFE Treaty, describing it as obsolete.[77] But it is unlikely in reality to dispense with such a central part of the post-Cold War European security architecture as regards monitoring conventional forces in Europe. The Russian General Staff has argued that the second phase of NATO enlargement has made it absurd and discriminatory for Russia to discharge its obligations under the CFE Treaty on flank limits for conventional arms.[78] Russia's main concern here has been about limits on its North Caucasian Military District (Moscow emphasizes that it has no intention to increase its border force in north-west Russia, the Leningrad Military District, in response to NATO enlargement to include the Baltic states).[79] The Baltic states in turn have stated that they will adhere to existing NATO policies, including an assurance that in the foreseeable future NATO would meet its common defence needs through infrastructure upgrades and capacity for reinforcement, rather than the permanent stationing of significant combat forces.

Military-to-military cooperation and defence reforms are a sensitive and problematic field that is more likely to reflect the state of the wider Russia–NATO relationship and Russian domestic military transformation than to act in itself as a catalyst to open out that relationship. The NRC agenda has emphasized the need for practical military cooperation and interoperability. In May 2004 a significant interoperability exercise was held in Russia, which included measures for operational cooperation in countering major terrorist attacks. This was conducted despite tension between the Russian Defence Ministry and General Staff over the agenda of joint exercises. At the end of 2003 the General Staff tried to stall a plan agreed between NATO and Russian Defence Minister Sergei Ivanov for over 100 of these exercises for 2004, 20 of them organized in Russia.

The new Russian Chief of General Staff, Colonel-General Yury Baluevsky, is more forthcoming in developing cooperation plans with NATO. However, he still opposes plans that could create pressure for real Russian defence reform or a wider military transformation. The goal of interoperability with NATO armed forces, he emphasizes, applies only to units preparing for joint tasks, such as peacekeeping and combating terrorism, and 'there is no reason to ensure full compatibility between all armed forces of Russia and NATO'.[80] In essence, little real progress over defence reform can be expected on the

Russian side without a fundamental reform of the Russian defence sector. This is an intractable problem and some analysts argue that the Russian military is unreformable, as it needs to be restructured root and branch.[81] Yet NATO officials have argued that democratic reform and control of the Russian armed forces are a sine qua non for the successful development of military cooperation with NATO (as well as the EU), which remains 'fraught with misperceptions and misunderstandings on both sides'.[82]

However, NATO–Russia seminars on defence reform have been held and a dialogue continues on the issue of force development, including the adaptation of armed forces to counter terrorist threats. In this context NATO stresses the need for Russia to develop forces that are interoperable, in a state of high readiness, rapidly deployable, well trained and well equipped – with many of the essential characteristics of special forces but not limited to special forces. But NATO's hope that Russia can create a new breed of forces cannot be encouraged by the Russians' lamentable record since the early 1990s in adjusting the structure of their armed forces to address new low-intensity, sub-state threats.[83] Russia has not abandoned its mass mobilization force structure. Russia and NATO seem to be constructing different armed forces, oriented to different conflicts.

Apart from structural issues, Russia's military practice, traditions and modus operandi remain very different from those of NATO. NATO's transformation objectives confront the problematic traditional Russian approach to the use of armed force. Indeed the prosecution of Russia's current policy in Chechnya ultimately limits the extent to which NATO states believe they can engage in live 'anti-terrorist' operations with Russian forces, for fear of legitimizing the Chechnya campaign in its entirety.[84] All this is most unpromising for the possibility, which is under discussion, of creating an integrated NATO–Russia military training centre for missions to address new challenges.

New threats and challenges in the Euro-Atlantic area, and the means to confront them, are explored by the NRC. So far, possible cooperation is confined to civil and military airspace controls (through the NRC Cooperative Airspace Initiative Working Group) and scientific exchanges (through the NRC Science Committee). However, the parameters for a wider convergence, or indeed divergence, of threat perceptions could be identified by a dispassionate analysis of the emerging threat environment.

RUSSIAN OFFICIAL THREAT PERCEPTIONS OF NATO AND NATO ENLARGEMENT

It is important to consider how far the new opportunities for cooperation with NATO have altered NATO's image in official Russian threat assessments. Since the creation of the NRC an impressive array of joint work has been conducted under its working groups. The evaluation of this activity by both NATO and Russian Foreign Ministry officials has been optimistic, and President Putin has expressed his satisfaction with the way this relationship has developed. In December 2003 a telephone hotline was established between NATO headquarters and the Russian Defence Ministry. Russia has also established a permanent liaison office at SHAPE headquarters.

But there remains a very provisional quality to this relationship. Meeting journalists and academics in September 2004, Putin called for a 'more transparent relationship with NATO and one with the character of real partnership'. He specified that 'we regard NATO not as an enemy', but was disparaging that 'it is not efficient militarily, rather it is a tool of politics', and claimed that 'as a result of internal processes the military in NATO are in search of a new opponent'.[85] Russian politicians also point to NATO activities in a variety of countries around the periphery of Russia. Mikhail Margelov, head of the Foreign Affairs Committee of the Federation Council, complained, for example, that 'NATO is circumventing Russia from the southeast as Partnership for Peace evolves into a military alliance'.[86]

These views are some distance, but not divorced, from the more scathing sentiments on NATO found among many Russian military leaders. They still seem torn between viewing NATO through the prism of old suspicions and adversarial threat perceptions, and regarding it as increasingly toothless and destined for soft security functions, while hard security tasks are appropriated by the United States with a few chosen allies. The first perception is exposed by elements of the Russian Defence Ministry 'White Paper', presented in October 2003 and perhaps drafted in large part by the General Staff.[87] This document contains a very positive appraisal of the NRC's achievements and its strategic importance for Moscow. But this coexists with a much darker view of NATO in general.

The document states: 'If NATO remains a military alliance with the offensive military doctrine it has at present, this will require a drastic reorganization of the Russian military's planning and principles of development of the armed forces.' It demanded that 'anti-Russian components' be removed from NATO military planning and from the political declarations of Alliance member states, and spelt out that the Russian Ministry of Defence does not plan to reduce the Russian armed forces below the level of about one million. Considerable emphasis is still placed on fielding a modern high-tech military capable of competing with NATO forces, rather than an appropriate force designed to respond to the very different risks posed by local conflicts and instability in and around Russia.[88]

For a leading Russian defence analyst, this document (together with the dialogue surrounding it), presented at a conference attended by Putin and senior Russian officers at which Defence Minister Ivanov set out the postulates of the White Paper, left 'no doubt that the United States and NATO are still viewed as the major enemy'.[89] Although it was not formally a new Russian military doctrine and may have been partly prepared with the forthcoming Russian elections in mind, Ivanov was pressed by NATO to clarify the White Paper. Questions were left that were reinforced a year later when more acrimony entered Russian–Western relations.

In a graphic expression of its concerns, Russia undertook a series of military manoeuvres in Russia and CIS countries connected with NATO enlargement eastwards in 2004, which indicate the possibility of using Russian troops in the Western strategic direction. It has promised to continue these exercises and to strengthen its military forces abroad.[90] In justification, Russian General Staff officers have pointed to the capacity of US tactical aircraft, operating from advanced NATO bases, to strike at key cities in European Russia.[91] However, this attitude is not consistent with the public position of the Russian political leadership that the real threats to Russian security arise from the south. Russia has refrained from the serious step of reinforcing its army groups in north-west Russia and Kaliningrad, despite its complaints about the fact that the Baltic states have not yet subscribed to the modified CFE Treaty. Moscow has talked of taking 'adequate countermeasures' to NATO enlargement, but in reality has not even modestly upgraded the defences of the Pskov region and Leningrad Military District.

It is true that some Russian commentators have argued provocatively that the deployment of tactical nuclear weapons in the Kaliningrad region, or perhaps the deployment of nuclear munitions in border areas, are the only options Russia retains to place NATO under military pressure.[92] The nationalist retired general Leonid Ivashov has called for negotiations with Minsk over the deployment of tactical nuclear weapons in Belarus, targeted on all NATO objects being constructed near Russian borders.[93] But there is no evidence that such destabilizing ideas have been seriously considered by the Russian leadership. Instead the Russian military command has made much of its commitment to joint operational planning with the Belarusian armed forces and has discussed deploying high-precision conventional weapon systems, S-300 'operational tactical complexes' with a range of 500 km, to the Belarusian national army and perhaps to Kaliningrad.

NATO enlargement is seen in Moscow as hardening anti-Russian currents in the Alliance as a result of the entry of new East European and Baltic states. Russian officials complain that 'the newly admitted members are trying to resolve their bilateral problems with Russia via Brussels, seeking to enlist the allied power and authority'.[94] A particular issue is the long-standing dispute between Latvia and Estonia, on the one hand, and Russia on the other, over the conclusion of border agreements and over the status of ethnic Russian minorities in these Baltic states. The NATO position is that it does not discuss the internal problems of NATO members in the NRC. But NATO enlargement in itself has brought with it potential new areas of friction in the new Russia–NATO border zone that could reinforce an anti-Russian mood in the new Alliance members. For example, in October 2004 Russia complained in the NRC that Lithuania and Latvia have been hampering Russian military transit to Kaliningrad following their accession to NATO and implied that this was contrary to their membership commitments in the NRC.[95]

This followed vocal Russian protests about the commencement of NATO airspace patrols along the borders of the Baltic states and Putin's complaint that in 'an exercise in negligence' the NRC failed to warn Russia of this pending development.[96] It is difficult to believe that Alliance policing of Baltic airspace was a surprise to the Russian leadership, and anyway the mission involves only four fighter aircraft. But Russian nervousness has also been reflected in complaints by the armed forces command about NATO AWACS reconnaissance flights from the airfields of the Baltic states that 'enable NATO to see deep into north-west Russia and Belarus'.[97] By November 2005 Russian officials claimed that NATO had assigned aircraft meant for the suppression and penetration of an enemy's air defence instead of traditional air-defence aircraft to patrol the airspace of the Baltic states.[98]

Moscow's reaction points to the potential for significant tension between the 'partnership' of the NRC and the traditional collective security function of NATO. This was highlighted by a Russian proposal to form a joint NATO–Russia air defence system. Although this idea is unlikely to proceed, Sergei Ivanov noted that it was an item for discussion by the defence ministers of Russia and NATO states at an NRC meeting early in 2006, as well as options 'for stepping up cooperation in the joint control of air space in the border regions between Russia and the NATO states'.[99] Clearly there are risks if border incidents occur, including in air space, during a psychological climate of suspicions and occasional recriminations between Russia and NATO's new member states. Russian Foreign Minister Sergei Lavrov has expressed concern about 'NATO's military activity along Russia's borders' and has called for 'auxiliary measures for trust, control and the prevention of dangerous actions'.[100] In a wider context Russia has proposed consultations on new threats to the new groupings of NATO in Eastern Europe, as part of the NRC process of joint assessment of new threats.[101]

NATO enlargement is the cause of another periodic complaint from the Russian military leadership: possible plans to relocate NATO bases and 'military infrastructure' from Germany to Eastern Europe. Moscow has been particularly keen that NATO should continue to refrain from deploying nuclear weapons and creating nuclear infrastructure in the territory of the newly admitted alliance members. NATO has offered assurances that no military hardware or armed forces in any substantial quantities will be deployed on a permanent basis on the territory of the new alliance members, and that these states will have only those armed forces that are realistically necessary to defend their territories.[102] But this has not allayed Russian concerns. Russian officials argue that the military infrastructure of the newly admitted NATO states is undergoing major modernization, and particularly point to the adaptation of airfields in the Baltic states for use by all types of combat aircraft and the expansion of the capacities of naval bases in these states.[103] Sergei Ivanov has warned explicitly that the formation of a substantial military base in the Baltic states would be interpreted as a threat to Russia.[104]

These anxieties should be moderated by on-site inspections that Russia is carrying out at the modernized NATO facilities in the Baltic states, in accordance with the 1999 Vienna Document of the Negotiations on Confidence- and Security-Building Measures. But Russian officials intend to carry out further inspections of this kind to rule out the possibility of a sudden substantial build-up of NATO forces near Russia's borders.

Against the background of the 2004 NATO enlargement, the extent of Ukraine's association with NATO has become a growing Russian concern. This was already a factor in the Russian–Ukrainian dispute in 2003 over the status of the Sea of Azov. An agreement of the two states late that year that this sea is an internal waterway for Russia and Ukraine guaranteed for Moscow that NATO vessels cannot enter the Azov region without Russian permission. Since spring 2004, however, Moscow has complained about a memorandum ratified by the Supreme Rada of Ukraine that permits NATO to move its troops to Ukrainian territory if 'the Alliance's common strategy demands this'. Moscow argues that Ukraine's readiness to allow its territory to be used for NATO operations without Russian agreement is at odds with the spirit of article 6 of the Russian–Ukrainian friendship treaty. This stipulates that neither side shall allow its territory to be used to the detriment of the security of the other.[105] Even NATO PfP exercises on Ukrainian territory, such as the Peace Shield-2005 exercise held in Crimea in July 2005, excite Russian criticism.

Under President Viktor Yushchenko Ukraine's relations with NATO have been reinforced and the vision of accession to NATO has become a primary Ukrainian foreign policy objective. The Ukrainian Defence Minister has claimed optimistically that Ukraine 'will be ready to join NATO at the beginning of 2008 in terms of preparedness of the Ukrainian armed forces and the security sector'.[106] This hope is encouraged by the Intensified Dialogue process between NATO and Ukraine, launched in April 2005, the formal precursor of a possible Membership Action Plan. The Ukrainian Foreign Minister and media have also suggested a membership date of 2008 or 2009, although such a date would be more realistic during Yushchenko's second presidential term (2009–14), if he is re-elected.[107] In response, many Russian commentators believe Moscow retains a trump card. They claim that NATO will not take the further step of accepting Ukraine into NATO while Ukraine's agreement with Russia enabling the Russian Black Sea Fleet to retain its base on Ukrainian territory in Crimea at Sevastopol remains in force – that is, to 2017. NATO argues that the presence of third party forces in a member state is not a problem in itself. But a crisis sparked off by political demonstrations in Crimea is quite likely and the possibility of Ukraine's entry into NATO at some stage still has the potential to cause considerable rancour in Russian–Western dialogue during Yushchenko's presidency. Russian leaders have warned that if Ukraine were to enter NATO, its defence industry ties with Russia would need to be cut. Accession to NATO would also 'erect a "Berlin Wall" between it [Ukraine] and Russia together with Belarus', declaimed one of Russia's most prominent parliamentarians and leading security specialists.[108] This kind of rhetoric is likely to grow.

Since Yushchenko assumed power, the Russian leadership has accepted in principle that Ukraine has the sovereign right to choose which international organizations it wishes to join. But there is little evidence yet of serious thinking in Moscow about the strategic alternatives that Russia would face in the event of Ukrainian integration into NATO.[109] This could exacerbate Russia's sense of 'encirclement' and strategic isolation. Or it could prompt a reassessment of Russian policy and conclusively put to rest Russian aspirations for alternative Russian-led integration processes emerging on the territory of the former Soviet Union. Moscow would also need to consider Ukraine's possible attitude to Russia if it were on the 'inside' of NATO (or indeed the EU). One possibility, though perhaps not a likely one, is that Ukraine would play the same role for Russia that Poland has played for Ukraine – explaining Russia's interests and perspectives and pressing for more intensive practical cooperation with Russia.

Beyond Ukraine, Russian officials have set themselves against 'NATO's mandate being extended to the Black Sea' through an expansion of its Active

Endeavour naval operation in 2006 (arguing that safe navigation in the Black Sea can be ensured by the local countries involved in the BlackSeaFor naval cooperation grouping).[110] They look warily at Moldova's proposal in June 2005 for a shift from PfP cooperation to the deeper relationship represented by an Individual Partnership Action Plan (IPAP) and resent President Voronin's request for NATO political support to achieve the withdrawal of Russian troops from Moldova.[111]

Moscow is also nervous that states of the South Caucasus are seeking eventual accession to the Alliance, and that their defence doctrines are being reviewed and adjusted to NATO doctrine so that a number of CIS countries could end up having a greater interoperability with NATO forces than with Russian forces. At the Istanbul NATO summit in June 2004 special emphasis was given to the prospects for NATO partnership with states in the South Caucasus and Central Asia. However, the Russian diplomatic response to this appears quite relaxed. The Russian Foreign Ministry has accepted that 'NATO actions are, essentially, designed to ensure military-political stability in the post-Soviet area', and that NATO and Russia have common tasks in countering new challenges in the region. These include preventing former Soviet territory from turning into a base area for international terrorist organizations or the proliferation of WMD, or into a channel for drug trafficking.[112] An NRC session in April 2005 went so far as to discuss prospects for the settlement of the Georgian–Abkhaz and Georgian–Ossetian conflicts, and in the following month a NATO–Russia parliamentary committee reportedly found common ground over settling the Nagorno-Karabakh conflict.[113]

At the same time Russian spokesmen have warned that cooperation with NATO could be jeopardized by 'rash actions linked, for example, with invitations to CIS countries to join NATO'.[114] Some leading Russian analysts already predict that in five years all the western republics of the former Soviet Union will join NATO.[115] Evidently Moscow is nervous that a group of CIS countries may push for Membership Action Plans towards NATO accession, but has no effective response. Defence Minister Sergei Ivanov has accepted that any Russian attempt to influence the process of any CIS country joining NATO would be futile. But he has stressed that in his view NATO accession by any of the CIS states will not be an issue for the next five to seven years, during which period NATO itself will change significantly as a result of the globalization of threats.[116]

It is less clear that senior Russian military officers have an equally sanguine view about the NATO role in Ukraine and beyond Ukraine in the CIS region. Schooled in Soviet training and war planning, they may focus more on NATO military capabilities. Yet despite their various concerns about NATO enlargement, there are many indications for them that NATO is moving away from its hard war-fighting role in Europe to at most peace support tasks on this continent. This is suggested by NATO's major commitment to Afghanistan, its training mission to Baghdad, the formation of the NATO response force with broad geographic missions (declared as operational by NATO in October 2004), and by continued divisions between NATO members over aspects of US policy. This softening of NATO's Europe function, even if article 5 commitments remain, may make it easier for Russia to reach pro forma cooperation agreements with NATO in the NRC. But then Moscow is less likely to rely on these agreements to address core traditional Russian security concerns.

TOWARDS ASSOCIATE MEMBERSHIP? AN AGENDA FOR DEEPER NATO–RUSSIA COOPERATION

In the light of the preceding analysis it is not clear whether Russia regards NATO or the NRC as a sufficiently effective institutional partner to privilege as the main channel in attempts to build bridges in terms of security policy across Europe and the Atlantic. Bilateral agreements with the United States in particular might displace an effort to bond with NATO. The growing focus on combating terrorism might also overwhelm the panoply of other security concerns that exercise European NATO states.

However, we should not dismiss the scenario of Russia proceeding on a trajectory towards some kind of 'associate membership' of NATO, or even developing an alliance with the Alliance as an outgrowth of the NRC (but bypassing the more politically challenging mechanism of developing an Individual Partnership Action Plan with NATO). For this to become possible a process of successful confidence-building would be essential. The new NATO members would need to become more relaxed about Russian intentions, and the Russian political and military leadership would need to conclusively set aside the image of NATO as a potential adversary. Senior Russian officials are aware that psychological hurdles would have to be overcome for deep cooperation with NATO. Colonel-General Viktor Zavarzin, the head of the State Duma Committee on Defence, has suggested that Russia would be interested in taking its relations with NATO 'to such a level of trust, and [in] finding such an algorithm of actions, which would not be inferior to the level of trust and cooperation among the members of the Alliance themselves'.[117] But this sidesteps the question of whether such trust can be generated if Russia does not accept the normative foundation that binds NATO members to common goals.

For Russia to proceed towards some kind of associate membership of NATO, it would be crucial, nonetheless, to develop ideas for NATO–Russia consultation, cooperation and in some cases joint decision and common action that might mesh Russia closer into the core of European security policy-making. Possible ideas that would assist such a process are being contemplated by Western and Russian specialists and can be divided into various fields.[118]

Military contacts and cooperation

Options include: to increase Russian involvement in NATO exercise planning and implementation, including the development of NATO peacekeeping doctrine and NATO Response Force employment doctrine; to establish a joint training centre in Russia focused on peacekeeping; to create a joint brigade focused on counterterrorist cooperation or on peacekeeping; and to promote joint activities between Russian military units in Kaliningrad and the Polish–German–Danish Corps; to explore opportunities for joint peace-keeping missions as a means to ensure the resolution of 'frozen conflicts' within CIS states; for Russia to create significant officer training opportuni-ties for NATO personnel in Russia, and in parallel for there to be increased Russian participation in NATO and NATO-related schools.

Engagement with NATO institutions

Options include: to review structures and tasks within NATO to consider how these might be revised or reallocated to make it easier to involve Russia; for Russia to more deeply engage NATO at SHAPE; and to establish a Euro-Atlantic Regional Security Strategy Group to enable NATO and Russia to develop their military-technical and political-military strategies in ways that are compatible with each other. In this way, inclusion could become the rule and exclusion the exception, so that NATO and Russia would increas-ingly counsel each other in any crisis either faces; Russia could progressively become associated with NATO transformation and Russia could share its transformation work with NATO.

Combating terrorism and related threats

Options include: to develop a Counter-terrorism Information Sharing Centre, under the NRC, including a mechanism for assessing terrorist threats and coordinating efforts and joint actions, with a particular focus on preventing the use of WMD by terrorists; and to take the lead in developing an international, counter-terrorist COCOM, resembling the West's Cold War Coordinating Committee on Multilateral Export Controls and centred on critical areas such as intelligence cooperation, border control, police coop-eration and financial controls. Cooperation in civil emergency preparedness could also be extended.

Defence industry and arms cooperation[119]

Options include: to create means for Russian firms to participate in the modernization of weaponry and to foster Russian firms' capacity to build and repair to NATO standards; to enhance cooperation in using Russian/Ukrainian transport aircraft for airlift in NATO military missions – this would be helped by a framework agreement on air transport that would provide access to military airlift.

There are natural limits to the extent of cooperation of this kind that can be achieved in a multilateral format, because of the sensitivity of many of these issues. The practicality of such far-reaching proposals will also depend greatly on the nature of military transformation in Russia and the overall political climate between Russia and NATO states. This partly reflects the new composition of NATO. NATO's absorption of the last round of accession states, particularly the Baltic states, is likely to result in more caution towards cooperative ventures between Russia and NATO that significantly increase Russian influence over NATO policies. Many of these ideas would also need to be coordinated with parallel NATO–EU and Russia–EU developments, if the overarching goal of drawing Russia more fully within the West and Western institutions is to be achieved. But it is important to note that such an agenda for cooperation should not be viewed as a channel for integration with the West or Europe; it is not subordinated to any specific process of transformation of Russia and is not dependent on such a process.

RUSSIAN MEMBERSHIP OF NATO?

This leaves the option of actual NATO membership as a possible means for Russian integration into Europe. There has been some debate in Moscow on the question of Russia joining NATO, with some in favour of raising this option 'in order to rationalize and simplify the terms of Russia–NATO relations and draw up a "road map" for deepening the partnership'. This perspective, which has not surfaced in official dialogue, depends on the transformation of NATO into a new format and would depend on radical changes in its systems of decision-making, planning and control, which would shift the emphasis from collective defence to collective security. Russian analysts have pointed out that the vision of Russia's eventual integration into a transformed NATO would enable Moscow to view any further wave of enlargement, such as to include CIS states, in a different way. It could be perceived 'as part of the wider transformation of the Western alliance into a European security organization with Russia'.[120]

In practice, however, such a transformation of NATO remains wishful thinking among such Russian analysts. Russia can hardly develop substantive policy on the assumption of NATO reinventing itself in the way required, regardless of the positive effects of the NRC since 2002, so Russian accession to NATO cannot seriously be contemplated on this basis.[121] Indeed, by 2005 even the scenario of a deep partnership between Russia and NATO appeared to be optimistic for the medium term, taking into account Russian evolving threat perceptions and domestic political developments. Given the attitudes of the Russian elite and policy-makers, the views of the new NATO members and the existing conditions for NATO membership, Russian entry into NATO is hardly likely in the coming decade and this must be understood in Moscow.[122]

But neither top NATO officials nor President Putin wish to wholly exclude this outcome.[123] On the Russian side this seems to reflect the view that an extended 'watching brief' should be maintained just in case NATO does in fact transform itself or degenerate into a very different entity. Over time, a member of the presidential administration suggested in spring 2004, and on certain conditions, 'it will not seem so senseless as even a couple of years ago'.[124] Putin replied equivocally to a question in October 2005 on the possibility that Russia would ever become a member of NATO. He noted that at the moment NATO is 'undergoing certain internal changes' and that 'we need to understand what we would be joining, if this issue arises, and what tasks we would tackle in this organization'.[125] Sergei Ivanov reflected Russian military opinion in bluntly noting that 'Russia is not keen to join NATO, very much as the alliance is not eager to see Russia among its members'.[126]

A core difficulty for Russia arises from NATO accession criteria. In 2002 the former US Secretary of State, James A. Baker III, downplayed this issue. He suggested that Russia qualified as eligible for NATO membership according to two broad and implicit criteria for admission: membership of the Atlantic community, that is to say the West; and sharing important security concerns with other members. However, of the five criteria that NATO specified in 1995 with which possible new members would need to conform, only one – good relations with neighbouring states (with the resolution of internal ethnic disputes) – is strictly relevant to the costs and benefits of admitting a new member to a military alliance. All the others are 'soft' criteria that assess the character of new members as expressed by their domestic arrangements.[127] Such criteria for admission to NATO express Western values and the need for candidate countries correspondingly to reorder their domestic political and economic affairs. These criteria are unlikely to be diluted for Russia and may represent insuperable hurdles for the country, since they are bound up with the core issues of identity and value formation.

During the current period of enlargement these criteria continue to define NATO's self-perception. In spring 2003 the president of the NATO Parliamentary Assembly conceded that Russia could become a NATO member in the future. But he reaffirmed that, as in the cases of Albania, Croatia and Macedonia, this would be conditional both on far-reaching military reform and on the introduction of principles usual in democratic countries.[128] The first requirement, structural military reform, is a particularly unwelcome challenge to the Russian military bureaucracy, since it would lead to losses among them in jobs, status and political influence. Russia's ambassador to NATO, Konstantin Totsky, has openly opposed Russia joining the Alliance, arguing that 'this would require a lot of time and substantial material resources'.[129] Russian analysts have noted that the Russian military has failed to use the experience not only of NATO, but also of East and Central European countries and the Baltic states, and that the issue 'concerns psychological distrust of Western advice and fears of losing identity'.[130]

The adoption of democratic principles, as a condition of accession to NATO, would require Russia as a baseline to implement further judicial reform and to curb corruption and organized crime. But crucially Russia would also have to effect substantial changes to its political arrangements in a direction contrary to the political system Putin is seeking to consolidate. These are challenges that Moscow can avoid through its current relationship with NATO through the NRC.

Furthermore, there is the issue of Russia's size and geographic diversity and the scope of its security interests. It has been suggested that this might partly be addressed by amending the NATO charter: first, to provide that an agreed purpose of the Alliance would be 'the maintenance of peace and stability on the Eurasian continent' – though this implies the challenge of extending security guarantees to Chinese borders; and, second, to provide that the Alliance could act with less than unanimous consent, so that nations could opt out of actions in which they did not wish to participate.[131] The latter revision would suit the tendency for coalitions of the willing to be formed, and allow Russia greater latitude in its policies. It would limit challenges to Russia's prized principles of sovereignty and strategic independence. But it could also offer the US too great a field for manoeuvre and would most likely be opposed by small new member states. Moreover, it would not address the basic need to absorb and dilute Russian 'great power' aspirations, or encourage Russia to assume the political and military constraints this involves, in a way that would allow the formation of a common NATO–Russia security culture. Russian leaders are unlikely to accept that their state should operate in NATO without special privileges under common rules as just one of many states, rather than as a 'power centre' in the Eurasian landmass. Without a fundamental change in the nature of the Alliance, Russian entry into NATO is an unlikely route, therefore, for Russian integration into Europe.

CONCLUSION

The instrumental relationship that Russia has developed with NATO during Putin's presidency has gradually expanded through exploring fields for cooperation that offer some mutual benefit and – crucially for Russia – do not appear politically challenging. The Russian leadership remains highly sensitive to perceived infringements of Russian sovereignty and continues to insist on developing relations with NATO, as with the EU, on the basis of 'equality'. This reflects lingering distrust and suspicion over NATO intentions but also nervousness that drawing close to the Alliance will encourage Western efforts to influence Russian internal policies, or result in some explicit conditionality, which could restrict the Kremlin's field for manoeuvre, especially in managing its domestic political arrangements. In fact the programme for cooperation with Russia advanced by NATO through the NRC, even if it is expanded considerably, is not subordinated to any specific process of transformation of Russia in political or economic terms and is not dependent on such a process. This assists the cause of developing pragmatic cooperation with Russia but strictly limits the capacity of the NRC to act as an agent to socialize Russia into the wider European community.

A wide field for pragmatic Russia–NATO cooperation has been sketched out in this chapter. But significant further progress even in some fields of the current NRC agenda, such as defence sector reform or planning a possible joint NATO–Russia peacekeeping operation, is difficult to envisage without changes in Russian military culture and attitudes on the use of force. These need to be rooted in greater pluralism and accountability in domestic politics rather than the reinforcement of 'statism'. In this respect it is notable that Russia has rejected the option of developing an IPAP with NATO. This is a mechanism, first introduced in 2002, aimed at offering NATO's partner states tailored support for the process of their democratic transformation in fields including political and security policy issues, defence and military issues, and civil emergency planning. Here a transformation agenda is clearly built into the relationship with NATO. But even if Russia remains averse to an IPAP, in essence NATO continues to regard democratic government as a requirement for long-term stability, for Russia as for other states.[132]

The new Central and East European members of NATO expect this kind of transformation agenda to remain a litmus test for any in-depth NATO engagement with Russia. A recent Polish study, for example, concluded that Russia needs to pursue such an agenda and harmonize it with standards applicable to Alliance member states, and that without 'a tangible community of values and basic interests, effective partnership and deepening cooperation between NATO and Russia is impossible'.[133] However, such progressive harmonization is not happening. As a process or exercise in sharing values, it cannot be substituted by recent efforts to present counter-terrorism as a new security paradigm for bonding Russia to NATO – still less for bonding Russia with the major European NATO states. The new NATO members in particular, seeking to consolidate their status in the enlarged Europe and its key security organization, are averse to Russia's claim that it deserves a special, privileged relationship with NATO based on its specific character and circumstances, regardless of its domestic policies. These differences significantly constrain the depth of Russia–NATO partnership, or 'partnership plus'.

Indeed, even Russia's current programme of cooperation in the NRC could sour if various potential 'spoilers' in the larger Russian relationship with the Alliance and its leading states are not effectively managed. These relate to the NATO presence and Russian conduct in post-Soviet geographic zones, especially Ukraine and the South Caucasus, the Russian use of force in Chechnya, or the use of force by Western states in other international conflicts in the absence of a relevant UN Security Council mandate.[34] Serious dissension in Russia–NATO relations (and within NATO) could arise from efforts to curtail Iran's nuclear programme. If Russia's hopes for cooperation with NATO begin to fade, then it could shift its emphasis to greater 'Eurasian' cooperation with China through the Shanghai Cooperation Organization as a putative counterweight to NATO. This would be no way to promote Russia's European security agenda, but might reflect frustration about the realization of that agenda.

These points indicate that Russia's rather limited engagement with NATO is unlikely during Putin's presidency or the medium-term future to spill over, from its current security concerns, into broader areas of functional integration with the member states of the Alliance that could erode and eventually even dispel the politico-security dividing lines between Russia and the enlarged Europe. NATO is not the vehicle for realizing this kind of neo-functionalist logic, associated in the past with the process of EU enlargement in Western and Central Europe. Actual Russian accession to NATO, even to a considerably transformed and more politicized NATO, would certainly hold much more promise of integrating Russia into the wider Europe because of the political and economic accession criteria that have to be met for NATO membership. But the very existence of these criteria, as argued in this chapter, is likely to preclude this outcome. In the coming decade there is little hope that Russia will be absorbed into the European mainstream through the shared values and habits of cooperation that common institutional membership in NATO would represent and reinforce.

This conclusion is reflected in the attitudes of the Russian foreign policy elite examined in this chapter. Those who seek a convergence of Russia with NATO and its leading states based on a value orientation are marginalized in Russian political life. The pragmatic collaboration with NATO that is broadly supported by the Russian leadership and an influential part of the political elite remains vulnerable to the overall state of Russian–Western relations. It can offer substantial benefits to Russia and its NATO partners, but it is neither a path towards Europeanization nor a sufficient means to overcome Russia's sense of exclusion from the institutional architecture of the enlarged Europe.

6

Russia and 'Europe': the public dimension

Stephen White

Foreign policy has not normally been a central concern in Russia's public life, any more than it is in that of most other countries.[1] Russia's vast landmass provides for a high degree of self-sufficiency, not least in natural resources. Foreign trade accounts for a relatively small share of GDP (in the early years of the new century, less than 12 per cent, compared with 19 per cent in the United States and 42 per cent in the United Kingdom);[2] and movement across national frontiers, although much greater than it used to be, remains difficult and limited. Nevertheless, Russia is much less isolated from the outside world than at any previous time in its history. Its president takes part in the work of the G-7 (which had to become the G-8), and chaired it in 2006; it is a member of the International Monetary Fund, and is moving towards membership of the World Trade Organization (WTO). At the same time its economy has been thoroughly penetrated by the US dollar, whose value in domestic circulation some time ago outstripped that of the rouble. Western brand names are an established presence on the high streets of major cities; affluent Russians take their holidays in Mediterranean resorts; its tennis players, particularly the female ones, sweep all before them on the international competition circuit.

Russia's domestic political agenda has reflected many of these developments, as well as the periodic crises that have convulsed the international community as a whole. The Yugoslav bombing campaign of 1999 led to demonstrations outside Western embassies; much larger numbers took to the streets in early 2003 as part of the internationally coordinated protest against the war that was about to take place in Iraq. And there are other, more institutionalized forms of public influence. Foreign relations, for instance, have not been a central issue in Russia's post-Communist elections. But the surge in the Communist vote in the Duma election of December 1995 was one of the circumstances that preceded the dismissal of Russia's pro-Western Foreign Minister, Andrei Kozyrev, early the following year. And changes in the composition of the Duma lead directly to changes in the leadership of its committees that deal with foreign relations – particularly, the Committees on International Affairs, National Security, Defence, and Relations with the Commonwealth of Independent States (CIS) and Russian diaspora – all of which have been headed since 2004 by representatives of the United Russia party. 'Linkage' of this kind is particularly apparent in relation to the continuing conflict in Chechnya, which both Russian and Western governments have not hesitated to place within a broader international context.

In exploring the domestic implications of Russia's international politics, we draw in this chapter on two bodies of evidence in particular. The first consists of nationally representative surveys, conducted between 2000 and 2005 as part of a wider exercise across the post-Soviet Slavic states that constitute Europe's new borderland. The second draws upon a series of focus group interviews conducted in 1999–2001, and again in 2006, in a number of 'typical' Russian locations outside the major metropolitan cities, which revolved around the same concerns (fuller details of both exercises are provided in our Note on sources, p. 181 below). We start, in the opening section below, by considering the public foreign policy agenda as it was articulated by the parties and candidates that contested the Duma and presidential elections of 2003–4. We relate this in the following section to the evidence that emerges from our surveys of the distribution of opinion on relations with 'Europe', and on Russia's international security more generally. The concluding section moves beyond statistical generalization to the thoughts and feelings of ordinary citizens, expressed in their own words.

FOREIGN POLICY: THE PUBLIC POLITICAL AGENDA

Classical models of democracy rest upon the assumption of an active and informed citizenry that makes a choice among the competing programmes of government that are put forward by political parties at general elections. It need hardly be said that Western countries, as well as post-communist Russia, depart in many respects from this ideal type. Nonetheless, political choices, for ordinary Russians, are organized in the form of political parties and presidential candidates, who may or may not have a party label, and these choices are made at regular elections to the State Duma and the presidency.

Under the law that governed the 2003 Duma election, parties or electoral blocs were required to publish a manifesto not less than ten days before polling took place (art. 57:10), and the law that applied to the 2004 presidential contest made a similar provision in respect of parties or electoral blocs that put forward candidates, although candidates themselves were free to choose the form and content of their own campaigning (arts. 49:9, 49:3).

The evidence of the programmes that were presented in the 1993 and 1995 elections had already suggested that Russian parties were becoming more 'Slavophile' on matters of state form, and more assertive on issues that were relevant to Russia's position in international affairs.[3]

Four parties or electoral blocs secured a party-list vote of more than 5 per cent at the Duma election of December 2003, and two other parties won 4 per cent or more. Taken together, these six won nearly 79 per cent of the party-list vote and 46 per cent of the vote in the single-member constituencies that make up the other half of the Duma, and took more than three-quarters of all the seats. They may reasonably be regarded as constituting the largest part of the organized political forces that constitute Russia's contemporary political spectrum, and as defining the central issues around which the public debate revolves. At the next Duma election, in December 2007, the entire contest will be organized around political parties of this kind, as the law adopted in 2005 has eliminated the single-member constituency section of the contest.[4]

The party that most accurately represented the position of the Kremlin itself, and that was indeed virtually defined by its support of presidential policies, was United Russia. This had been formed at the end of 2001 on the basis of a merger between the Unity party and its main challenger, Fatherland–All Russia, and emerged the clear winner in December 2003 with nearly 38 per cent of the party-list vote. United Russia spoke in its election manifesto of the formation of a 'belt of friendship' based upon the other members of the Commonwealth of Independent States, and of an 'anti-terrorist regime' that would embrace Chechnya just as much as those who had been responsible for the 9/11 outrages in New York and Washington, but which would rest upon the foundations of international law and recognize the particular responsibilities of the United Nations. United Russia also favoured a 'sensible and coherent migration policy' that would allow fellow nationals to return to Russia; the introduction of a visa-free regime with the countries of the European Union by 2008, on the basis of the Schengen agreement; and the maintenance of 'friendly relations' with the United States.[5]

There were, in fact, many common elements across the party programmes, particularly with regard to the closer integration of the former Soviet republics and the conduct of relations with other countries that respected Russia's national interests (including the position of the Russian-speaking diaspora). The Communist Party's manifesto was the only one that spoke of the need to restore a Soviet form of government, and it gave more emphasis than others to the nationalization of economic resources, but it was also concerned to restore Russia as a powerful state, and to reconstitute a divided Russian nation. All the country's natural resources, promised the Communists, would be taken into public ownership. So would the energy and defence industries and the railways, all of which were of strategic significance. State orders would be used to support domestic producers and to raise living standards. Internationally, all obstacles would be removed to the unification of Russia, Belarus and Ukraine into a 'single union state', to take place on a 'voluntary, democratic basis'. And every effort would be made to restore Russia's standing in the wider world, so as to avoid 'complete colonization' and the 'sad fate of Serbia or Iraq'.[6]

The newly formed Rodina (Motherland) party took an unexpected fourth place in the election, with just over 9 per cent of the party-list vote. Its programme shared many of the same national-patriotic assumptions but introduced additional elements, including a particular emphasis upon the moral and cultural dimension. The domestic economy would be protected from unfair competition; the state itself would exercise control over the 'basic infrastructure', including mineral resources and sectors that were of strategic or social significance; and Russian negotiators would be instructed to undertake an 'active defence of the interests of the national economy on the international arena', including in their negotiations with the World Trade Organization. Steps would also be taken to stop the illegal export of capital, and to 'de-dollarize' the economy more generally. There was a similar emphasis, as with the other parties, upon the reintegration of the former Soviet republics, including the completion of the formation of a union government with Belarus as the first step towards a broader association. Rodina struck a distinctive note in its call to defend the 'traditional values of Russian culture' from what it described as 'psychological aggression and "screen terrorism"', and in its suggestion that the state itself commission work of a 'high artistic and moral level'.[7]

The other party that reached the 5 per cent threshold was the right-wing nationalist Liberal Democratic Party of Russia under its half-buffoon, half-sinister leader Vladimir Zhirinovsky. The LDPR put forward its entire party programme, a lengthy document that set out most of the priorities with which the party had been associated for more than a decade. It shared much of the 'national-patriotic' consensus, but within a larger philosophical framework that ranged over entire civilizations. The LDPR claimed to be a 'party of genuine patriots', whose aim was to restore Russia as a great power, or even as the 'world superpower', in keeping with its geopolitical mission. This meant, in the first instance, strengthening the unity of the Russian state itself, and then reunifying the other former Soviet republics around it. The LDPR had supported the attempted coup of 1991 that sought to prevent the break-up of the USSR, and welcomed the union treaty between Russia and Belarus as a 'first step' towards the reconstitution of a Russian state within its 'natural boundaries'. The LDPR was also committed to the protection of Russians in the 'near abroad', in the Baltic republics, Central Asia, Kazakhstan and elsewhere, and called for the Russian government to take the appropriate steps against countries that conducted a 'policy of genocide' in relation to their Russian-speaking minorities.

These general priorities led to a number of specific policy prescriptions. Internationally, cooperation with the United States should continue, particularly in relation to terrorism (although it was in many ways a response to the United States' own bid for global hegemony). But the LDPR opposed NATO's enlargement towards the east, and rejected any of the 'vassal' obligations that Russia might be asked to assume as part of a broader framework of cooperation. The party looked forward to the formation by Russia and other countries of an 'eastern bloc' that would offer an effective counterbalance to NATO, and called for a review of existing treaty commitments of a kind that might no longer be conducive to national security. The LDPR looked east as well as west, in the belief that Russia should promote its own interests wherever it was practicable to do so. In this connection, the LDPR called for a partnership with Japan, in spite of the continuing territorial dispute, and with China, in spite of the 'ethnic aggression', both taking place in the Russian Far East; but it was more cautious about the prospects of a better relationship with an expansionist Turkey.[8]

The other distinctive element in the public agenda comprised the liberal, or pro-Western, parties Yabloko and the Union of Right Forces, although neither of them reached the 5 per cent threshold that was necessary for representation in the new Duma. Yabloko's election manifesto gave relatively little attention to foreign affairs, apart from suggesting that the future of Chechnya be considered by an international conference under Russian presidency.[9] But its programme set out a much more detailed position, including goals that were explicitly modelled on those of Russia's western neighbours. Yabloko sought to establish a stable democratic order, including a state based on the rule of law; a socially oriented market economy; an authentic civil society; a modern system of security; and a 'post-industrial strategy within the frame-work of the European path of development'. Russia, Yabloko believed, was indeed a 'European country in its historical destiny, its cultural traditions, [and] its geographical situation', with a potential that could be realized only by 'making creative use of the values of European civilization'. Yabloko was accordingly a supporter of Russian membership of the EU (not, admittedly, an immediate prospect) and of other European organizations.[10]

Yabloko's companion on the liberal wing of the political spectrum was the Union of Right Forces, formed in August 1999 shortly before the Duma election of that year. Its programme, as modified in 2001, committed the party to a range of liberal democratic values, including freedom of speech and association, the separation of powers, decentralization, the rule of law, private property, equal rights, and tolerance of diversity.[11] Its election manifesto called directly for the 'integration of Russia into Europe, its structures and institutions, [and] for the equalization of the level and quality of life of Russians and Europeans'.[12] However, the URF fell even further short of the 5 per cent threshold in the Duma election than Yabloko had done, and its three single-member deputies joined United Russia in the new parliament; neither party nominated a candidate in the presidential election, and indeed their future existence began to be questioned. There was certainly no indication in their electoral fortunes that a substantial constituency was available for the pro-Western values with which both parties were explicitly associated.

Putin himself was not the candidate of a political party in March 2004, but stood formally as an independent. His 'programmatic address', presented at Moscow University a month before the polls, gave little attention to foreign affairs, but he was more forthcoming in his responses to a series of questions from his carefully selected audience. He shared their sense of loss about the collapse of the Soviet Union – a 'massive tragedy' from which none of the newly independent nations had gained any advantage. But there was no alternative but to accept the situation that actually existed, and it did at least allow Russia to insist that its own legitimate interests were treated with the same respect as the interests of the other republics that had formerly been part of the USSR. Another question dealt with the way in which Russian policies were perceived abroad, and the extent to which they were supported. There were still powerful forces, Putin acknowledged, that regarded Russians in much same way as they had been regarded during the Cold War, but there were also 'healthy forces' that were broadly speaking 'our partners', and it made most sense to work with them so that the 'ice of mistrust' could gradually be broken. He insisted that Russia's own armed forces were a source of international stability in this connection, and promised that they would receive the resources they needed.[13]

There was, in fact, a substantial measure of agreement across all the parties and candidates, whether they were nominally 'left' or 'right', 'nationalist' or 'centrist'. The collapse of the USSR was widely regretted, and there was virtually unanimous agreement that Russia should do everything possible to encourage closer reintegration with the former Soviet republics, and in the first place Belarus. Closer relations with Europe and North America had great importance, particularly for liberals, but so too had relations with Russia's Asian neighbours, particularly for nationalists and communists. Russia should at the same time be more assertive in defending its national interests, and supporting its fellow nationals in other countries; this was partly a matter of military spending and equipment, but it was also bound up with issues of demography, language and religious faith, and the protection of Russian moral and cultural values from the harmful influences of other countries. More generally, every effort should be made to maintain a multipolar world, based upon the principles of international law and the organizational framework of the United Nations, and to resist the global hegemony of the United States.

A 'EUROPEAN CHOICE'?

Perhaps the most immediate of these foreign policy choices was the relationship with 'Europe', and it was certainly the one that raised the most pressing questions of national identity. Indeed, there had been a debate since at least the time of Pushkin and Chadaev about whether Russia was best understood as a European society, or as a distinctive and perhaps unique social formation. Russians spoke an Indo-European language. Their religion was Christian. Their state had been part of the European balance of power since at least the early eighteenth century. Their royal house had dynastic connections with its counterparts elsewhere on the continent – Nicholas II even bore a striking physical resemblance to his British cousin, George V. But most of the state sprawled across Asia, its religion was a part of Eastern rather than Western Christianity, and its historical trajectory had been marked by centuries of foreign domination and bureaucratic despotism. At least for Samuel Huntington, this distinctive experience marked out a distinctive Slavic-Orthodox civilization, and a society and culture that 'had little resemblance to those developed in Western Europe under the influence of very different forces'.[14] Where did Russians place themselves in terms of such choices? And what, if anything, did this imply for their relationship with the economic and military associations that bound together most of their European neighbours?

We included questions of this kind in our national surveys between 2000 and 2005, using large and representative samples of the Russian voting-age population. We asked, first of all, whether Russians thought of themselves as Europeans. The results are set out in Table 6.1. As we can see, only a quarter of our respondents in 2005 thought of themselves 'to a significant extent' or even 'to some extent' as Europeans; more than half 'never' did so. Nor was this explained by whether our respondents actually lived in geographical Europe, or (like about a quarter of their fellow nationals) in what was geographically Asia. Of those who lived anywhere in Russia, just under 9 per cent thought of themselves to a significant extent as European; of those who lived in geographical Europe, no more than 10 per cent did so. These levels of European identity were substantially lower than those we found in 2000, when as many as half of our respondents thought of themselves 'often' or 'sometimes' as Europeans; and they are consistent with the findings of other researchers that Russians conceive of 'Europe' in terms of values and ideals at least as much as territory, and are accordingly less likely to think of themselves as Europeans than their geographical location might entitle them to do.[15]

Table 6.1: Russians and a European identity, 2000, 2004 and 2005

Percentage of respondents who thought of themselves as Europeans:	2000	2004	2005
'To a significant extent'	18	9	7
'To some extent'	34	21	18
'Seldom'	28	13	14
'Not at all'	19	47	54
Don't know; no answer	2	10	7

Source: Authors' surveys; figures show the percentage who selected each option. Question wordings were, in 2000, 'Do you regard yourself as a European? Yes, unconditionally; yes, on balance; no, on balance; not at all'; in 2004–5, 'Do you think of yourself as a European?' with the options shown. Further details of the surveys are provided in our Note on sources.

Table 6.2: Russians and their identities, 2004 and 2005

	Primary identity		Secondary identity		Primary + secondary		[European Russia only]	
	2004	2005	2004	2005	2004	2005	2004	2005
European	4	4	6	4	10	8	12	9
Eurasian	3	1	4	2	7	3	7	2
Soviet citizen	8	8	5	6	13	13	11	13
Citizen of one's country	45	46	27	30	72	76	74	76
Citizen of one's region	9	8	22	21	31	29	29	27
Resident of one's town/settlement/village	31	33	34	34	65	69	65	72
Other	1	1	0	1	1	2	1	2

Source: Authors' surveys. Figures show the percentage that chose each separate option; the European Russia columns show those who opted for 'European' as a primary or secondary identity. The question wording was, 'Which of the following do you think of yourself as first of all? And secondarily?' (Options were read out;

Table 6.3: Russian assessments of the European Union, 2000, 2004 and 2005

	2000	2004	2005
Very positive	5	9	9
Rather positive	16	35	40
Rather negative	7	6	8
Very negative	4	3	3
Don't know	69	46	40
Refused to answer	0	1	1

Source: Authors' surveys; column percentages.
Question wordings were, in 2000, 'What, on the whole, is your impression of the aims and activities of the European Union?'; in 2004 and 2005, 'What is your attitude towards the aims and activities of the European Union?'

Questions of this kind are clearly no more than a first approximation of the nature and distribution of a complex and polyvalent phenomenon.[16] Accordingly, in 2004 and 2005 we asked a second question in which our respondents were asked to select a primary and then a secondary loyalty from a list that was provided by our interviewers. Deliberately, these questions were designed to reproduce the form in which 'Europeanness' has been tested for many years in the Eurobarometer that is sponsored by the EU Commission. Our results are set out in Table 6.2; they are broadly consistent with the pattern of responses that emerged from our earlier question. Overwhelmingly, Russians identify themselves as Russian citizens, or as residents of their local community (these two between them represented more than three-quarters of all responses). Substantial numbers identified themselves

Table 6.4: Russia and EU membership, 2000, 2004 and 2005

	2000	2004	2005
Strongly in favour	12	18	19
Somewhat in favour	35	34	37
Somewhat against	9	9	12
Strongly against	2	6	7
Don't know/No answer	41	34	25

Source: Authors' surveys; column percentages; for 2000, 'neutral' responses have been coded as 'don't know'.
Question wordings were, in 2000, 'From the economic point of view, do you think it would be desirable for Russia to join the European Union, which includes the main countries of Western Europe?'; in 2004 and 2005, 'What view would you take of the possibility of our country becoming a member of the European Union?'

as citizens of their region (constitutionally, a doubtful concept). But very few saw themselves primarily or even secondarily as 'Europeans', fewer even than saw themselves as Soviet citizens. And, again, this pattern of responses was almost uniform across the country, whether our respondents actually lived in geographical Europe or not.

We asked, in separate questions, about attitudes towards the European Union itself, and about the possibility that Russia itself might become a member.[17] We set out our results in Tables 6.3 and 6.4. In relation to the 'aims and activities' of the European Union, Russians who had an opinion were generally very positive – and increasingly so, as compared with responses to the same question five years earlier. But at least as striking was the very high proportion of respondents who felt unable to offer an opinion of any kind, a response that reflects the substantial numbers who lacked even the most elementary factual knowledge of the EU and its activities. We asked, for instance, how many of our respondents could identify the EU headquarters from a list of five European capitals. Barely more than a third (39 per cent in 2005) picked Brussels (a fifth would have done so if the choice had been entirely random), and half of them felt unable to offer an opinion of any kind (we were also offered 'Davos', 'New York' and 'Washington'). Equally, no more than 39 per cent in 2005 were able to identify the EU as an 'economic and political association of the countries of Western Europe', given a list of four options; the next most numerous group (28 per cent) had no idea, and 16 per cent thought it was 'an association of all the European countries, including our own', evidently confusing it with the Council of Europe.

We asked, finally, about the possibility of Russian membership of the European Union, and about the consequences it might be likely to have. There was certainly strong support for membership in principle (not, of course, that it is currently on offer): more than half took this view in 2005, slightly more than in 2000 and 2004. A similar level of support has been apparent in other investigations, although there have been considerable variations over time. The All-Russian Centre for the Study of Public Opinion (VTsIOM), for instance, found that 36 per cent of its respondents in early 2004 were in favour of full EU membership, and that 45 per cent would vote in favour if the issue were placed before them in a referendum.[18] The Public Opinion Foundation reported similarly that between 52 per cent and a remarkable 73 per cent of its respondents between 2001 and the end of 2003 believed Russia should 'make every effort to become a member of the European Union', but by the summer of 2005 the level of support for a hypothetical membership had fallen back to 48 per cent and there were 'more and more "Eurosceptics"'. Perhaps surprisingly, opposition to membership was particularly marked among the better off and better educated, and among Muscovites.[19]

We asked, in follow-up questions, what our respondents thought would be the most likely consequences of EU membership. In every case, positive evaluations were much more common than negative ones. Most of all, it was thought that EU membership would assist Russia's economic development (51 per cent in 2005) and its political stability (50 per cent). There was less certainty that it would help to keep down prices (27 per cent) or sustain levels of employment (25 per cent), and least of all that it would help to sustain personal incomes (17 per cent). But in every case substantial numbers, and sometimes the largest numbers of all, had no opinion (between 25 and 34 per cent across the various questions), or thought there would be no effects at all (from 14 per cent, in the case of economic development, up to 38 per cent, in the case of personal incomes).[20]

These were views that were representative of the country as a whole: how did they vary – did they, in fact, vary at all? – by social group, or in other ways? As we might have expected with such high levels of uncertainty, there were relatively modest differences in all respects. Males, for instance, were more likely to favour European Union membership than females, but they were also more likely to oppose it (fewer were undecided). A higher level of education tended to increase support for membership, but had more effect on reducing the level of unwillingness to offer an opinion. The over-60s, as might have been expected, were less enthusiastic about the prospect of membership, but they were no more likely to oppose it, and the most obvious effect of older age was to raise the proportion that was unwilling to answer the question. Similarly, there was little variation across the parties, although United Russia supporters were the most positive about membership and Communists the least enthusiastic. Those who favoured EU membership were also more likely to 'feel European' and to locate EU headquarters in Brussels, but not by large margins; they were much more likely to approve of the aims and objectives of the EU, but this was scarcely a separate issue.[21]

Summing up, Russians' attitudes to 'Europe' are very positive – where they exist. This includes both their assessment of the European Union as an international association of states, and their attitude towards the (hypothetical) possibility of Russian membership. Attitudes of this kind, moreover, appear to be consistent over time. But what is more immediately apparent is the strikingly large numbers who have no opinion, or who decline to answer the question; and of those who do, the loose association between support for EU membership and the kinds of social characteristics that typically underpin such choices in the Western democracies, a finding that has its counterpart in the literature on Russian voting behaviour.[22] Indeed, it is likely that these two conclusions are related, and that attitudes towards EU membership will not be powerfully affected by the usual demographic variables as long as the prospect of membership is remote and relatively large numbers do not believe it will significantly affect their various interests.

A CHANGING SECURITY ENVIRONMENT

Relations with 'Europe' are obviously no more than a part of Russia's external environment, and so we went on to ask about the countries that were seen as 'friendly' or 'unfriendly' on a more broadly global basis. Alexander III, it is said, took the view that Russia's only real friend in the outside world was the Prince of Montenegro.[23] The evidence to date has suggested a more positive picture, of a people who are 'remarkably well disposed towards the outside world, and more inclined to see friends abroad than enemies'.[24] On the evidence of the surveys conducted for the Public Opinion Foundation in 2001, the friendliest of all foreign countries was thought to be India (83 per cent thought it well disposed towards Russia, compared with just 4 per cent who thought it hostile), followed closely by Finland (77 per cent and 8 per cent respectively). At the other extreme, more than half (52 per cent) thought the United States was hostile towards Russia, and fewer than a third (32 per cent) thought it friendly; the most unfriendly countries after the United States were thought to be Iraq, Iran and America's faithful ally, the United Kingdom.[25]

Our own evidence, as of the first half of 2005, is set out in Figure 6.1. The figures are strikingly similar. Once again, India heads the list of the friendly, followed by Finland, France and Germany. Northern and neighbouring countries, generally, are well regarded, and most of all Finland, seen historically as 'our partner',[26] and associated with images of a clean and healthy natural environment, covered in lakes and forests. Finland, before the revolution, had been a grand duchy within the Russian Empire, and its peripheral areas had been close enough to St Petersburg to form part of its dacha zone. The Winter War of 1939–40 had evidently left little impression, except among the older age-groups, and the predominant view in the early years of the new century was of a country that was prosperous and well favoured, associated with outdoor sports and high-quality commodities, and the homeland of Father Christmas.[27] Norway and Sweden are also prominent among the 'friendly' nations; and so were current or historical allies in Asia – Vietnam and North Korea. Spain and Canada were also well regarded, as were European countries generally.

We also asked about perceptions of the other former Soviet republics, all of which (apart from the Baltics) are members of the Commonwealth of Independent States, and some of which have entered closer forms of association (see Figure 6.2; Turkmenistan considers it is no longer a full member).

Figure 6.1: Russia's friends and foes, selected foreign countries, 2005

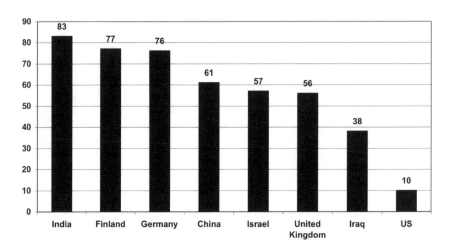

Source: Authors' survey. The figures show the percentage that perceived a given country as 'very' or 'somewhat friendly' minus the percentage that perceived the same country as 'very' or 'somewhat unfriendly'.

There is a close relationship, as we might expect, between a perception of 'friendliness', and the closeness of these various ties, and a common Slavic identity. Belarus, the most closely associated of all the former Soviet republics, was seen as the 'friendliest', and scarcely less so than India; the other 'friendly' republics were Armenia, Azerbaijan, Kazakhstan, Kyrgyzstan and Uzbekistan, all of them perceived as about as friendly as the major European countries of the 'far abroad'. There was a more cautious view of Ukraine and of the other Central Asian countries, and especially of Moldova and Georgia (where existing tensions had evidently been exacerbated by the runaway success of a pro-Western candidate, Mikhail Saakashvili, at the 2004 presidential election). In respect of Georgia, all the same, opinion was evenly balanced; it was only in respect of the three Baltic republics that a clear majority held them to be 'unfriendly', indeed much more so than any of the countries of the 'far abroad'.

We explored these attitudes in further questions, and ones that gave attention to the former Soviet republics as well as to the wider world. With which foreign countries, for instance, was it most important for Russia to have good relations? In the view of our 2005 respondents, it was most important of all to have a partnership with the countries of Western Europe (35 per cent), with Belarus (19 per cent) and the other former Soviet republics (10 per

Figure 6.2: Russia's friends and foes, CIS member countries, 2005

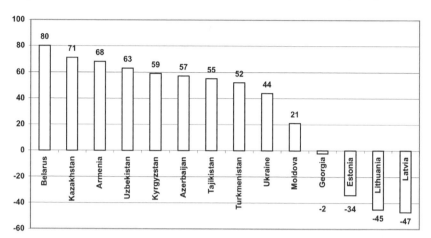

Source: Authors' survey. The figures show the percentage that perceived a given country as 'very' or 'somewhat friendly' minus the percentage that perceived the same country as 'very' or 'somewhat unfriendly'.

cent), and only then with the US (8 per cent). There was substantial support for the idea that the members of the Commonwealth of Independent States should merge their separate identities (39 per cent), and nearly as many thought they should at least cooperate more closely (38 per cent); just 4 per cent thought the CIS had outlived its usefulness and should be dissolved. In relation to Belarus particularly, a majority thought the two countries should form a single state (51 per cent), although a substantial minority (37 per cent) thought both should retain their independence. A very clear majority (66 per cent), as in our earlier surveys, thought it was a 'great shame that the Soviet Union no longer exist[ed]'.[28]

The most 'hostile' country outside the former Soviet republics, in the view of our respondents, was the United States, although there were almost as many who thought of it as 'friendly' or 'very friendly' (42 per cent) as those who thought of it as 'very' or 'fairly unfriendly' (45 per cent, down from 52 per cent five years earlier). As these findings suggested, the Russian image of the United States has varied considerably over time – more positive in the immediate aftermath of 9/11 and the 'war on terror', more negative during the bombing campaign in Kosovo and again after the US-led invasion of Iraq in early 2003.[29] But it is striking that in virtually every inquiry of this kind, the United States is regarded as the most hostile of all the larger foreign countries, and particularly when it is compared with the European countries that are members of NATO, some of which (such as Britain) have also played a full part in the war in Iraq. After the Baltic countries and the United States, the countries most likely to be regarded as hostile in 2005 were Iraq, Iran, Japan and China; but even in these cases, no more than a quarter thought they were hostile and a clear majority thought they were friendly.

The same impression emerged from other questions: for instance, whether any of a list of countries and organizations represented a threat to Russian security (see Table 6.5). By a considerable margin, the United States was the most likely to be regarded as a threat of this kind, although less so in 2005 than in 2004. NATO itself, on balance, was not regarded as a hostile force, nor was China, although in both cases a substantial minority took a different view. The European countries, individually and collectively, were not thought to represent a threat to Russian security; and this was overwhelmingly the perception of Russia's largest Slavic neighbour, Ukraine. Perceptions of the United States, however, were similar to those we obtained in our earlier investigations (also shown in Table 6.5). The United States has in fact consistently been regarded as the country or organization most likely to be a threat to Russian national security. We asked several other open-ended questions, one of which invited our respondents to suggest which 'country, countries or coalitions' represented a 'particular threat to Russian security'. The largest proportion of all (40 per cent) made no suggestion, and 8 per cent thought 'nobody'; but otherwise the most substantial numbers once again identified the United States (21 per cent), followed some distance behind by China (6 per cent).[30]

Table 6.5: Perceived threats to Russian security, 2000, 2004 and 2005

Country/organization	'Large' or 'some threat'			'Little' or 'no threat'		
	2000	2004	2005	2000	2004	2005
US	48	48	41	50	40	48
NATO	–	32	30	–	48	53
China	24	31	31	74	51	59
Germany	14	19	7	83	66	83
European Union	22	13	10	74	67	74
Iraq	24	9	20	73	78	68
Ukraine	9	6	9	89	82	80

Source: Authors' surveys. The figures show percentage agreement; don't knows and no answers account for residuals.

Question wordings were, in 2000, 'In your view, do any of the following represent a threat to Russian security?'; in 2004 and 2005, 'In your view, , what threat to the security of our country is represented by the following countries or organizations?'

Overall, we found relatively clear and consistent patterns. The closest and friendliest of all, in the view of our respondents, were the other Slavic republics, notably Belarus, and the other former Soviet republics that are members of the CIS (particularly Kazakhstan, with its large Russian-speaking minority).[31] Neighbours, allies and former allies were also likely to be seen in positive terms (above all India and the Scandinavian countries, particularly Finland); other European countries were generally seen in positive terms as well, but less uniformly (France and Germany were thought to be more friendly than the United Kingdom, but all of them more friendly than Poland, and the Baltic republics were seen as the most hostile of all). There was some caution about Iraq, Iran, Japan and China, although the balance was generally favourable. But there was a much less favourable view of the United States; it was important to maintain good relations, but the US was seen by a considerable margin as Russia's most hostile foreign counterpart, and much more so than the NATO alliance as a whole. Similarly, more Russians thought they should relate their choice of foreign policy to Western Europe (74 per cent) or Ukraine, Belarus and the other former Soviet republics (60 per cent) than thought they should orient themselves towards the United States (46 per cent) or, least of all, Iraq, Libya, Cuba and North Korea (27 per cent).[32]

RUSSIA AND NATO

External security, in the post-Cold War period, is still defined for ordinary Russians by their relationship with the NATO member countries. NATO is certainly much better understood than the European Union – which is hardly surprising, given the length of time for which it has represented the main external threat to Russian security. Nearly half (49 per cent) of our respondents were able to identify it as a 'US-led military union with Western Europe', compared with about 16 per cent who identified it as a 'trade and economic union between Western Europe and the US', or as a 'peacekeeping agency of the United Nations' (13 per cent); 22 per cent were unable to offer an opinion. Substantial proportions (26 per cent) were unable to suggest any reason for NATO's existence; but the largest proportion thought it was a 'platform for expansion to the east' (33 per cent), nearly a fifth (19 per cent) thought it was a 'legacy of the Cold War', and no more than 22 per cent subscribed to the view that NATO has itself been seeking to propagate, which is that its contemporary purpose is to 'strengthen international security'. This was reflected in the view of a clear majority that NATO should be considered an 'aggressive' (53 per cent) rather than a defensive (28 per cent) alliance.[33]

In our earlier investigations we explored the extent to which the threat from NATO was thought to have increased following the entry of three formerly communist regimes in Central Europe, the Czech Republic,

Hungary and Poland, all of which became members on NATO's fiftieth anniversary in 1999. About a quarter (28 per cent) in our survey the following year thought the expansion of the alliance represented some kind of security threat to Russia, but larger numbers (35 per cent) took the opposite view, and still larger numbers (37 per cent) had no opinion. In our 2005 survey we asked about the entry of the three Baltic republics, Latvia, Lithuania and Estonia, all of which joined in May 2004 as part of a bigger wave of enlargement and which were the first former Soviet, and not simply communist-ruled, states to enter a Western military alliance. Again, opinion was relatively relaxed: for 32 per cent, it represented some degree of threat to Russian security, but nearly half thought the threat was either slight (37 per cent) or non-existent (18 per cent), and 14 per cent had no idea. There was understandably more concern about the possibility that Ukraine, under the presidency of Viktor Yushchenko, would develop closer relations with the European Union and NATO (41 per cent thought this would be detrimental to Russian interests); but 43 per cent thought it would make no difference, or might even have a positive effect.

We tested these attitudes further by asking our respondents to consider the possibility of NATO membership for Russia itself – a possibility that has occasionally been raised officially and which both Yeltsin and Putin appear not to have precluded, at least in appropriate circumstances.[34] Once again, a substantial proportion (nearly a quarter in 2005) had no opinion, and the most substantial proportion of all regarded it with indifference; but considerable numbers either approved of the principle of membership with various degrees of enthusiasm, or – more often – disapproved of it (see Table 6.6). As compared with our survey in 2000, there had been relatively little change, but such movement as had taken place was generally away from, rather than towards, the possibility of membership (supporters outnumbered opponents in 2000, but were outnumbered by them five years later). This was in spite of the fact that relations between Russia and NATO had meanwhile moved, at least formally, towards much closer forms of cooperation.

NATO supporters were less directly representative of the Russian public than those who supported membership of the European Union. But again, there were relatively few differences across the genders, age groups, or educational and income levels. Males were more inclined than females to oppose the idea of NATO membership, but they were also more likely, if only marginally, to support it (a larger proportion of females were undecided). Education had relatively little effect, although respondents with lower levels of education were less enthusiastic; those with higher levels of self-assessed income, by contrast, were more positive than others. Age made a further contribution, in that respondents over 60, who had spent more of

Table 6.6: Attitudes to Russian membership of NATO, 2000, 2004 and 2005

	2000	2004	2005
Very good	8	6	5
Quite good	28	23	17
Neither	–	–	33
Not very good	18	26	18
Very bad	10	12	6
Don't know	32	33	22
Refused to answer	4	1	1

Source: Authors' surveys; column percentages.

Question wordings were, in 2000, 'In your view, would Russia's security be increased if it joined NATO?' (respondents who indicated that it would 'have no effect' were coded as 'don't knows'); in 2004 and 2005, 'In your view, if Russia became a member of NATO would its security be increased?'

their lives in the Soviet Union at a time when the Cold War was still the defining feature of its international environment, were less likely than others to support the idea of NATO membership and more likely to oppose it. A logistic regression analysis, not reported here, confirmed that age and income were statistically related to support for membership, once other factors had been taken into account. Gender, age, education, income and urban residence, however, taken together, explained only 1.2 per cent of the variation. Attitudes, in other words, are still relatively formless.[35]

Support or otherwise for NATO and its activities was in any case much less apparent than the concern that has developed in relation to a variety of rather different security threats that have emerged since the end of the Cold War (Table 6.7). It was characteristic of these newer and 'softer' security threats that they were less directly attributable to Russia's external environment; rather, they crossed the domestic as well as international agenda. All of them, indeed, related in some degree to the continuing dispute with Chechnya, which Putin has consistently presented as a much more general challenge to Russia and the Western countries. Chechnya, in fact, was rarely mentioned when we asked our respondents to identify the 'countries or coalitions' that represented a 'particular threat to Russian security' (just 3 per cent in 2005). As to the outcome of the conflict, no more than a quarter (27 per cent) of our respondents in 2004 thought the federal government would eventually prevail, and fewer (23 per cent) thought that efforts should continue to be made to subordinate the rebellious republic; substantial numbers thought Chechnya should simply be allowed to secede (19 per cent), and a further proportion (14 per cent) thought it had already done so. But there was no disguising the level of popular concern about the threat of terrorism, which

Table 6.7: Russian attitudes to new security threats, 2004 and 2005

	Very serious		Quite serious		Not very serious		Not at all serious	
	2004	2005	2004	2005	2004	2005	2004	2005
Terrorism	77	78	18	19	2	1	1	1
Illegal drugs trade	72	74	21	20	4	3	1	1
Islamic fundamentalism	46	49	28	28	12	11	3	3
International crime	45	46	31	32	16	14	3	3

Source: Authors' surveys. Figures show row percentages; don't knows and no answers account for residuals.

The question was, 'As you know, the threat to national security from some forces may be more serious than from others. How serious, in your view, is the threat to Russian security from the following?'

Putin has always identified as the origin of the Chechen conflict, and there was strong support for the measures that were introduced in the aftermath of the Beslan hostage-taking crisis of September 2004.[36]

Overall, our survey evidence suggests a much higher level of 'name recognition' for NATO as compared with the European Union, but considerable levels of hostility or at least of caution in relation to the possibility of a closer association. At the same time there were relatively few who saw NATO as a substantial and immediate threat to Russian security, many fewer than those who thought the United States was such a threat, and very large numbers indeed who regarded a range of newer security threats, including terrorism and Islamic fundamentalism, as of more immediate concern. There is evidently some basis here for pragmatic forms of cooperation, or even for a more broadly based 'coalition of the willing', although rather less for a common security space in which all parties share a common perception of their threat environment, and a common set of interests to whose defence they are equally committed.

IDENTITY: THE VIEW FROM BELOW

Surveys provide us with evidence of the distribution of opinion that is not available from other sources. But given the limitations of the survey method, particularly in relation to complex questions of identity and perception, we thought it essential to complement our quantitative evidence with a series of focus groups in which ordinary citizens had an opportunity to set out their attitudes in words of their own choosing. Focus groups, as Kruger has pointed out, 'tap into real-life interactions of people and allow the research to get in touch with participants' perceptions, attitudes, and opinions in a way that other procedures do not allow';[37] they are particularly appropriate for exploring 'controversial, sensitive and complex topics', although the results will not necessarily lend themselves to generalization.[38] Our focus groups took place in two waves, in 1999–2001 and again in 2006, in 'typical' Russian locations that were for the most part outside the major cities, with about eight participants in each case. They followed a list of questions we had provided, which paralleled the questions we had included in our surveys, and normally lasted two hours; the proceedings were recorded, and then made available in electronic and transcript form (further details are provided in the Note on sources, p. 181; quotations are drawn, unless otherwise indicated, from the first wave of discussions).

We began, in most cases, by exploring perceptions of 'Europeanness'. Not surprisingly, all kinds of views were expressed. Some were simply indifferent, like Zhenya in Moscow: 'I don't give a damn whether we're Europeans or Asians. I know there are things I like to do and I should do them ... And what they call me afterwards – an Asian, an African or a European – is all the same. We have our culture and we should defend and develop that culture.' But, for many, Russia was in the last resort a European country – even in the Khanty-Mansi autonomous region in Siberia, where one of our focus groups took place.

> We're more like a European country [remarked Tanya, a 21-year-old house-wife]. We have European films and fashions. We see and wear everything from there. And we develop the same way they do, only more slowly. They're more developed. But look at the narcotics that came from the West. And more and more narcobusiness is developing here as well, like a fashion from the West. We take everything from there.

As one of our participants in Yaroslavl pointed out, while most of Russia's territory was in Asia, most of its population was in Europe; and what population there was in Siberia had mostly settled there at some time over the previous 50 years, in the course of industrialization. Not only this, but relations with Russia's Asian neighbours were distant for purely geographical reasons, separated as they were by deserts, mountains and steppes. The changes that had taken place with the demise of the USSR had also made a difference, in the view of one of our Arkhangelsk participants. 'Before, when there was a Union and many Asian republics, there was more reason to call us an Asian country ... But then they separated off, and we became more European.'

The opposite view was also widely supported, particularly in Khanty-Mansi. 'I think we've lost a lot having taken so much from the West', remarked Tanya, a 36-year-old biologist. She went on:

We're completely different. When we do everything the Western way, it's just a mess. We're an Eastern people all the same. We're our own people, but the West is further away from us, and our mentality, than the East. It seems to me that our roots are in the East. Yes, people live well in Europe, better than us. But there's a lot more that we aren't able to understand. Even their business ... We have a lot of businessmen that drink like fish. We can't sustain a [Western] rhythm ... We have to learn from Europe, but remember that we're completely different.

Ilya, a 27-year-old sociologist who was on the staff of the district administration, took a similar view. Russia was

undoubtedly Asiatic. It was, and remains so. A community of people with pronounced communal, collective, archaic values ... right up to the communal flats and dormitories in which half the country is still living. Many things that are topical for the West just don't interest us. Things that are connected with accumulation, with the rational achievement of objectives. Russians are much more contemplative, much less activist. So Russia is an Asiatic country, with all the traits that are characteristic of Asians. It was just the elite that tried to introduce all the elements of European culture, but they only caught on in the big cities. So that only Novosibirsk, Sverdlovsk, Moscow and Leningrad [*sic*] have really embraced liberal values. All the rest of Russia is cut off from that.

Most often of all, our respondents thought they were European as well as Asian, a 'kind of synthesis'; or neither of these, but a new and distinctive community. Some could draw on their own experience. One of our 2006 participants, from a town in the Kaluga region, had visited Europe herself in the Soviet period, as part of a tourist group. She had been very impressed by the way ordinary people lived their lives. 'We don't live like that. Everything is orderly there, everything is looked after. And what have we here? Nothing of the kind!' Russia, she concluded, was neither Europe nor Asia, but a 'separate civilization'. Many, indeed, resisted the idea that they had to choose at all. Russia, explained one of our Yaroslavl participants, had 'always advanced along its own path, and to equate it or even compare it with any other European countries [was] impossible'. For another of our Khanty-Mansi participants, Russia was a 'special country', with its 'own culture'; as for choosing between Europe and Asia, 'I just can't do it!' Wasn't it a kind of inferiority complex, asked an Obninsk policeman in another of our 2006 discussions, that assumed they had to copy someone else? Russians were 'special', and this was the basis of their strength and values. One of our Novgorod participants put the point in terms that might have been borrowed from Alexander Blok. Russians, he insisted, weren't Scythians, or Asians, or

Europeans – 'We're just Russians.' And the country itself was 'just too big to tuck away somewhere. It is, because it's Russia! Don't try to confine it to Europe, or Asia!'

It was clear, for many of our participants, that any self-definition of this kind had to take account not just of individual perceptions, but of the way in which large numbers of the population had moved around the country in the course of their working life. Vladimir from Dolgoprudny, for instance, thought of himself more often as an Asian than a European, as he had been born in the Far East, but both his grandfathers had come from European Russia, one from Orenburg and the other from Ryazan. Another Dolgoprudny participant had been born in Tashkent but his godparents were Armenian, and he had lived on the outskirts of Moscow since the age of 16: 'I always feel the influence of three cultures.' As Svetlana in Khanty-Mansi explained, 'We're all mixed up by blood. Any one person can have four or five different ancestries. So the people in my own district are quite particular … We're tempered here by our Siberian frosts. We're not Europeans; still more so, not Asians. We're just ourselves, a friendly people. And those who visit us notice – "What strange people you are, you're so kind".' For some, this dual identity meant that Russia could act as a kind of 'bridge' between East and West, not just interpreting one culture to the other but (for instance) taking part directly in negotiations between the US and Iran, or between the West and Yugoslavia.

Not only were individuals divided in their cultural allegiances – different parts of the country also looked in different directions. People who lived in Khabarovsk, for instance, as one of our Novgorod participants explained ('I've been there'), leant naturally towards Japan. The way they thought and the goods they bought were often Japanese; and when they went to Moscow or St Petersburg they spoke of 'travelling to the mainland'. Their image of their place in the world was much more closely associated with China, Japan and Korea than with anywhere in Europe. Our focus group in Vladimir, not far from Moscow, was equally confused. Were the people of Vladimir itself, for instance, Europeans? It depended on who they were: in some cases they were simply 'peasants', in other cases they were 'Eurasians', or even 'Centrals'. In the view of our Vladimir participants, it wasn't even clear that Muscovites were Europeans, rather than (for instance) Eurasians. It was a different matter in the Baltic republics, where local people had 'lived all their lives closer to Europe' and had a 'European mentality'. The Balts, for another of our participants, were really an 'offshoot of the German-speaking world'. In Kaliningrad, for instance, it was 'immediately clear that it's in Europe. It's very different from central Russia in its living standards, and in its lifestyle. It's the former Königsberg.'

The stronger the sense of a distinctive culture, the more likely it was that our participants would insist on Russia's 'special path' towards the future. 'Only our own path will save us,' declared a Moscow engineer. 'Either we'll be swallowed up by Europe and become its appendage, or we'll be swallowed up by Asia and will also turn, you could say, into a colony.' Some quickly became philosophical, like Viktor, a Khanty-Mansi businessman, who saw Russia, in Dostoevskian terms, as Europe's only hope of salvation. Russia, in his view, was a

> genuinely unique civilization, a subculture of its own. It's between East and West, which is reflected in its political system, and in the economy. All the same, the way things are developing, it's clear that the future of Europe lies in a union with Russia. We're seeing the decline of Europe, however para-doxical that might seem. And if Russia's spirituality isn't introduced into Europe, it will perish. In what ways? In its simple human values. Don't we see slaves in Europe? Don't we see Fascist and Nazi tendencies? That's the death of Europe, that's its decline. If Europe and Russia move towards each other, if they form a union, Europe will have a future. If it doesn't happen, Europe will be the greater loser.

The more Europe fell under the diktat of America, the more evident would be its decline; but Russia was on a higher spiritual plane than Europe or America, where rationalism had taken extreme forms – 'Achieve your goal by any means.' Russian culture could moderate this extreme rationalism, and then Asia as well as Europe would move towards it.

RUSSIA AND 'EUROPE'

In this varied and sometimes threatening world, what kind of relations should Russia maintain with 'Europe' – with its member states, and with the European Union as an institution? What, for a start, is the European Union? Many admitted they had a rather hazy impression. 'The European Union – is that the "common market"?', asked Viktoriya, a housewife with a higher education from Novgorod. 'I can't make much sense of it. Are we supposed to pay some kind of money to it? How is it different from the Paris Club or the London Club? Or from the Group of Seven?' Natal'ya from Khanty-Mansi, an office worker with a higher medical education, admitted that she found the EU a 'fairly abstract conception'. Others were less hesitant, but not always better informed. Tamara in Moscow, for instance, assured the other partici-pants that the European Union had been founded in 1998, but that its origins went much further back, to the period immediately after the First World War. Or even earlier, to the Napoleonic wars, when the French emperor had conquered the whole continent and aimed to make it a single country. 'Now Napoleon's ideas have been converted into the European Union.'

Which countries were members? There was general agreement that it embraced the more developed European countries, including Britain, Germany and France, indeed the 'whole Schengen zone'. But there were other views as well, including many that clearly confused the European Union with the Council of Europe. Among a group of junior officers, for instance, there was some confidence that Turkey was a member of the EU, and that Ukraine was trying to join, although it had not been accepted. Many, including one of our junior officers and one of our younger participants in Yaroslavl, were sure that Russia itself was already a member, in spite of attempts to expel it. One of our participants in Novgorod was equally sure that Russia was already a member; after all, 'they wouldn't be able to manage without us'. Another of the junior officers explained that the European Union had been willing to offer Russia the right to attend its meetings, without the right to speak; but as 'comrade Zhirinovsky' had pointed out, 'without us they're nothing, because they have nothing to discuss, apart from us'. Another view was that the EU was a group of seven countries, 'and we're to be the eighth'. On the other hand, Tamara, from Moscow, was sure that Britain was not a member; and another insisted that Britain had applied to join the EU, but had not been accepted. In Arkhangelsk we were told that Greece had also been refused membership on account of its human rights record and economic performance.

What should Russian relations be with the European Union, whether or not it was accurately defined? And was its wider expansion in Russia's interests or not? There was generally very strong support for closer, but mutually advantageous, relations. For some, it was security considerations that mattered most of all. There had been so many wars, as one of our participants from the Kaluga region explained: but to what purpose? As a Podol'sk participant pointed out, in another of our 2006 discussions, the emergence of international terrorism meant that Russia and the EU had 'common enemies'; if Russians had a hostile relationship with Europe, they would be less able to deal with their 'real enemies'. Another participant, a Yabloko sympathizer from the town of Kaluga itself, saw the relationship with the European Union as a means of guaranteeing at least 'some kind of democracy, some kind of human rights'; it was a 'guarantee against dictatorship'. Why should they be embarrassed to learn from other countries that had a longer experience of democracy? And there were practical advantages. If it hadn't been for the European Union, asked one of our Obninsk participants, how many people would have died because of a lack of medicines? Russia, for instance, had no supplies of insulin of its own. 'All the most important medicines that help people, they're all from Europe.' In Novgorod, the view was that Russia and the West were just 'obliged' to be on friendly terms: where else could the West invest its capital, or sell its commodities? 'We need Europe, and Europe needs us.' In Yaroslavl it was pointed out that it would be easier to move across frontiers if Russia were a member of the EU, with less need to worry about visas or currency. In Novgorod the view was that there would be economic and technical advantages if Russia became a member, but not cultural and moral advantages, as Russian culture was already at a higher level than in Europe or North America.

There were also more cautious voices. It might, for instance, be a good idea to consider membership, but at a later stage. Russia, explained one of our Novgorod participants, had not yet caught up with the EU countries. Europe had very strong legal traditions, unlike Russia. There was no respect in Russia for private property; and there was a high level of corruption. 'In principle, honest business in Russia is still impossible.' It was also too soon for Russia to contemplate free trade and free competition. Once the borders were open, remarked one of our junior officers, European technologies would simply crush local industry. Russian goods were not competitive on world markets; and they would lose the markets they had managed to retain in Iran, Iraq and other developing countries. It would make more sense to maintain good relations with the EU, but not to consider membership. There was a similar view in Novgorod, where it was pointed out that the European Union was oriented towards small countries that had already begun to merge, not to the circumstances of a very different country like Russia. A similar union among the CIS countries would be helpful, and this should certainly cooperate with the EU. But membership, in any event, was hardly an early priority. It was far more important, in the immediate future, to improve their economic relations with Belarus, Ukraine and Kazakhstan.

Indeed there were greater dangers than this. In Arkhangelsk, for instance, there was no doubt that the EU's real aim was to turn Russia into a raw materials appendage, and a means of getting rid of goods they were unable to sell elsewhere. In Khanty-Mansi, there was still greater concern about the EU's 'economic expansion and political aggression'. The EU just wanted Russian resources, agreed another participant. Russia had more gold and diamonds than all of South America, and more oil than the 'entire East'. Foreigners, in particular, should not be allowed to acquire Russian oil, as they would just export it and keep the profits in their own countries. Investment in oil and gas, for our Novgorod participants, was 'the last stage in the robbery of Russia', which would lead to a 'loss of sovereignty and security'. The Russian gas industry, for the moment, allowed them to have some influence in the world, political as well as economic. But if they lost it, they would lose everything. Foreign investment was not just unnecessary, but very harmful: why would foreign countries have any interest in developing Russia as a serious competitor? 'The European Union is just trying to rob us,' as one of our Yaroslavl participants explained, expressing a view that was widely shared. What, asked one of our Obninsk participants in 2006, did the EU need this constant expansion for? 'So as to take even more territory from Russia.' Already Ukraine had been detached. If things went any further, 'we won't even have trousers left'.

RUSSIANS AND THEIR SECURITY ENVIRONMENT

What, finally, about the wider security environment? And about the possibility of an association with the NATO alliance in particular? There were close relations with many countries in the current period, our participants explained. For instance, with Germany, where there was a 'very big émigré population', and with Israel, where much of the population was Russian-speaking ('half the USSR is there') and where their Christianity had its origins. The Scandinavian countries had been Russia's 'northern partners' since at least the days of Rurik and the Varangians. Many other Russians had emigrated to Canada or the United States, but kept up their links with the motherland. There were closer contacts with Western than with Eastern Europe, but cultural exchanges with Poland and the Czech Republic continued, Bulgarians had all been 'brought up on Russian fairy tales', and Russians still went there on holiday. India, Iran and Iraq were all 'potential allies', similar in their mentality, who had never represented a military threat; you could always work with them and find a basis for agreement. Greece, Turkey and Israel were 'our tourist resorts'. There were even contacts with Latin America, for instance with Brazil and Mexico: 'We have relations literally every day – we watch their television serials,' as we were told in Arkhangelsk.

But closest of all were the other members of the CIS, and the other Slavic republics in particular. 'We still relate to them in the same way as to our own people,' we were told in Moscow. Ukrainians, for instance, were essentially the same community. They had several times separated off, but always returned in the end. Where else were they to go? Even if (then) President Kuchma built a Berlin wall along the frontier, 'that doesn't mean that the day after tomorrow we won't be friends'. There were 'spiritual and historical roots' in common, and they were 'close to us by blood'. Belarus in particular, as our focus group in Vladimir put it, was 'almost Russia'. As we were told in Dolgoprudny, closer relations were very desirable, even a fully-fledged union. It would make life much easier, as so many Belarusians lived in Russia and Russians in Belarus. It had become very difficult even to visit friends there. These difficulties were hard to understand – after all, Russians and Belarusians had been interacting for a long time. If the two countries failed to combine, perhaps not exactly as before, life would be full of practical difficulties. There was general agreement with this view, 'provided only that the president is Lukashenko, not our one' (at this time Boris Yeltsin).

There were big divisions between ordinary people and the ruling group in Belarus and particularly Ukraine, however, although the prevailing sentiment in both countries was strongly pro-Russian. And, besides, each of them was really 'two countries': in Ukraine, the west had historically been anti-Russian, and in Belarus there was a historically Lithuanian territory that was much more pro-Western than the rest of the country. Moldova, also, had long-standing associations with Russia: it was Orthodox, like Romanians and Serbs, and a bridge between Russia and the West. But Central Asia and the Caucasus, as one of our Khanty-Mansi participants explained, were a 'sort of geopolitical buffer between Russia and the Islamic countries', and the Caucasus itself had to be disaggregated, as we were told in Novgorod. Armenians were closer to Russia than any of the others – they were poor, persecuted, and Christian. But Georgians had 'always considered themselves an elite', and Azerbaijan showed no wish to join a reconstituted union; and the Baltic republics would find a more natural home in the European Union, where 'no one would even notice them'.

One of the most widely shared assumptions was in fact that Russia had rather few friends in the outside world. The strategic partnership with China, for instance, might well be a delusion: China had always been a potential opponent, and now it was being supplied with Russian armaments. There were 1.2 billion of them, and they 'had to live somewhere'. There were 'sort of Slavic brothers' in East-Central Europe, but they had still to define their new allegiances. Turkey was pushing Russia out of the Black Sea area, and even India, seen as the most well-disposed of all foreign powers, had a different culture and could enter into no more than temporary alliances. Indeed Russia had 'no friends at all', as one of our Novgorod participants told us. 'A friend', explained one of our Dolgoprudny participants, 'is someone who comes unselfishly to your assistance at a difficult moment. But if our state ha[d] a difficult moment of this kind, not a single state [would] come and help us.' 'Nobody loves us,' complained Tamara in Moscow. There was 'no love for us in any European country and never will be', remarked another of our Novgorod participants. Russia had 'no real friends left'; even Belarusians and Ukrainians were pursuing policies that served their own interests: 'They are not friends in the genuine sense of the word.'

What about the main threat to Russian security in this friendless world, the NATO alliance? Attitudes were generally very cautious, and much more so than in relation to the European Union. After all, NATO was more or less the same as the United States – 'even children know that'. NATO had been established in 1947 after the Western countries had declared a Cold War on the USSR, and Churchill had made his famous 'iron curtain' speech. The Warsaw Treaty Organization had been set up in response, and for many years there had been a military balance. But why was it still in existence, when the Warsaw Treaty Organization had collapsed and there was no longer an external threat? Was it, perhaps, for peacekeeping purposes? But the United Nations already assumed this kind of responsibility. NATO's armed forces should have been placed under the command of the United Nations, and renamed. But this hadn't happened, as otherwise they would have lost the ability to dictate their own decisions. NATO's aims, for one of our Arkhangelsk participants, were actually clear enough: it had become an instrument for US expansion, aiming at nothing less than 'world domination'.

As for NATO expansion, it was simply a means of extending the territory under its control without any loss of central authority. The new members would have no influence whatsoever, one of our Moscow contributors insisted; it was all about gaining access to their territory. The Baltic countries, and Azerbaijan, would hardly wish to make war on Russia – but they would be in a tiny minority, 'and no one will even ask'. NATO bases would be occupied by American troops, with a NATO commander, and American law would operate within them, not the law of the country in which they were located. The whole thing was 'very dangerous', in the view of our participants. The expansion would bring NATO up to Russia's own borders. No longer would Poland represent a buffer between Russia and Germany. And what, for instance, if NATO were to use the strategic air bases in Georgia as a platform for a hypothetical military attack? The whole process might begin peacefully enough, but then a politician could appear who might attempt to exploit the situation for his own purposes.

Among our junior officers, there were some who went as far as to believe in a 'special programme for the break-up of Russia'. Already the USSR had been forced to separate into its constituent republics; now the CIS countries were being divided into isolated principalities such as Ukraine and Belarus, which had been strong when they were united but were now weak and divided. There had been an economic embargo, and the rouble had been tied to the dollar, making it a dependent currency: 'In other words, we now depend on the dollar, and they can do whatever they like with our economy.' Factories were being closed down, and workers reduced to a 'cheap labour force'. The clever and well educated had emigrated, and young women were moving into prostitution. Meanwhile a small clique dependent on the US had enriched themselves through the process of privatization, and were helping to turn the country into a 'raw materials appendage' under the control of foreign powers. The dismemberment of Yugoslavia was just a 'dress rehearsal' for the attempt to dissolve the Russian state for the benefit of the same interests.[39]

What kind of relations could Russia have with NATO in these circumstances? For a few, in our 2006 discussions, there were positive reasons for a closer association. It was, at least, doing something about the Islamic threat, one of our Kaluga participants suggested. 'If we don't do that now, Islamic extremism and fanaticism will take over the world, and then it will be too late.' Things had changed, added one of our Podol'sk participants. NATO used to be a hostile bloc, but now it was 'neutral' – Putin had even suggested that Russia might join it. But these were minority opinions. NATO, another Kaluga participant suggested, was not so much against the Islamic threat, but against Russian influence in the Islamic world, and especially in the Middle East. From the outset it had been conceived as a counterweight to the USSR, and to Russia. It couldn't be believed, in any circumstances. Better to keep them as in the Soviet period, suggested one of our participants from the Kaluga region: 'at a distance and in our sights'. Otherwise, continued a colleague, 'they'll sit on us and take our wealth, our oil, and everything we have'. 'Thank God we have plenty of nuclear weapons', commented another participant, 'enough for everybody. Let them just try to set foot on our territory!' There were very similar sentiments in other 2006 focus groups. NATO expansion was 'very dangerous', for another of our Podol'sk participants; 'the way they invaded Yugoslavia, they could invade us'. NATO just pretended to be interested in good relations, commented another; 'what they really want is to get closer to our borders, to point their rockets at us, and control what we're doing'. NATO was a 'very dangerous organization', for one of our Obninsk participants; it was completely under the control of the Americans, who wanted to 'seize the whole world and control everything, everywhere'. The Cold War, commented one of our participants from the Bryansk region, a teacher in her twenties, 'really [hadn't] ended'. Another of our Bryansk participants, a pensioner in her sixties, went as far as to suggest that the threat from NATO was 'no less than the threat from Hitler'.

Across our focus groups, as well as our surveys, there was evidently a loose grasp of the specifics of 'Europe', but a better understanding of the NATO alliance – clearly, for most of the previous period, a more visible adversary. There was deep regret that the USSR had been allowed to collapse, and a widely shared belief that the former Soviet republics should reintegrate as closely as possible, starting with union between Russia and Belarus. There were broadly positive assessments of Russia's European neighbours, including France and Germany, but most of all of their closest neighbour, Finland. There was broad support for a closer association with European institutions, but concern that this should be on the basis of an equal partnership. There was even more concern in relation to the United States, which was still seen as the foreign power that was least well disposed towards them and the greatest conventional threat to their security. The survey evidence suggested a generally benign view of the external world; our focus groups placed more emphasis on Russia's international isolation, and on the domestic problems that underpinned them. It was this sense of isolation that perhaps more than anything else was strengthened by the dramatic change of regime in Ukraine at the end of 2004. Very few, in our focus group discussions, thought there was any prospect of an 'Orange Revolution' in Russia itself, or indeed in Belarus; but relations with their largest neighbour had certainly worsened.

7

'Russia in Europe' or 'Russia and Europe'?

Roy Allison

The extent of Russian 'inclusion' in Europe remains contentious and unre-solved, whether we assess the policy content of Russian engagement with the EU and NATO, the perspectives of the Russian political elite or perceptions in Russian public opinion at large. Efforts continue to move Russia 'closer to Europe', and to bridge divisions by developing enhanced partnership rela-tions, by sustaining dialogue and by promoting normative and policy conver-gence between Russia and these key European institutions. But such efforts are fragile and could quite easily become deadlocked. They depend on coher-ence and vision in Western policies towards Russia, and on the condition of broader international political relations, as well as on Russia's domestic political evolution.

This concluding chapter investigates a number of key issues and themes that will help to determine whether in the medium term Russia is likely to be part of Europe – 'Russia in Europe' – or separate from the architecture of the enlarged Europe – 'Russia and Europe'. Particular attention is devoted to the shift towards a more testy Russian relationship with the EU just before and during Putin's second presidential term. Earlier the Russian political elite was apparently indifferent to EU enlargement but very hostile to NATO enlargement. During Putin's second term the Russian elite – except for some military officers and nationalist politicians – has appeared more concerned about the consequences of EU enlargement and about future relations with the EU than about NATO. This is likely to be reversed, however, if Ukraine were to sign a Membership Action Plan with NATO or take other decisive steps towards accession to the Alliance. Indeed Ukraine's political and foreign policy trajectory since autumn 2004 has become an increasingly important factor in influencing Russia's own relationships with European institutions.

The chapter initially analyses the impact on Russian foreign policy of new challenges, especially those posed by the Orange Revolution in Ukraine and pressures for more democratic accountability in the CIS region. How might this affect Russian interaction with the enlarged Europe? Then we address the central problem of how to manage the tension between Western efforts to promote 'European' values in policy towards Russia, which Moscow increasingly rejects, and the practical need to promote Russia–EU cooperation based on joint interests. Finally, we suggest medium-term scenarios for Russia–EU and Russia–NATO relations that highlight policy dilemmas ahead. *see NGO note 41 article.*

NEW CHALLENGES IN THE FOREIGN POLICY ENVIRONMENT

During Putin's second term Russian foreign policy on the periphery of the enlarged Europe has shown itself to be defensive and reactive rather than prudent and strategic. This has contributed to growing rancour in Russia's European policy and, in the case of the dispute over Ukraine's presidency during 2004–5, to the most serious stand-off between Russian and Western positions in East/Central Europe since President Boris Yeltsin found himself unable to prevent NATO's air campaign over Kosovo. The controversy over Ukraine has overshadowed the enlargements of the EU and NATO as a source of possible new political 'dividing lines' in Europe.

Russia's failure to prevent Viktor Yushchenko's triumph in the Orange Revolution in Ukraine led to claims in Moscow, as during the Kosovo campaign, that Russia was losing its strategic 'positions' and that Western states and institutions pursue large geopolitical designs on Russia's borderlands. But the wider concern in the Russian leadership has been that a Western-promoted democratization agenda, sweeping through Western-leaning CIS states, could challenge regime security even in Russia itself. This reinforces the status quo objectives of Russia's 'integration' agenda – integration on Russian terms in the 'CIS space' in an attempt to keep CIS states in a condition short of full sovereignty and to maintain Russian primacy in this 'space' – and pits it against the revisionist vision of a 'wider Europe' favoured by the EU.

This EU conception of a wider Europe includes Ukraine and, in the form of the European Neighbourhood Policy, also Moldova and the states of the South Caucasus – states that are searching for ways to reinforce their Euro-Atlantic ties. The European neighbourhood that features in EU documents is a neighbourhood shared with Russia and is inconsistent with conceptions of deep CIS integration. Russia perceives this as a challenge, but has found it difficult to respond. In the Europe-wide context, a well-placed Russian analyst lamented, in spring 2005, that the main problem for Russian policy is the lack of strategic vision: 'In the absence of a strategic aim we are doomed to retreats and unilateral concessions.' In five years, he forecast, 'all the

interrelated re: CIS, Europe, etc
↳ Russian integration v. EU neighbourhood

161

western republics of the former USSR will join NATO and will move into the zone of EU attraction.'[2] This prospect is conceivable and is deeply troubling to Putin's political elite.

But in debate among Russian analysts and policy-makers after the 'defeat' in Ukraine and in the context of Ukraine's subsequent drive towards NATO, there is some understanding that Russia needs more than a strategic vision to compete with the West's banner of democratization and to gain the cooperation of CIS countries, particularly those on EU borders. It is an issue of how and whether Russia can or should try to act as a centre of political attraction and a reference point for post-Soviet identities. Analysts close to the Kremlin, such as Gleb Pavlovsky, maintain that Russia appears in the 'Euro-East' as 'the initiator of a new form of European unity', and that Western democratic institutions 'cannot be fully accepted in the Euro-East'. They offer no definition of what the distinct values of the 'Euro-East' should be, although the concept seems to draw on traditional views on Eurasianism.[3] The nationalist ideologue Alexander Dugin, who has long argued that Russia's identity is inherently Eurasian rather than European, writes of a contest and choice for European and CIS states between the orientations of Euro-Atlanticism and 'Euro-continentalism' – the latter representing 'autonomy' from US influence.[4] Others, however, do not see the problem in terms of a division in European identity and the way this should be expressed politically. They specify the core challenge instead to be reforming the Russian political and economic system itself. If Russia lacks an economically and politically attractive model, they affirm, then other CIS countries necessarily will reorient themselves towards the EU.[5] Where Russia will find itself positioned in relation to Europe and its key institutions will fundamentally depend, therefore, on the domestic orientation of the country.

In practice, Russia–EU policy has struggled to surmount the ill will caused by the diametrically opposed positions adopted by the two sides on the nature of the crisis that followed the second round of the Ukrainian presidential elections in November 2004. These differences were clearly expressed during the Russia–EU summit on 24 November and in the rhetoric of Russian officials during the crisis. While the EU envoy, Javier Solana, the Polish President, Alexander Kwasniewski, and the Lithuanian President, Valdas Adamkus, were actively involved in mediating in Kiev, Putin's adviser on EU affairs, Sergei Yastrzhembsky, referred to the overthrow of the earlier Serbian and Georgian regimes and declared: 'We can see the same hand, probably the same resources, the same puppet masters, and the scenarios are very similar.'[6]

In this psychological atmosphere it is not surprising that Russian strategists have identified further Western machinations behind the plan announced by the Georgian and Ukrainian presidents in August 2005 to create a Commonwealth of Democratic Choice to unite 'all democratic states in the Baltic, Black Sea and Caspian regions'. Presidents Mikheil Saakashvili and Viktor Yushchenko envisaged their initiative being used to 'turn the region into a space of democracy, stability and security, fully integrated into the democratic Euro-Atlantic community'.[7] This challenges policies of inclusion in Russian-dominated CIS structures. Even if the Georgian/Ukrainian initiative remains a broad statement of political intent and exhortation, as is likely, and does not lead to serious efforts to create a counter-organization to the Commonwealth of Independent States, it strengthens expectations that values espoused by the EU and NATO will become more accepted in a broad zone of countries to the west of Russia. Russian security specialists are generally agreed that the new Commonwealth idea is intended to serve as a kind of 'ante-chamber' designed to facilitate the road to NATO membership for Ukraine and Georgia. In a similar vein, on proposing an Individual Partnership Action Plan between Moldova and NATO in June 2005, the Moldovan President, Vladimir Voronin, affirmed the country's goal of 'joining a common security system in the Euro-Atlantic space'.[8]

The image of a consolidating group of countries on Russia's western flank, driven by a distinctly different political and foreign policy philosophy from that of Russia, was reinforced in May 2006 in Vilnius by leaders of the Baltic, Black Sea and Caucasus regions at a conference entitled 'Common visions for a common neighbourhood'. A key discussion theme was the commitment of Western countries to promote the 'completion of Europe' through the integration of countries in Europe's East – Ukraine, Moldova, Georgia and Azerbaijan – and work through Euro-Atlantic institutions towards that goal. Most Russian commentators interpreted this gathering as further proof of an anti-Russian cordon of Western-aligned states, driven perhaps more by the US than by the EU, and strongly reinforced by Ukraine's ambition to enter NATO within a few years.[9]

Russia is anxiously aware, however, that the EU mediation effort over the crisis surrounding the Ukrainian elections, and EU concerns over the Russia–Ukraine gas dispute in 2006, were prominent examples of the EU's deepening engagement in its shared neighbourhood with Russia and greater involvement in conflict settlement in the region. This has occurred despite the lack of agreement about this role so far in the Russia–EU dialogue and irrespective of Russian belief in the commonalities that define the 'CIS space'. Russia has been most reluctant to accept that the shared Russia and EU neighbourhood embraces a wide political zone of interest to the enlarged EU, which mandates cooperative approaches to conflicts beyond technical issues of border management. This was clear during the negotiations for the road map for a Russia–EU Common Space in External Security: the agreed draft adopted Russia's preferred term, 'regions adjacent to EU and Russian borders', rather than the EU's 'common neighbourhood'. Russian leaders are similarly reluctant to accept that NATO has legitimate objectives in deepening partnership relations with the western CIS states.

Moscow's default position towards these states has been that CIS 'integration processes' are unavoidable, and it warns that the EU's Wider Europe and ENP initiatives should not contravene these processes. However, thrown on the defensive by the outcome of the elections in Ukraine, by summer 2005 Foreign Minister Sergei Lavrov argued that Russia and the EU should share the task of integration so as not to confront their neighbours 'with a choice between Russia and the EU'. He proposed that 'this joint policy should proceed from the recognition that integration processes in the East and West equally contribute to the formation of a greater Europe without dividing lines'.[10] On this basis, specific fields of cooperation could be developed. Vladimir Chizhov, then Russian Deputy Foreign Minister, has foreseen a possible EU role in cooperation with Russia in regulating 'frozen' conflicts. Russia would not take part in EU operations, but it was ready to lead or co-lead, together with the EU, possible crisis response operations in Transdniestria or the South Caucasus.[11] However, to the extent that the modalities of this cooperation would be aimed at retaining Russia's dominant role in the area, it is unlikely that the local states, or perhaps the EU, would agree to such a format for crisis regulation.

The concept of 'greater Europe' advanced by the Russian leadership implies the existence of a European macro-region, within which there exist separate but in some way complementary integration dynamics centred on the EU and Russia.[12] The concept does not presuppose a basic division in European identity, as does the claim that a 'Euro-East' exists as the counterpart of the EU; it merely papers over fundamental differences about democratic transformation that are deepening between Russia and states to its west. Nor does it correspond to the EU's approach to integration or to its policy to neighbour states, and it is contrary in particular to the strategy of the new member states in the EU and NATO.

The divergence is apparent in Polish efforts to develop an 'Eastern Dimension' to EU policy, which is premised on the idea of Europe as composed of 'concentric circles' (with a hierarchy and clear subordination to a single political centre, in Brussels), not 'Olympic' ones (with a plurality of different poles of influence and power).[13] Polish interest in an EU Eastern Dimension that involves a networking concept of regional cooperation, particularly with Ukraine, and that is sceptical of Russia's European credentials has not developed into a formal EU strategy towards Russia. But the concentric circles approach is the basis of the ENP and has only been fudged by the road maps

164

on EU–Russian 'common spaces'. NATO partnership p
Ukraine and Moldova similarly route back to Brussels ar
complement Russia-centred CIS security integration.

Looking ahead, Ukraine's policy since the Orange Reve
ularly significant in challenging Russian predictions about
and Moscow-centred) integration processes in the 'great
Commonwealth of Democratic Choice initiative may make little headway,
and the suspicions of many Russians that Ukraine has become an instrument
of Western states in the strategic weakening of Russia and in its distancing
from Europe may prove to be unfounded or at least exaggerated. However,
the possibility that Ukraine will expressly include countries such as Moldova,
the South Caucasus states and perhaps Belarus in its zone of national interests and develop policies on that basis has to be taken seriously, and this
would be quite contrary to the exclusivist and now discredited Russian view
of its 'near abroad'.

Attitudes to Belarus are a litmus test of Ukrainian and Russian interpretations of their European choice. The current Ukrainian leadership inclines
towards EU views on the authoritarian rule of Belarusian President Aleksander
Lukashenko, who was re-elected in March 2006, even if Kiev needs to maintain
working relations with Minsk. Russia, in contrast, describes EU and OSCE
assessments of Belarusian elections as biased, downplays political repression in
Belarus and accepts the legitimacy of Lukashenko's election and presidency.[14]
After the Orange Revolution, the scenario of a future political crisis in Belarus,
perhaps prompted by widespread popular unrest, in which Russia intervenes
to support Lukashenko or another favoured candidate for the leadership in
defiance of EU and Western protests, cannot be discounted. Such a scenario
would compel Ukraine to dissociate itself further from Russian regional policies and would reinforce divisions between Moscow and Brussels.

Yet for all the initial enthusiasm after Yushchenko became President and
Kiev's interest in the EU's European Neighbourhood Policy, most Ukrainian
officials realize that their country cannot aspire to EU accession in the short
or medium term, even if a fast-track accession into NATO is conceivable.
Foreign Minister Borys Tarasyuk shows considerable optimism in suggesting
that Ukraine will begin talks on a future framework treaty with the EU
in 2006, will adopt this framework agreement in 2008 and will become an
EU member around the year 2015. He is also optimistic in suggesting that
Ukraine has a good chance of adopting a Membership Action Plan in 2006
and becoming a NATO member three years later.[15] These goals are influenced by the agreement in August 2006 between Yushchenko and Viktor
Yanukovych (Yushenko's adversary in the 2004–5 presidential contest) that
brought Yanukovych back to the political centre stage as prime minister.

, would permit Ukraine to enter NATO only after a nationwide refer-
.ndum. Yanukovych retains good relations with Putin. But even without this
policial channel Ukrainian–Russian trade, and economic and energy relationships, are likely to remain highly important for Kiev for the medium
term and therefore to constrain any dramatic and conclusive reorientation of
the country into the Euro-Atlantic fold. For this reason, Russia may hope to
shelve indefinitely the vexed issue of how Ukraine will be positioned in the
regional geometry of its western neighbourhood.

Moscow will continue to interpret any EU commitment to democratization in its eastern neighbourhood or in Russia itself as a foreign policy challenge, despite its formal support for the principles of democracy and good
governance as objectives to guide Russia's rulers. This leaves a fundamental
dilemma: can Moscow reinforce and deepen its strategic relationship with
the EU, and with the NRC, beyond a certain stage if divergent normative
visions separate Russia and its Western partners and overshadow efforts to
develop pragmatic, interest-based cooperation?

VALUES, INTERESTS AND PRAGMATIC POLICY

When Putin commenced his second term as president, the options for
deeper engagement of Russia in Europe and EU policy frameworks were
viewed by many European diplomats and specialists as being limited by an
intensifying controversy over whether values or interests should predominate
in the Russia–EU dialogue and in efforts at functional cooperation. Since
then Russian officials have made clear that regardless of the language of
earlier Russia–EU documents and communiqués in the 1990s on 'common
European values' (or Russian commitments as a member of the OSCE and
Council of Europe), they will now resist the incorporation of such values
into the Russia–EU relationship, since Moscow perceives them as determined exclusively in the EU zone and simply proclaimed by EU officials for
Russia to adopt. This includes but goes beyond the controversy over the role
of Western states and institutions in democracy promotion.

By 2004 the official Russian position was that Russia would participate
in European affairs 'not as an object of "civilizing influences" on the part of
other states or groups thereof, but precisely as an equal among equals'.[16] Putin
still talks of shared values that determine Russia's democratic and European
choice, but this position is frequently qualified by the assertion that values
such as democracy should reflect Russian traditions. Russian officials now
present this as one of the features of a new guiding concept for the state
– 'sovereign democracy'. EU states in turn have expressed growing concerns
about political and security developments within Russia.[17]

166

"Sovereign democracy"

The controversy over values vs interests

Values are at the heart of the EU's identity; they define the institutionaliza-
tion of Europe in civic terms. Their paramount importance is confirmed in
the Treaty on European Union, which came into force in 1993, in the Treaty
of Amsterdam, which came into force in 1999, and in the formulation of the
Common Foreign and Security Policy. They express the commitment of the
EU to foster democracy, respect for human rights, the market economy and
the rule of law in its external relations and in bilateral relations with all third
countries. The EU has never laid out what defines the 'European' character of
these values, as compared with their universal character. But evidently the EU
has had higher expectations from Russia on this issue than partners on other
continents because of Russia's geographic proximity and historical/cultural
associations with Europe.[18] Moreover, the EU set almost the same objectives
for democracy in its Partnership and Cooperation Agreement with Russia as
it does in its Europe Agreements with the accession states.

The ambitions of the EU were reflected in the Common Strategy of the
European Union on Russia, accepted by the European Council in 1999. This
welcomed 'Russia's return to its rightful place in the European family … on the
foundation of shared values enshrined in the common heritage of European
civilization'. This fulsome and optimistic statement implies that Russia strayed
off its European course during the Soviet period (though even the Soviet
leader Leonid Brezhnev had paid lip service to the idea, emphasized later by
Mikhail Gorbachev, that 'Europe is our common home').[19] Shared values, the
Common Strategy hoped, would be the basis of transforming Russia into a
state, economy and society on the European or Western model.

This hope has faded during the Putin presidencies.[20] A comprehensive 'Communication from the Commission to the Council and European
Parliament on Relations with Russia', presented in February 2004, explicitly
confirmed that these values had weakened in Russia. In fact research has
shown not only that this applies to Russian official policy but that these
values are not firmly rooted or ascendant in Russian society.[21] By 2004 the
European Parliament Committee on Foreign Affairs, Human Rights and
Common Security and Defence Policy was also forthright in its criticism
of Russia over human rights. Despite this unpromising situation, the EU
Commission's Communication reaffirmed that 'Russian convergence with
universal and human values will to a large extent determine the nature and
quality of our partnership'.[22] This helps explain the launch of Human Rights
Consultations by the EU and Russia in 2005, where counter-terrorism and
the war in Chechnya feature on the agenda (as well as Moscow's concerns
about the treatment of Russian minorities in the Baltic states), though
arguably Russia views this dialogue as going through the motions. It is true

that the promotion of common values is referred to in the EU–Russia Road Maps for the Common Spaces. But their text leaves undefined whose values these would be.

At the same time the EU's neighbourhood strategy has come to be interpreted by Moscow, on the one hand, as a challenge to its 'CIS integration' agenda and, on the other, as undermining its partnership with the EU. The ENP has been explicit in its intention to create a ring of countries sharing the EU's fundamental values and objectives and to forge cooperation that would involve a significant measure of economic and political integration. The ENP envisages a process by which neighbour countries grow closer to the EU by 'approximating' its values and standards in order to increase prosperity and security in the neighbourhood. It creates a 'hub and spoke' model for its relations with the neighbours, similar to the one it created with the Central European countries (that model, at least, had the real incentive of EU accession).[23] From another perspective it forms one of the concentric circles for EU policy that could form the basis of an Eastern Dimension for EU policy (see above). The Action Plans of the ENP give pride of place to democracy, human rights and the rule of law.

The ENP and the above-mentioned EU documents left unclear how EU–Russia relations would be conducted or what kind of partnership could be sustained if there is no Russian convergence with the values promoted by the EU (or open divergence), but EU interests still necessitate cooperation with Russia.

In fact EU documents, such as the Common Strategy on Russia, always had sections on 'common interests' or 'common objectives', which have reflected a duality in approach: 'to spur Russia towards the very principles that guided the EU or western democracies and to cooperate with Russia in meeting common challenges from the outside world'.[24] This kind of expedient need for cooperation is revealed in a passage of the 2004 Communication, which recommends that the Council 'move away from grand political declarations and establish an issues-based strategy and agenda'. It also proposed that EU–Russia summits should have an 'objectives paper', which 'should clearly draw "red lines" for the EU, positions beyond which the EU will not go'.[25]

These recommendations are common sense to many senior EU officials. Chris Patten, the former EU Commissioner for External Affairs, has been particularly blunt – calling it 'nonsense' to suggest that relations with Russia could be based on common values.[26] In fact EU member states vary in the emphasis they place on pragmatism in relations with Russia, and all ultimately are agreed that the EU's relationship with Russia cannot be value-free and purely strategic.

The UK presidency of the EU in 2005 openly adopted a pragmatic policy towards Russia: interests were considered to be at the heart of the relationship and values were represented as one of the interests in dealing with Russia. EU cooperation with Russia was sought in areas where strong mutual interests were identified: energy, counter-terrorism, business and economic affairs, Iran, the G-8 presidency, counter-proliferation and counter-narcotics. This agenda closely matches the list of serious problems identified by centrist Russian politicians for a Russia–EU discussion 'on an equal footing'.[27] But the EU presidency rotates. Finland's EU presidency in the second half of 2006, like that of any of the new EU member states, could be expected to emphasize EU policy on values in its external relations rather more, while seeking specific areas for practical cooperation with Russia such as a reinvigoration of the 'Northern Dimension'.

Energy was a particularly important dimension of dialogue with Russia during the UK's presidency of the EU – symbolized by the formation of an EU–Russia forum on energy cooperation – and it remains central to any discussion of EU interests with respect to Russia.[28] The growing reliance of the EU zone on Russian energy raises controversial issues of EU energy security, as discussed in Chapter 3, which is of particular concern to Central European and Baltic states. Broadly, EU policy seeks to diversify energy sources away from Russia. But this is inconsistent with the actual policies of some member states, such as Germany, which are set to increase their reliance on Russian supplies. In 2005 Russian officials chose to interpret the decision to construct the trans-Baltic North European Gas Pipeline, a project which Moscow strongly supported despite the objections of those EU countries outflanked by the pipeline route, as a triumph of EU pragmatism, arguing that 'economic considerations ... outweighed political gamesmanship'.[29] In fact, despite concerns over Russia's approach to energy security, the EU's input into energy relations with Russia so far has been secondary; key discussions are held between member states themselves and Russia.

It could be argued that presenting EU–Russia differences over Russian domestic policies simply as a clash of values is counterproductive, since the EU's promotion of the rule of law, a market economy or good governance and democracy in Russia is done not out of high moral principle but because these are perceived to work better than alternatives and ultimately to serve Western interests. They are expected to lead to a better environment for Western trade and investment and a more effective, predictable Russian policy-making process.[30] However, some EU states emphasize the normative basis for policy development significantly more than others, and EU policy in the field of human rights, including the EU approach to Chechnya, clearly has a normative aspect that cannot be defined just in terms of expediency.

'Common spaces' for Russia and the EU?

Even if values still underlie the EU's relationship with Russia, both parties seem to accept that this relationship will become relatively more pragmatic and issue-oriented. So does this create the basis for more policy convergence around a set of core priorities? Does the concept of 'common spaces' help advance such priorities? The May 2005 Russia–EU summit in Moscow adopted a single package of 'road map' documents that are intended 'in the long term' to create a Common Economic Space, a Common Space on Freedom, Security and Justice, a Common Space on External Security and a Common Space on Research, Education and Culture.[31]

The road maps are described as conforming to the framework of Russia's current PCA and as setting out shared objectives for Russia–EU relations as well as the actions necessary to realize these objectives. The documents note the importance of cooperation becoming more results-oriented. However, they are stronger on symbolism and declaratory goals than substance and operational clauses (with the partial exception of the Space on Freedom, Security and Justice – see below). They are political not legal documents, so they are not legally binding. They also lack implementation mechanisms. The road maps are bureaucratic and, like the larger relationship between the parties, seem unable to project a strategic vision for Russia–EU cooperation. The common spaces concept does not offer the macro-incentive of EU membership for Russia at some stage in the future, nor does it clarify what alternative the parties are ultimately striving towards.

The road map most concerned with the high politics of foreign policy, the Common Space on External Security, formally appears important for the concerns of this volume, since it agreed that attention would be given to enhancing cooperation primarily in 'the regions adjacent to the EU and Russian borders'. However, for one Western specialist the document is more notable for what is absent than for what it contains. In his view such a space should be premised on the following: agreement on what is and is not included in the common space – the basic agenda needs to be agreed; a foundation of harmonious rather than divergent values; common definitions of developments in the space – the parties should agree on the nature of major trends in this space, and especially what constitutes a crisis; shared working institutions and mechanisms that allow for joint or coordinated measures in the common space; and shared aims in the space and common interests.[32] Our previous discussion of the foreign policy challenges that Russia perceives in the shared neighbourhood shows decisively that these basic premises are absent.

There are fundamental lacunae in the road maps, which reveal the gulf between Moscow and Brussels. For example, the Common Economic

Space makes no mention of the term 'free trade', even as a long-term objective. Moreover, how can this EU–Russia space be reconciled with Russia's favoured project among CIS states, the Single Economic Space? Russia's insistence on the principle of being an 'equal partner' in the relationship with the EU appears to explain why the document defining the Common Economic Space is unable to make explicit references to EU law, which 'leaves the substance on the long catalogue of technical standards and regulatory norms hanging in the air'. The Common Space on Freedom, Security and Justice has only a brief symbolic reference in its preamble to adherence to common values of democracy, rule of law and human rights. The Common Space on External Security, in turn, discards the EU terminology of the 'common neighbourhood'.[33]

Russian specialists have been sceptical of the road maps. In 2004, before they were signed, a specialist group that lobbies for closer Russia–EU relations forecast that it would take at least 20 years to realize the Common Economic Space, and this long-term outcome would also depend on Russia creating a stable, effective and reasonably competitive market economy. Common spaces for internal and external security were viewed as a 'remote prospect'.[34] Since the May 2005 summit most Russian analysts have viewed the road maps as insidious in purpose or vacuous in content and certainly no reliable pathway to deep partnership with the EU.[35] One view (which exaggerates the real influence of these documents) is that the Common Economic Space is disadvantageous for Russia, since it tends towards a model of 'integration without membership', so that 'while the EU obtains a strong instrument to influence Russian domestic affairs and legislation, Moscow remains deprived of decision-making rights related to the process of integration with the EU, a fact that may generate more friction, rather than deepening integration'.[36] Others are dismissive of the whole diplomatic exercise which culminated in the road maps, arguing that these documents represent a simulation of policy, a means of filling the strategic void, and that crucially they fail to define whether Russia and the EU are neighbours or strategic partners.[37]

It is unreasonable, however, to write off the road maps as just a bureaucratic smokescreen for the failure of Moscow and Brussels to identify deeper common purposes. Given the seriousness of the obstacles for any deeper rapprochement or substantive partnership between Russia and the EU, as described in Chapters 3 and 4, any programme hoping to outline the contours of the future relationship and suggest proposals for cooperation inevitably would be an effort to paper over the cracks and maintain dialogue rather than to reach conclusive agreement on principles.

A more selective, pragmatic partnership?

Putin's Russia and the enlarged Europe

The immediate challenge is how Russia–EU relations will proceed on the expiry of the Partnership and Cooperation Agreement in December 2007. As noted in Chapter 3, some Russian specialists envisage an Agreement on Special or Advanced Association (or Advanced Partnership), which would amend or replace the PCA and aim at the gradual integration of Russia in the EU; others suggest boldly that a new document or package of documents could establish a 'strategic union' (community) between Russia and the EU, where the relationship would be restricted to selective cooperation.[38] In fact the PCA can be prolonged on an annual basis after its expiry (this automatically happens under article 106 if neither party gives notice of withdrawal at least six months before it expires) and in terms of practical policy this is more likely to happen than the adoption of a transformed agreement. It would take years to negotiate any new framework, and if a new agreement needed to be ratified it would be an even longer process. Russia will wish to know what is to replace the PCA before it abandons it.[39]

Russian ambivalence over the process of Russia–EU relations rests on a deeper uncertainty over the substance of 'partnership'. By the middle of Putin's second presidential term, as observed at the end of Chapter 3, most leading Russian analysts of the EU were questioning whether it is meaningful to talk of a strategic partnership between Russia and the EU – in conditions when the two parties lack clear common strategic aims and political positions. One foresees a continuation of 'selective and pragmatic partnership in areas of mutual interest'. To raise the relationship to a new level the parties should 'combine the development of specific, functional and results-oriented cooperation, with a gradual introduction of the principles of strategic partnership'.[40] — what need.

Another specialist, doubting that a rapprochement between Russia and the enlarged EU will be formed for the next 10–15 years on the basis of the projects for a Wider Europe or a strategic partnership, suggests that Russian–European relations will be characterized by small-scale, down-to-earth forms of cooperation, including cross-border programmes connected with the challenges of enlargement. Projects could be designed to enhance specialized areas of activity on both sides of the border. The relationship would be based not on integration but on the complementarities of certain sectors of the two parties' economies, 'as well as on openness in those areas that do not touch on the basic working principles of the political and economic systems'.[41]

This suggests a fairly modest profile of EU engagement with Russia in the next decade or so, rather than, for example, any grand planning for a Russia–EU Strategic Partnership Agreement.[42] Indeed the evidence in this volume, particularly Chapter 3, supports the view that progress in the relationship would be better ensured by focusing on practical, issue-oriented and low level forms of cooperation in specific sectors based on mutual interests rather than on grand programmatic goals. Consequently, the road map documents to create Common Spaces are unlikely to result in progressive convergence and harmonization in the fields concerned, but in consent to work by similar rules in specific areas where mutual benefits can be derived.[43]

For example, the road map for the Common Space of Freedom, Security and Justice contains numerous points for concrete cooperation between Russian security agencies and the growing number of EU agencies, such as Europol, Eurojust, FRONTEX, and the anti-terrorism special representative. Common interests could provide the bedrock for future initiatives for this 'space'. An active EU–Russia dialogue can be expected on the facilitation of human contacts (linked especially to the Kaliningrad issue), border issues, migration issues and various soft security challenges. However, the political framework for this dialogue – which will suggest to Moscow whether Russia is viewed as part of the problem or part of the solution in this Common Space – is a sensitive aspect and may influence the chances for progress.

More emphasis on pragmatic, interest-based EU–Russia cooperation will require the EU to scale down its expectations over the process that should accompany and define this relationship. Individual large EU member states may well moderate their hopes about Russian transformation in their bilateral dealings with Moscow and probably have already done so. But it may be difficult for the EU to achieve this as a body, since it does not act as, nor can it be represented as, a traditional international institution operating through interstate bargaining. Instead, the EU presents itself as an essentially post-sovereign international institution that promotes one-sided transformation, harmonization and gradual integration with its own norms and values, but not with its institutions.[44]

As described earlier, this is contrary to the thrust of Russian policy under Putin, with its emphasis on equality in interstate relations, national sovereignty and state consolidation. It runs counter, especially, to any Russian assertion of its separate values and identity. If this dichotomy continues to prevail, then such cooperation as is possible will occur between two very different entities, divided by 'hard' Schengen borders, with divergent political, economic, social and legal norms.[45]

This is a discouraging prospect for politicians in European states and Russia who agree on the need to prevent the formation of 'new dividing lines' that would frustrate Russia's 'European vocation'. At the same time Russian leaders consider that NATO enlargement has reinforced 'old dividing lines', despite cooperation under the NATO–Russia Council. Russia defines the priorities of this collaboration in very practical tasks: in May 2005, for example, in ensuring the compatibility of counter-terrorist and peacekeeping units, and in organizing 'joint control of air space'.[46] In reality the very progress of the NRC agenda reflects the fact that it lacks any overt objective of Russian domestic transformation and does not seek to monitor Russian domestic conduct. This allows the NRC to sidestep the entire values-versus-interests controversy, but also means that NATO cannot serve as an instrument for more fundamental convergence between Russia and Europe outside the sphere of pragmatic military-security issues. Values may bind existing NATO members and be built into IPAP agreements with other post-Soviet partner states, but except in the most general form they are not the substance of Russia–NATO communiqués or institutional ties.

The NATO–Russia relationship, anyway, can hardly be expected to develop a meaningful normative dimension, certainly in the medium term, if hostility to the Alliance is widespread in Russia. The NATO Secretary-General publicly claimed in 2004 that 'opinion polls show that around 60 per cent of Russian citizens consider NATO a potential threat'.[47] Our own survey results suggest that Russians are less exercised about NATO; only 30 per cent of Russian respondents in 2005 perceived NATO as a 'large' or 'some' threat, and around half of respondents viewed NATO as 'little' or 'no threat'. But various polls show a clear majority of Russians consider NATO to be aggressive rather then defensive, and the interviews among the Russian political elite discussed earlier in this volume confirm the existence of an ingrained distrust of NATO. For the Russian leadership this mood is now wedded to fears of Ukrainian accession to NATO and of the complicity of NATO countries in efforts to promote 'coloured revolutions' among CIS states.

In conclusion, Russia is likely to reinforce its determination to focus on practical interests to obtain specific benefits from its relationships with the EU and NATO and to define its European policy agenda strictly in these terms. The EU will be under pressure to adjust to this reality, to avoid an impasse with Moscow and to define a relationship beyond the expiry of Russia's PCA. Further, Russia will contest the legitimacy of Europeanization as a process of accommodation (by Russia) to a set of values and norms, though it may pay lip service to normative commitments it has already undertaken in agreements with Western partners. This should not impede pragmatic cooperation, for example over energy, but it does not seem a path that would offer Russia more inclusion in Europe, regardless of the proclaimed Russia–EU commitments to the common spaces. Nor does it bode well for Russia's objective of a 'greater Europe' that includes Russia. Indeed, does it not risk another period of Russian self-exclusion or dissociation from Europe?

SCENARIOS FOR FUTURE POLICY

In assessing this crucial question, we can gain insights from scenarios for the development of Russia–EU relations, for the medium and longer term, beyond the expiry of the Russian PCA in December 2007. Such scenarios are analytical constructs that present alternative trajectories for Russia based on an extrapolation of current Russian (domestic and foreign) and EU policies and on assumptions about the determinants of these policies.

Looking forward, an important determinant is whether Putin's strategy towards the West, which we define in this study as part of a policy of pragmatic nationalism, will continue to reflect a drive for greater Russian assertiveness and independence in foreign policy choices. Related to this, will Russia's perception of itself as more than just a European country, but rather as a power with wide regional and even global interests, become further entrenched and reinforce a dynamic of competition with Western states in the CIS region and even beyond? These are core questions for the medium term, since Russia would need to renounce some of its sovereignty in exchange for some degree of integration with the EU, if this is sought, and perhaps also for deeper partnership with NATO. If this does not happen, then Russian cooperation with the core institutions and the states of the enlarged Europe is not likely to proceed further in the medium term than some cautious adaptation where required by mutual interests and relations of dependence, as suggested by our previous discussion of interests versus values.[48]

Russian–Western competition in the CIS region is identified as a key issue in revealing scenarios for medium-term Russia–EU relations developed in January 2005 by a workshop with participation from leading Russian specialists and some officials.[49] As mentioned in Chapter 3, most participants at this event considered that it would be possible to place Russia's EU membership on the agenda as a long-term, 15–20-year, objective. But opinion was divided over the aims and policy Russia should adopt during the next decade or so. The starting point was general agreement that if current tendencies were to persist, including in Russia's internal development, then CIS states to the west of Russia would integrate into the Euro-Atlantic military and political system within a few years and would seek EU membership. The outcome would be a deep division along the boundaries of Russia's western regions. To avoid this, they argued, Russia would need not only to choose a developmental model for the country, but crucially also to define a strategic goal for its relations with the EU.

Only two options were believed to exist for the medium term. First, a form of Russia–EU strategic interaction that could culminate in Russian accession to a new European Union. Second, a form of cooperation between two independent centres of power that would not imply formal integration, but could include some harmonizati   slations of the two parties. These outcomes, it was noted, coul   influenced by the policies of states in the enlarged Europe. Two alternative perspectives are offered on EU integration dynamics.

One group in the workshop (the minority) proposed that, in the interests of Russian modernization, the theoretical issue of Russia–EU membership should already be raised and the prospect of a higher level of Russia–EU integration should be mooted. A steady rapprochement with the EU is necessary, it was argued, since the EU would be more predictable and attractive than Russia's other would-be partners, and since Russia's acute demographic crisis and growing technological lag would inevitably reduce its role as an independent global centre of power.[50]

This scenario of rapprochement is appealing to Western states. However, the possibility of actual Russian accession to the EU seems beyond any policy horizon, since there is little 'pull' in the form of support by EU states for even medium-term Russian membership (taking Russia's domestic political trajectory into account and the EU's need for its own internal consolidation). There is also little 'push' from Russian elites intent on preserving Russian sovereignty and resisting EU leverage in Russian domestic policies.[51] The EU may find it difficult to envisage offering a seat to Russia in its own institutions, but equally Russian politicians make clear that Russia would never accept a 'junior status' in the EU. Russian Deputy Foreign Minister Vladimir Chizhov clearly spells out official thinking: Moscow seeks 'mutually beneficial rapprochement' between Russia and the EU, but 'Russia has never intended to join the EU. We do not need it and do not consider it a task meeting modern realities.'[52] Given these concerns and others, as noted in Chapter 3, it is hardly surprising that in recent years few in Russia have considered Russian accession to the EU as realistic in the foreseeable (medium-term) future.

A second group of participants in the January 2005 workshop argued that a crisis of confidence and EU–Russia systemic differences, as noted above (as well as the EU's need to digest its new members), prevent EU–Russia relations from being raised to a higher level of integration. They considered 'integration without membership' (along the lines, for example, of EU–Norway or EU–Switzerland relations) as being the most disadvantageous for Russia of various models of institutional relations that the EU builds with its external partners. This option has been raised by some Russian specialists but has attracted little support in Moscow.[53]

The supporters of this second view in the workshop, who seem to represent pragmatic nationalist thinking, affirmed that the Russian priority should be to adapt to international, as opposed to European, legislation through access *[handwritten margin notes: "pragmatic nationalism}", "Int'l priorities, EU", "Put[...]"]*

to the WTO. Russia should sign a new long-term treaty with [...] would provide for close economic and political relations betweer [...] ally independent economic and political actors on the world stag [...] also recommended that Russian relations with the EU should te[...] lowered in the hierarchy of Russia's foreign policy priorities.

These proposals encourage greater strategic autonomy and dissociation in Russia's relations with the EU. Russia would seek to balance its relations with the EU with its relations with other 'power centres'. But in reality it would not be easy to conclude a new 'balanced' Russia–EU treaty relationship of the kind suggested, so the proposal to downscale relations between Brussels and Moscow is risky. What the workshop participants had in mind was a kind of interim period, which would give the two sides the opportunity to achieve a higher level of integration at some time in the future, proceeding from a relatively clean sheet. But, in fact, a long pause in properly functioning Russia–EU relations could ensue.

The root problem, however, is not one of process. One of the organizers of the scenarios workshop has argued that EU–Russia rapprochement is now clearly limited by a divergence in values, that the political elites in Russia and the EU may live in one civilization but exist in different time zones: the former 'seeks to join the Old World of fifty or a hundred years ago' while contemporary Western Europe is developing a new 'post-European' system of values.[55] This reformulates the dilemma posed earlier in this chapter, but it also overstates the cohesion of EU outlook and the commitment of EU states to post-sovereign identities – as indicated by the crisis over the EU Constitutional Treaty since mid-2005.

Responding to the systemic crisis over the EU Constitutional Treaty, some more liberal Russian thinkers, in line with the minority view of the January 2005 workshop, have suggested that a window of opportunity has opened up for true cooperation and rapprochement with Europe for several reasons.[56] They argue that the weakened Europe is unlikely to become a global geopolitical leader in the near future, and may become more interested, therefore, in fostering relations with Russia and generally more susceptible to external influences; the model of development of the EU as a quasi-federation is now unlikely, and this makes it more conceivable, if in the remote future, for Russia to join this entity; and Moscow can use the ongoing search by the EU for a new development strategy to revise its overall relationship with Brussels. This assessment would be viewed sceptically by those representing the majority opinion of the January 2005 workshop, although they might hope that Russia now has more opportunity to extract the new long-term EU–Russia treaty, between 'independent actors' that they advocate. On the other hand, one of the workshop participants argued later that, faced with the need to resolve its crisis of confidence, the EU will hardly be likely to discuss a long-term vision for Russia's position in Europe. This EU internal focus could then 'force Russia beyond the boundaries of "political Europe"'.[57]

A quite different response to the EU's constitutional problems is found among more nationalist Russian strategists, who argue that the EU will ultimately unravel if it continues its policy of 'reckless expansion' and that Russia has a chance to 'recoup' perceived geopolitical losses. According to one analysis, Europe's future lies 'in the creation of two unions – a West European one and an East European (Russian) one – which would balance each other and compete in a friendly way'.[58] This kind of prediction contradicts the official Russian commitment to a single 'greater Europe', not to mention the concept of common spaces. But if the greater Europe idea is not fleshed out through the development of practical cooperation and Russia's statist domestic political trajectory continues, then Russian policy-makers may increasingly be attracted to a more nationally self-assertive and uncompromising vision of Moscow's future relations with the enlarged Europe.

Scenarios on the depth of Russian engagement with NATO were presented in Chapter 5: accession to NATO, 'associate membership', more limited pragmatic cooperation through the NATO–Russia Council, or a possible alienation of Russia from NATO as a result of a revival of traditional threat perceptions or of disputes on the periphery of the enlarged NATO.

The first of these scenarios is shown to be unrealistic, except in the unlikely eventuality – which is linked to some traditional Russian hopes – that NATO is transformed radically into a collective security organization. However, there are no signs of NATO's abandoning its core collective defence identity.

The second outcome, some form of Russian associate membership of NATO, is not inconceivable, although it is likely to be resisted by the new NATO members and would be deterred by an erosion of the larger Russian–Western political relationship. According to Russian commentators, the Russian Security Council has discussed the idea of Russia's 'indirect' membership in NATO. This would be expressed in a joint document officially proclaiming Russia and NATO as 'allies'. But it seems this would be essentially a political statement – Russia would seek involvement in all spheres of NATO activity except collective defence.[59] The option of some kind of Russian associate membership of NATO, or less ambitiously just the gradual extension of the current agenda of cooperation in the NRC, would offer diverse, practical security policy links between Russia and European NATO members. But it would probably offer no more than limited influence on decision-making in other fields in the enlarged Europe.

Finally, the scenario of deepening Russian alienation or dissociation from

NATO remains possible, especially if we take into account the vicissitudes of post-Cold War Russian relations with NATO. This could reflect a more entrenched Russian policy of national self-assertion and growing acrimony over NATO relations with CIS states. It would be accompanied by a Russian determination to avoid the constraints on sovereign decision-making, especially towards CIS states, that might be expected if Moscow were to acknowledge NATO as the core of a system of security governance in Europe. Russia would then rely even more on bilateral channels for promoting Russian security interests in Europe.

Further afield, Russia might then seek to develop coalitions to 'counterbalance' NATO, for example through the Shanghai Cooperation Organization (SCO), which brings together Russia, China and Central Asian states and is exploring options for greater military cooperation. It seems unlikely that Russia could persuade its SCO partners to agree to this role, and Russian officials have denied that the SCO is being 'established as a bloc, a counterweight to NATO in the East'.[60] But the geopolitical instinct in Russian security thinking could still give rise to hopes about 'Eurasian' balancing structures, if current NATO–Russia relations were to degenerate.[61] In an extreme form such hopes are fed by the nationalist argument that Russia could become the core of a Eurasian anti-American alliance system.

Moscow is aware, however, that the objectives and structure of NATO are in flux, that the European concerns of NATO are declining and its extra-European role and functions are growing, even as its new East/Central European member states seek to influence NATO policy towards Russia – and that Russia can do little to influence these processes despite its involvement in the NRC. At the same time Russia feels unable to influence the ESDP and is defensive about broader EU intentions in the shared neighbourhood.

All this fuels traditional Russian concerns about exclusion from the top table in European security affairs, especially since the OSCE, in which Russia has membership rights, is viewed by Moscow as ineffectual and tarnished by its focus on deficiencies in the electoral conduct of CIS states. One response is to call for changes in the geometry of the current dialogues in international institutions. 'We need to jettison the old formats,' urged Konstantin Kosachev, chairman of Russia's State Duma's International Affairs Committee. He suggested that security issues should be discussed within a US–Russia–EU troika.[62] But this proposal for a new framework with co-decision-making rights for Russia and no clear position for NATO seems more rhetorical than substantive. Alternatively, Russian officials envisage 'a common European space of security', arising from the harmonization of two parallel processes with Russia: the transformation of NATO, and the form the ESDP and deepening EU partnership with Russia.[63] Foreign I gei Lavrov and the NATO Secretary-General Jaap de Hoop Scheffer have discussed expanding the agendas of NATO–EU, NATO–Russia and EU–Russia dialogues and bodies, and advancing cooperation in key regions, beginning with the Balkans.[64]

This suggests a policy of gradually engaging Russia through a network of relations, including special institutions (existing and to be formed), that would act in synergy and unite Russia and its partners in Europe. If we are optimistic and rely on the cumulative benefits of institutionalism, then we could hope, in the words of a liberal Russian analyst, that 'rather than badges of exclusiveness and clearing shops for mutual grievances, these institutions will be used as vehicles for an ever deeper inclusion and involvement of Russia in the common councils with the West, while at the same time helping Russia accept those councils and their agendas as Russia's own'.[65] All this could be supported by the lower-level practical substance and interaction of the Russia–EU relationship.

However, this is an unlikely trajectory for Russian relations with the enlarged Europe. The objectives, modus operandi and potential of Russia–EU and Russia–NATO relations differ significantly. The expectations built into EU policy, in particular, increasingly clash with Russia's internal political evolution and this raises the threshold for cooperation in the 'common spaces' or any other programmatic format. Putin and his entourage indisputably defer to realism rather than institutionalism in their approach to European institutions and processes; they give pride of place to interests rather than norms of cooperation, let alone values.

To be sure, for various reasons national interests could drive Russia towards increased rapprochement with the enlarged Europe, and the European orientation, which forms part of the divided Russian political identity, could also be reinforced. But a dominant assumption among Russian foreign policy-makers under the second Putin administration seems to be that Russia can be a partner of the EU or NATO only as 'an independent centre of power'; or, in the words of a leading pragmatic nationalist commentator, 'a centre of power which is inclined towards Europe, but still independent and self-sufficient'.[66] For at least the medium term this aspiration is likely to remain at the root of Russia's semi-detached status – on the periphery of the enlarged Europe, and outside its core institutions, but searching for greater inclusion within it.

A note on sources

We have drawn in the chapters in this book on a wide variety of sources, most of them collected specially for the project on 'Inclusion without Membership? Bringing Russia, Ukraine and Belarus closer to "Europe"', which was funded by the UK Economic and Social Research Council under grant RES-000–23–0146 to Stephen White, Roy Allison and Margot Light. Our sources are of several kinds.

INTERVIEWS

We aimed in the first instance to interview a substantial cross-section of the foreign policy-making community in each of the three countries. We targeted six groups particularly: (i) relevant figures within the presidential administration and (ii) Ministry of Foreign Affairs, together with (iii) leading members of parliamentary committees whose business is connected with foreign and security affairs, (iv) party leaders and spokespersons, (v) representatives of the defence and security sector, and (vi) private business. In addition, we consulted widely with local specialists, and with representatives of the mass media. In all, we aimed to carry out 110 elite interviews of this kind, of which 60 were to be in Russia. We conducted most of these interviews ourselves in the course of research visits in 2004 and 2006; we followed a standard sequence of questions, tape recorded when we were permitted to do so (in nearly every case), and prepared a summary of our own at the earliest subsequent opportunity. Interviews were conducted on a 'Chatham House Rule' basis, in that statements could be quoted but not attributed to a named individual. Most interviews were in Russian, a few in English. In addition, we commissioned a Russian colleague, Dr Olga Kryshtanovskaya of the Institute of Sociology of the Russian Academy of Sciences, to conduct a further series of interviews following the same questions, of which we were provided with a complete transcript.

Independently of the project, all of the authors were able to make sometimes extended visits to Russia during the period of the research in order to consult the

.est possible range of printed materials, and to take part in further interviews
.nd group discussions with Russian leaders. These included discussions with the
Minister of Defence, Sergei Ivanov, and the Russian President.

SURVEYS

There is no satisfactory substitute for mass surveys in establishing the distribution of opinion across a population, and our project funded two representative surveys in Russia, as well as related exercises in Belarus and Ukraine.
Our surveys were conducted by the UK-based agency Russian Research,
under the supervision of Dr Igor Galin. Fieldwork took place between 21
December 2003 and 16 January 2004, immediately following the Duma election, and between 25 March and 20 April 2005. The number of respondents
was 2,000 in each case, selected according to the agency's normal sampling
procedures; it was representative of the population aged 18 and over, using a
multistage proportional representation method with a random route method
of selecting households.

Interviews were conducted face to face in respondents' homes. The sample
was then weighted according to sex, age and education in each region. There
were 97 sampling points, and 150 interviewers were employed in both cases.
Local fieldwork supervisors checked a 20 per cent sample of each interviewer's
returns and, where it was thought to be necessary, all returns. In each territorial
unit, local fieldwork supervisors conducted a further 100 per cent paper question-
naire control to ensure that returns were complete and that all answers had been
recorded correctly. The standard logical checks were used during data entry and
cleaning. We have also drawn for comparative purposes on national surveys that
were conducted for the authors and other scholars in 2000 (available through
the UK Data Archive, reference SN 4550) and in 2001 (available through the
UK Data Archive, reference SN 4464). Our own data and a full documentation,
including the text of both questionnaires, will also be made available through
the UK Data Archive.

FOCUS GROUPS

In a further part of the project we conducted a series of focus groups, which
were designed to allow participants to discuss the issues with which we were
concerned in their own terms and in direct interaction with local moderators.
Groups had between six and ten participants, who took part in a discussion
that typically lasted two hours, and which was organized around a series
of key questions. These were intended to parallel the elite interviews: accordingly we asked about understandings of 'Europe', whether Russia was
'European' or something else, about perceptions of the European Union and
NATO, about the kind of relationship that Russia had and should have with
both organizations, and about relations with the former Soviet countries that

are now members of the Commonwealth of Independent States.

Our focus groups were conducted in a series of locations, for the most part in urban areas outside the 'two capitals', under the auspices of either the Institute of Applied Politics in Moscow, or the Department of Qualitative Research at the All-Russian Centre for the Study of Public Opinion (VTsIOM), also in Moscow, which is directed by Aleksei Levinson.

A first series of focus groups took place between 1999 and 2001 in Moscow, Dolgoprudnyi (near Moscow), Vladimir, Khanti-Mansiisk in western Siberia, Novgorod, Yaroslavl, and Arkhangelsk. Full texts have been deposited in electronic form and hard copy at the UK Data Archive, reference SN 4747. A second series took place during 2006 in Sosensky, a small town in the Kaluga region; in Kaluga itself; in the town of Podol'sk, in the Moscow region; in the town of Klintsy, in the Bryansk region; and in the 'science city' of Obninsk, the first in the world to have a working nuclear power station, which is also in the Kaluga region.

DOCUMENTARY SOURCES

We provide details of our printed sources in the endnotes to each chapter. We attached particular importance to primary sources of various kinds, including diplomatic documents (a full selection is available up to 2004 in the Foreign Ministry's monthly *Diplomaticheskii vestnik* and for the period since 1990 in its annual collection *Vneshnyaya politika Rossii: sbornik dokumentov*, first published in 1992). Foreign Ministry statements of various kinds are available at its website *www.mid.ru* (accessible in English as well as Russian), and Ministry of Defence statements at its website *www.mil.ru*; the Presidency maintains a separate website, *www.kremlin.ru* (which is also accessible in English as well as Russian). Official statistics, when we use them, have generally been drawn from the statistical yearbook *Rossiiskii statisticheskii ezhegodnik*. European Union documentation may most conveniently be found at *www. europa.eu.int*, and NATO documentation at *www.nato.int*.

Journals and newspapers were also important, including, for instance, the monthly journal *Mezhdunarodnaya zhizn'* (International Life) (published in English as *International Affairs*), the bimonthly journal *Rossiya v global'noi politike*, which has appeared since late 2002 (an English-language version is published as *Russia in Global Affairs* and is available online), the quarterly journal of the Institute of Europe, *Sovremennaya Evropa* (Modern Europe), and the monthly journal of the Institute of the World Economy and International Relations, *Mirovaya politika i mezhdunarodnye otnosheniya* (World Politics and International Relations). Important sources for discussions of military and security matters include *Nezavisimoe voennoe obozrenie* (Independent Military Gazette) (a weekly supplement to the newspaper *Nezavisimaya gazeta*), and the Defence Ministry's monthly publications *Armeiskii sbornik* (Army Collection) and *Voennaya mysl'* (Military Thought). *Rossiis-kaya gazeta* (daily) gives full coverage of the official viewpoint, and includes large numbers of official documents. *Izvestiya, Kommersant* and *Nezavisi-maya gazeta* (all daily) are more independent; *Krasnaya zvezda* (Red Star) is the daily organ of the Ministry of Defence.

The *Current Digest of the Post-Soviet Press* (Columbus OH, weekly) covers newspapers and journals and is available online as well as in printed form; the BBC monitoring service (on subscription – *www.bbc.monitoringonline.com*) provides comprehensive coverage of broadcast as well as printed material.

Notes

1 THE PLACE OF EUROPE IN RUSSIAN FOREIGN POLICY

1 Iver B. Neumann, *Russia and the Idea of Europe* (London: Routledge, 1996), p. 12.
2 Vyacheslav Morozov, 'V poiskakh Yevropy: rossiiskii diskurs i okruzhayushchii mir', *Neprikosnovennyi zapas,* No. 4, 2003, pp. 7–8.
3 See, for example, N. Polyvanov, 'Austria, neutrality, Europe', *International Affairs,* No. 8, 1973.
4 Speech by Romano Prodi, President of the European Commission, 'After reform: a future strategy for europe as a whole', International Bertelsmann Forum 'Europe Without Borders', Berlin, 19 January 2001. *http://europa.eu.int/rapid/pressReleases-Action.do?reference=SPEECH/01/14&format= HTML&aged=0&language=EN&g uiLanguage=fr,* accessed 25 February 2006.
5 The number of people in Russia who understand the inner workings of the EU and who understand the details of internal EU development, and hence of economic and trade issues, are still said to number only about 20. See, for example, 'Yevro-peiskaya strategiya Rossii: noviy start', *Rossiya v global'noi politike,* Vol. 3, No. 2, March/April 2005, p. 181.
6 According to Joseph Nye, '"High" politics is symbol-laden, emotive, and based on attitudes characterized by greater intensity and duration than "low" politics, which is consequently more susceptible to the rational calculation of benefits associated with economic problems.' J.S. Nye, 'Patterns and catalysts in regional integration', *International Organization,* Vol. 19, No. 4, Autumn 1965, p. 871.
7 For some representative discussions of NATO–Russia relations, see J. L. Black, *Russia Faces NATO Expansion: Bearing Gifts or Bearing Arms?* (Lanham MD: Rowman and Littlefield, 1999); Richard J. Krickus, *Russia in NATO: Thinking About the Unthinkable* (Copenhagen: Danish Institute of International Affairs, 2002); Anatol Lieven and Dmitri Trenin, eds, *Ambivalent Neighbors: The EU, NATO and the Price of Membership* (Washington DC: Carnegie Endowment for International Peace, 2003); Lawrence S. Kaplan, *NATO United, NATO Divided: The Evolution of an Alliance* (Westport CT: Greenwood Press, 2004); Wade Jacoby, *The Enlargement of the European Union and NATO: Ordering from the Menu in Central Europe* (Cambridge: Cambridge University Press, 2005); Martin A. Smith, *Russia and NATO Since 1991* (London: Routledge, 2006). See also Tuomas Forsberg, 'Russia's relationship with NATO: a qualitative change or old wine in new bottles?', *Journal*

of Communist Studies and Transition Politics Vol. 21, No. 3 (September 2005), pp. 332–53.

8 President Yeltsin made this remark in a speech to the Budapest summit of the CSCE in 1994. See Andrei Kozyrev, 'Partnership or cold peace?', *Foreign Policy*, No. 99, Summer 1995, pp. 3–14. For the advice to the Russian government, see, for example, Sergei Karaganov, *Nezavisimaya gazeta*, 3 February 1995.

9 The Founding Act on Mutual Relations, Cooperation and Security between NATO and the Russian Federation can be found on the NATO On-Line Library, Basic Texts, at *http://www.nato.int/docu/basictxt/fndact-a.htm*, accessed 24 January 2006.

10 For an analysis of Russian policy towards the Bosnian conflict, see Jim Headley, 'Sarajevo, February 1994: the first Russia–NATO crisis of the post-cold war era', *Review of International Studies*, Vol. 29, No. 2, 2003, pp. 209–27.

11 *Krasnaya zvezda*, 10 May 1999.

12 *Krasnaya zvezda*, 16 March 1999. The new strategic concept and the Membership Action Plan are published in *The Reader's Guide to the NATO Summit in Washington*, 23–25 April 1999 (Brussels: NATO Office of Information and Press, 1999).

13 See, for example, the article by Viktor Chernomyrdin in *Moscow News*, 28 May 1999.

14 Allen Lynch, 'The evolution of Russian foreign policy in the 1990s', *Journal of Communist Studies and Transition Politics*, Vol. 18, No. 1, March 2001, p. 174.

15 For some representative discussions of EU–Russia relations, see Dmitri Trenin, ed., *Russia and European Security Institutions: Entering the 21st Century* (Washington DC: Carnegie Endowment for International Peace, 2000); John Pinder and Yuri Shishkov, *The EU and Russia* (London: Kogan Page, 2002); Lieven and Trenin, eds, *Ambivalent Neighbors* (see note 7 above); Oksana Antonenko and Kathryn Pinnick, eds, *Russia and the European Union* (London: Routledge, 2005); Alexander J. Motyl, Blair A. Ruble and Lilia Shevtsova, eds, *Russia's Engagement with the West: Transformation and Integration in the Twenty-First Century* (Armonk NY: M. E. Sharpe, 2005); Debra Johnson and Paul Robinson, eds, *Perspectives on EU–Russia relations* (London: Routledge, 2005); O. Buturina and Yu. Borko, eds, *Rasshirenie Yevropeyskogo Soyuza i Rossiya* (Moscow: Delovaya literatura, 2006). See also Graham Timmins, 'Strategic or pragmatic partnership? The European Union's policy towards Russia since the end of the Cold War', *European Security*. Vol. 11, No. 4, Winter 2002, pp. 78–95.

16 For the text of Russia's PCA agreement, see *http://europa.eu.int/comm/external_relations/ceeca/pca/pca_russia.pdf*, accessed 20 January 2006.

17 EuropeAid Financial Statistics, tables summarizing the allocation of TACIS resources, 1991–2002, Table 1, *http://europa.eu.int/comm/europeaid/projects/tacis/financial_en.htm*, accessed 1 February 2006. Russia also participates in cross-border and regional programmes funded by TACIS. For details of TACIS programmes in Russia, see 'The EU–Russia Cooperation Programme/TACIS Russia', *http://www.delrus.cec.eu.int/en/p_260.htm*, accessed 1 February 2006.

18 The EU's Common Strategy on Russia is published in *Official Journal of the European Communities*, L157/1, 24/06/1999.

19 David Gowan, *How the EU Can Help Russia* (London: Centre for European Reform, 2000), p. 11.

20 'Strategiya razvitiya otnoshenii Rossiiskoi Federatsii s Yevropeiskim Soyuzom

na srednesrochnuyu perspektivu (2000–2010 gg)', *Diplomaticheskii vestnik*, No. 11, 1999, pp. 20–28. For an interesting comparison between the two strategies, see Marek Menkiszak, *Russia vs. the European Union: A 'Strategic Partnership' Crisis* (Warsaw: Centre for Eastern Studies, January 2006), Appendix III, pp. 67–8.

21 Cologne European Council, Presidency Conclusions, Annexes to the Presidency Conclusions, Annex 3, CAB 150/99, p. 33, *http://ue.eu.int/ueDocs/cms_Data/docs/pressdata/en/ec/57886.pdf*, accessed 1 February 2006.

22 'Kontseptsiya natsional'noi bezopasnosti Rossiiskoi Federatsii' (The Concept of National Security of the Russian Federation), *Nezavisimoe voennoe obozrenie*, 14 January 2000; 'Voennaya doktrina Rossiiskoi Federatsii' (The Military Doctrine of the Russian Federation), *Nezavisimaya gazeta*, 22 April 2000.

23 'Strategiya razvitiya otnoshenii', pp. 21, 22.

24 For further details about EU–Russia trade, see European Commission, Trade Statistics, *http://trade-info.cec.eu.int/doclib/html/113440.htm*, accessed 3 February 2006.

25 See Helsinki European Council, Presidency Conclusions, Annex 2, 10 and 11 December 1999, *http://europa.eu.int/council/off/conclu/dec99/dec99_en.htm#annexII*, accessed 4 February 2006. The sanctions were removed after six months.

26 See, for example, the article by Konstantin Ugodnikov and Aleksei Chichkin, 'Yevropa grozit zabit' okno v Rossiyu', *Rossiiskaya gazeta*, 28 January 2000.

27 *Rossiiskaya gazeta*, 4 April 2001.

28 Oksana Antonenko, 'Putin's gamble', *Survival*, Vol. 43, No. 4, 2001, pp. 49–59.

29 In particular, Putin hoped that President Bush would soften his uncompromising stance on the abrogation of the ABM treaty and development of Ballistic Missile Defence (BMD).

30 The Joint Statement and Joint Declaration can be found at EU–Russia Summit, Brussels, 3 October 2001, Annexes 2 and 4, at *http://europa.eu.int/comm/external_relations/russia/summit_10_01/dc_en.htm*; retrieved 13 February 2006. The EU's Political and Security Committee (created in 2000) consists of senior national representatives of EU members and European Commission officials.

31 Commission of the European Communities, Communication from the Commission to the Council and the European Parliament, 'Wider Europe – Neighbourhood: A New Framework for Relations with our Eastern and Southern Neighbours', COM (2003) 104, Brussels, 11.3.2003, p. 3.

32 *Itar-Tass Weekly News,* 9 November 2004.

33 *Rossiiskaya gazeta*, 21 March 2003.

34 Dov Lynch, *Russia Faces Europe*, Chaillot Paper No. 60 (Paris: Institute for Strategic Studies, 2003), p. 35.

35 Declaration by Heads of State and Government of NATO Member States and the Russian Federation, 28 May 2002, *http://www.nato.int/docu/basictxt/b020528e.htm*, accessed 13 February 2006.

36 Dmitry Danilov, 'Russia and European Security', in Dov Lynch, ed., *What Russia Sees*, Chaillot Paper No. 74 (Paris: Institute for Strategic Studies, 2005), pp. 79–97. For an example of the early sceptical views, see the remarks by Oleg Chernov, Deputy Secretary of the Russian Security Council, quoted in Lynch, *Russia Faces Europe*, p. 36.

37 These are the terms we employed in an earlier project ('The Outsiders: Russia, Ukraine, Belarus, Moldova and the New Europe', Project Grant L213252007),

adopting the typology first proposed in Neil Malcolm, Alex Pravda, Roy Allison and Margot Light, *Internal Factors in Russian Foreign Policy* (Oxford: Royal Institute of International Affairs/Oxford University Press, 1996). See Margot Light, Stephen White and John Löwenhardt, 'A wider Europe: the view from Moscow and Kyiv', *International Affairs*, Vol. 76, No. 1, January 2000, pp. 77–88. Although most analysts agree on the criteria that should be used to distinguish between views about Russian foreign policy, they disagree about the number of distinctions that need to be made, and they use a variety of different terms to characterize different groups of views. For other classifications, see Alexei Arbatov, 'Russia's foreign policy alternatives', *International Security*, Vol. 18, No. 2, 1993, pp. 5–43; Renée de Nevers, *Russia's Strategic Renovation*, Adelphi Paper 289 (London: IISS/Brassey's, July 1994); William Zimmerman, 'Slavophiles and Westernizers redux: contemporary Russian elite perspectives', *Post-Soviet Studies*, Vol. 21, No. 3, pp. 183–209; Andrei Tsygankov, 'New challenges for Putin's foreign policy', *Orbis*, Vol. 50, No. 1, 2006, pp. 153–65.

38 See, for example, 'A transformed Russia in a new world', *International Affairs* (Moscow), No. 4–5, 1992, pp. 85–104; A. Zagorsky et al., *Posle raspada SSSR: Rossiya v novom mire* (Moscow: MGIMO, 1992).

39 See, for example, 'Ideologiya mirovogo pravitel'stva', *Den'*, No. 2, 1992; 'Yevraziiskoye soprotivleniye', *Den'*, No. 2, 1992; Gennady Zyuganov, *Geografiya pobedy: osnovy rossiskoi geopolitiki* (Moscow: S.N., 1997); A. Dugin, *Osnovy Yevraziistva* (Moscow: Arktogeya, 2002).

40 See, for example, S. Rogov, *Nezavisimaya gazeta*, 6 March 1992; A. Pushkov, *Moskovskie novosti*, 1 March 1992; Council on Foreign and Defence Policy, 'Strategiya Rossii v XXI veke: analiz situatsii i nekotorye predlozheniya', *Nezavismaya gazeta*, 18 June 1998.

41 RIA Novosti, 28 November 2005, in *BBC Summary of World Broadcasts. Former Soviet Union*, *http://bbc.monitoringonline.com*, Mon FS1 FsuPol gyl.

2 THE DOMESTIC MANAGEMENT OF RUSSIA'S FOREIGN AND
SECURITY POLICY

1 *Izvestiya*, 2 January 1992, p. 3.

2 Ibid., 22 February 1992, p. 3.

3 *Vneshnyaya politika Rossii: Sbornik dokumentov. 1990–1992* (Moscow: Mezhdunarodnye otnosheniya, 1996), pp. 216, 218.

4 *Izvestiya*, 11 November 1992, p. 1.

5 Ibid., 2 January 1992, p. 3.

6 *Rossiiskaya gazeta*, 31 December 1999, p. 5.

7 Quoted in Roi Medvedev, *Vladimir Putin – deistvuyushchii prezident* (Moscow: Vremya, 2002), p. 157.

8 See 'O polnomochnom predstavitele Prezidenta Rossiiskoi Federatsii v federal'nom okruge', *Sobranie zakonodatel'stva Rossiiskoi Federatsii* (hereafter *SZ*), No. 20, 2000, item 2112, 13 May; and 'O poryadke formirovaniya Soveta Federatsii Federal'nogo Sobraniya Rossiiskoi Federatsii', *SZ*, No. 32, 2000, item 3336, 5 August.

9 These remarks are generally attributed to Putin's radio broadcast on 18 March 2000; according to *Segodnya*, 20 March 2000, p. 1, he said only that oligarchs would

'not exist as a class'.

10 The term first became widely used in the early 1990s: Gasan Guseinov, *D. S. P.: Materialy k Russkomu Slovaryu obshchestvenno-politicheskogo yazyka kontsa XX veka* (Moscow: Tri kvadrata, 2003), p. 502.

11 Olga Kryshtanovskaya and Stephen White, 'Putin's militocracy', *Post-Soviet Affairs* Vol. 19, No. 4, October–December 2003, pp. 289–306, at p. 294.

12 Peter Baker and Susan Glasser, *Kremlin Rising: Vladimir Putin's Russia and the End of Revolution* (New York: Scribner, 2005), p. 252.

13 Ibid., quoting Viktor Cherkesov, another former top official in the Leningrad secret service, who had been prominent in the repression of dissidents during the 1970s.

14 OSCE, Office for Democratic Institutions and Human Rights, *Russian Federation: Elections to the State Duma, 7 December 2003, OSCE/ODIHR Election Observation Mission Report* (Warsaw: ODIHR, January 2004), pp. 1, 16.

15 Based on the revised final results, published in *Vestnik Tsentral'noi izbiratel'noi komissii Rossiiskoi Federatsii*, No. 8, 2005, pp. 215–19; single-member results have been derived from *Vybory deputatov Gosudarstvennoi Dumy Federal'nogo Sobraniya Rossiiskoi Federatsii. 2003. Elektoral'naya statistika* (Moscow: Ves' mir, 2004). Turnout was a modest 55.8 per cent, lower than in any Duma election since 1993, and 4.7 per cent and 12.9 per cent in the party-list and single-member contests, respectively, voted 'against all' parties and candidates. By February 2006 the United Russia fraction had increased even further and stood at 307 (the current membership is listed at *www.duma.gov.ru*).

16 *Rossiiskaya gazeta*, 30 December 2003, p. 1.

17 *Moskovskie novosti*, No. 1, 2004, p. 8.

18 See for instance *Kommersant*, 6 February 2004, pp. 1, 4 (a seven-year term was proposed by a member of the Ivanovo regional assembly and by the Chuvash president; the governor of Bryansk region suggested five years).

19 *Rossiiskaya gazeta*, 16 March 2004, p. 2.

20 *Nezavisimaya gazeta*, 13 February 2004, pp. 1–2 (see further Chapter 6 of this volume).

21 *Izvestiya*, 25 February 2004, p. 1.

22 See the instructive biography in A. A. Mukhin, *Samurai prezidenta. Proekt-2008* (Moscow: Tsentr politicheskoi informatsii, 2005), pp. 179–201.

23 *Nezavisimaya gazeta*, 2 March 2004, pp. 1–2; Olga Kryshtanovskaya in *Moskovskie novosti*, No. 8, 2004, p. 5.

24 *Kommersant*, 10 March 2004, p. 10.

25 Regional officials were set 'targets', just to make sure; see, for instance, *Russkii kur'er*, 12 March 2004, p. 3.

26 OSCE, Office for Democratic Institutions and Human Rights, *Russian Federation: Presidential Election 14 March 2004: OSCE/ODIHR Election Observation Mission Report* (Warsaw: ODIHR, June 2004), p. 1.

27 *Vremya novostei*, 16 March 2004, p. 2. For the results themselves, see *Vybory Prezidenta Rossiiskoi Federatsii. 2004. Elektoral'naya statistika* (Moscow: Ves' mir, 2004).

28 *Vremya novostei*, 2 September 2004, pp. 1–2.

29 Ibid., 9 September 2004, p. 3.

30 *Nezavisimaya gazeta*, 7 September 2004, p. 1.

31 *Rossiiskaya gazeta*, 14 September 2004, pp. 1, 3.

32 *Vremya novostei*, 21 May 2004, p. 4; for the text of the law, see *Sobranie zakono-datel'stva Rossiiskoi Federatsii*, No. 27, 2004, art. 2710, 28 June.

33 *Sobranie zakonodatel'stva Rossiiskoi Federatsii*, No. 50, 2004, art. 4950, 11 December.

34 Ibid., No. 15, 2005, art. 1277, 4 April.

35 Ibid., No. 21, 2005, art. 1919, 18 May.

36 For the text of the amendment, see *SZ*, No. 52, 2004, art. 5272, 20 December.

37 *Izvestiya*, 1 June 2005, pp. 1–2; the sentence was later reduced to eight years (*Vremya novostei*, 23 September 2005, pp. 1, 3).

38 *Rossiiskaya gazeta*, 17 January 2006, pp. 10–11.

39 See, for instance, Olga Kryshtanovskaya in *Russkii kur'er*, 6 October 2004, p. 3. Another suggestion was that Putin should become the leader of the dominant party, United Russia, with Sergei Ivanov moving to the presidency, and the Moscow mayor, Yury Luzhkov, taking over the premiership; see Roi Medvedev, *Vladimir Putin: vtoroi srok* (Moscow: Vremya, 2006), pp. 341–2. For a suggestion that the constitution should be amended to remove the prohibition on three or more consecutive terms, see, for instance, *Kommersant*, 11 August 2005, p. 2.

40 Discussions of this kind had been encouraged by some cryptic remarks in Putin's address to the Federal Assembly in 2003: *Rossiiskaya gazeta*, 17 May 2003, p. 4.

41 *Rossiiskaya gazeta*, 31 December 1999, p. 5.

42 *Nezavisimaya gazeta*, 25 February 2005, p. 1.

43 Arch Puddington, 'Global survey 2006', at *www.freedomhouse.org*, accessed 10 February 2006.

44 See, for instance, Stephen Holmes, 'Superpresidentialism and its problems', *East European Constitutional Review*, Vol. 2, No. 4/Vol. 3, No. 1, Fall 1993/Winter 1994, pp. 123–6; Oleg Rumyantsev, *Osnovy konstitutsionnogo stroya Rossii* (Moscow: Yurist, 1994), p. 123; G. V. Dëgtev, *Stanovlenie i razvitie instituta prezidentstva v Rossii: teoretiko-pravovye i konstitutsionnye osnovy* (Moscow: Yurist', 2005), p. 220.

45 Quoted in Konstantin Kosachev, 'Vneshnepoliticheskaya vertikal'', *Rossiya v global'noi politike*, Vol. 2, No. 3, May–June 2004, pp. 25–34 (p. 28).

46 The present composition of the Security Council is set out in a presidential decree of 24 April 2004 (*SZ*, No. 17, 2004, art. 1653); its permanent members include the Prime Minister, the speakers of both houses of the Federal Assembly, the ministers of Defence, Internal Affairs and Foreign Affairs, the directors of the FSB and SVR (foreign intelligence), the head of the presidential administration and the Secretary of the Security Council; there are also 13 ordinary members.

47 The present structure of the presidential administration is set out in a presidential decree of 2004 (*SZ*, No. 13, 2004, art. 1188, 25 March 2004).

48 A. A. Mukhin, ed., *Federal'naya i regional'naya elita Rossii. 2003: kto est' kto v politike i ekonomike* (Moscow: Tsentr politicheskoi informatsii, 2004), pp. 569–70. Both Prikhod'ko and Yastrzhembsky hold the senior rank of 'assistant', rather than 'adviser'.

49 See 'Reglament Soveta Federatsii Federal'nogo Sobraniya Rossiiskoi Federatsii', *SZ*, No. 7, item 635, 30 January 2002, art. 24, as updated on the Federation Council's website (*www.council.gov.ru*).

50 See 'Reglament Gosudarstvennoi Dumy Federal'nogo Sobraniya Rossiiskoi

Federatsii', *SZ*, No. 7, item 801, 22 January 1998, art. 20, as updated on the Duma's website (*www.duma.gov.ru*).

51 *Rossiiskaya gazeta*, 1 April 2004, p. 3.

52 The treaty ratification process is given detailed consideration in W. E. Butler, *The Law of Treaties in Russia and the Commonwealth of Independent States: Text and Commentary* (Cambridge: Cambridge University Press, 2002).

53 *Kommersant*, 23 October 2004, p. 2.

54 Ibid., 13 May 2005, p. 3.

55 *Nezavisimaya gazeta*, 8 February 2006, p. 3.

56 Kosachev, 'Vneshnepoliticheskaya vertikal'", pp. 26–8.

57 Ibid., pp. 28–30.

58 Ibid., pp. 30–4.

59 *Rossiiskaya gazeta*, 12 January 2005, p. 5.

60 See Thomas Gomart and Tatiana Kastueva-Jean, eds, *Russie. Nei. Visions 2006* (Paris: IFRI, 2006), p. 51.

61 'Yevropeiskaya strategiya Rossii: novyi start. Situatsionnyi analiz pod rukovodstvom Sergeya Karaganova', *Rossiya v global'noi politike*, Vol. 3, No. 2, March-April 2005, pp. 172–84 (at pp. 181–4).

62 'O raspredelenii obyazannostei mezhdu dolzhnostnymi litsami administratsii prezidenta', 20 April 2004, as amended on 26 March and 29 July 2005, *www. kremlin.ru*, consulted on 8 April 2006.

63 Aleksei Mukhin, *Praviteli Rossii: Staraya ploshchad' i Belyi dom* (Moscow: Algoritm, 2005), pp. 90–91, 13. Like Baturin, Troshev holds the junior status of 'adviser' (sovetnik) rather than 'assistant' (*pomoshchnik*).

64 *Sobesednik*, July 2004, cited in A. A. Mukhin, *Samurai prezidenta. Proekt – 2008* (Moscow: Tsentr politicheskoi informatsii, 2005), p. 62.

65 Ibid.

66 Aleksei Mukhin, *Putin: blizhnii krug prezidenta* (Moscow: Algoritm, 2005), p. 133.

67 A. A. Mukhin, *Nevsky – Lubyanka – Kreml'. Proekt – 2008* (Moscow: Tsentr politicheskoi informatsii, 2005), pp. 70, 72.

68 'O Ministerstve oborone RF', *SZ*, No. 34, 2004, item 3538, 23 August.

69 'Ob oborone', *SZ*, No. 23, 1996, art. 2750, 31 May; the amendment of article 13 is reported in *Rossiiskaya gazeta*, 15 June 2004, pp. 1, 3.

70 For a comprehensive review, see Bettina Renz, 'Russia's "force structures" and the study of civil–military relations', *Journal of Slavic Military Studies* Vol. 18, No. 4, December 2005, pp. 559–85.

71 Mukhin, *Nevsky*, p. 94; *Novye izvestiya*, 20 July 2004, pp. 1–2. The General Staff regulations are in *SZ*, No. 46, 1998, item 5652, 11 November, as subsequently amended.

72 *Kommersant*, 20 July 2004, pp. 1, 3.

73 *Izvestiya*, 22 March 2006, p. 3.

74 'O voenno-promyshlennoi komissii pri Pravitel'stve Rossiiskoi Federatsii', *SZ*, 13/2006, art. 1360, 20 March 2006.

75 *Kommersant*, 10 May 2006, p. 2.

76 *Rossiiskaya gazeta*, 10 March 2006, p. 12.

77 Ibid., 17 February 2006, pp. 1, 11.

78 *SIPRI Yearbook 2005. Armaments, Disarmament and International Security* (Oxford: Oxford University Press, 2005), pp. 361, 367, 373.

79 Brian D. Taylor, *Politics and the Russian Army: Civil–Military Relations, 1689–2000* (Cambridge: Cambridge University Press, 2003), p. 260.

80 Cited in *Mosnews.com*, 26 February 2006, accessed 10 April 2006.

81 For these discussions, see, for instance, Jennifer G. Mathers, 'Outside Politics? Civil–Military Relations During a Period of Reform', in Anne C. Aldis and Roger N. McDermott, eds, *Russian Military Reform 1992–2002* (London: Cass, 2002), pp. 22–40.

82 Olga Kryshtanovskaya and Stephen White, 'Inside the Putin court: a research note', *Europe-Asia Studies*, Vol. 57, No. 7, November 2005, pp. 1065–75.

83 *Kommersant*, 29 November 2005, p. 2.

84 *Komsomol'skaya pravda*, 29 September 2004, p. 4.

85 *Ekspert*, 4 April 2005, p. 72.

86 *Rossiiskaya gazeta*, 11 May 2006, p. 3.

87 Fradkov's successor as Russia's ambassador to the European Communities, for instance, Vladimir Chizhov, is associated with a hostile attitude towards the European Neighbourhood Policy; see Gomart and Kastueva-Jean, eds, *Russie*, p. 50 (note 60 above).

88 *Vremya MN*, 13 July 2001, p. 11.

89 Just 20 per cent, for instance, felt 'sympathy' for Mikhail Khodorkovsky in early 2006; see *www.levada.ru/press/2006020705.html*.

90 In his address to the Federal Assembly in 2005, for instance, Putin called the demise of the USSR the 'biggest geopolitical catastrophe of the century': *Rossiiskaya gazeta*, 26 April 2005, p. 4.

91 See Stephen White, Neil Munro and Richard Rose, 'Parties, Voters, and Foreign Policy', in Vicki L. Hesli and William M. Reisinger, eds, *The 1999–2000 Elections in Russia: Their Impact and Legacy* (Cambridge and New York: Cambridge University Press, 2003), pp. 51–72.

3 RUSSIAN POLITICAL ENGAGEMENT WITH THE EUROPEAN UNION

1 We define foreign policy elites as people who have an active interest in foreign policy and who occupy positions in which they either influence, or attempt to influence, Russia's foreign policy choices or are affected by those choices.

2 See Chapter 1.

3 This is not unique to Russia, of course, as a cursory glance at the quality press in EU member states demonstrates.

4 V. Likhachev, 'Rossiya i Yevropeiskii Soyuz', *Mezhdunarodnaya zhizn'*, No. 12, 2002, p. 30.

5 Mikhail Gorbachev, *Perestroika i novoye myshleniye dlya nashi strany i dlya vsego mira* (Moscow: Politizdat, 1987), p. 200. In fact, the phrase 'common home' was used by Ilya Ehrenburg as early as 1949 (see Konstantin Dushenko, *Russkiye politicheskiye tsitaty ot Lenina do Yel'tsina* (Moscow: Yurist, 1996), p. 20, and Leonid Brezhnev used it in a speech in the Federal Republic of Germany in 1981. See 'Rech' na obede v dome Pravitel'stvennykh Priemov "Redut" (FRG)', in L. I. Brezhnev, *Leniniskim*

kursom, Vol. 10 (Moscow: Izdatel'stvo politicheskoi literatury, 1982), p. 324.

6 *http://www.kremlin.ru/eng/text/speeches/2003/05/31/1949_46509.shtml*, accessed 20 July 2005.

7 See, for example, the statements quoted by the historian and political scientist, Vyacheslav Morozov, in his article 'V poiskakh Yevropy: rossiiskii politicheskii diskurs i okhruzhayushchii mir', *Nepriskosnovennyi zapas*, No. 4, 2003, pp. 3–4.

8 Aleksandr Dugin, 'Rossiya – yevropeiskaya strana?', *Izvestiya*, 22 April 2005.

9 Aleksandr Chubaryan, 'Yevropa edinaya, ne delimaya', *Rossiya v global'noi politike*, April/June 2003, p. 27.

10 Ibid., pp. 5–8, and see Iver B. Neumann, *Russia and the Idea of Europe* (London: Routledge, 1996).

11 Dmitri Trenin, 'Russia–EU partnership: grand vision and practical steps', *Russia on Russia*, Issue 1, Moscow School of Political Studies, February 2000.

12 *Zavtra*, 17 September 2003, *Sovetskaya Rossiya*, 14 September 2004.

13 *Zavtra*, 17 September 2003.

14 Russia in a United Europe Committee (RUE), *Russia and the European Union: Options for Deepening Strategic Partnership* (Moscow, 2002), p. 38.

15 See, for example, Igor Leshukov, 'Russia and Europe: a crisis with a honeymoon flavor', *Russia Profile*, 16 May 2004. *http://www.russiaprofile.org/international/article.wbp?article-id=138F68DB-4FB1-459A-B28B-5431AEA80032*, accessed 1 July 2005.

16 It was predicted that it would take from two to four years for new members to acquire the equipment necessary to join the Schengen zone.

17 Joanna Apap et al., 'Friendly Schengen borderland policy on the new borders of an enlarged EU and its neighbours', *CEPS Policy Brief*, No. 7, November 2001, p. 2.

18 Nadezhda Arbatova, 'Rasshireniye ES na vostok: politicheskiye posledstviya dlya Rossii', *Mezhdunarodnaya politika*, No. 1, 2003.

19 Vladimir Ryzhkov, 'Introduction', in Russia in a United Europe Committee (RUE), *Schengen: Novyi Bar'er mezhdu Rossiei i Yevropoi?* (Moscow: RUE 2002), p. 6.

20 V. V. Kotenev, in ibid., p. 26.

21 Vladimir Chizhov, *Bezvizovyi rezhim mezhdu Rossiei i ES: ot utopii k real'nosti* (Moscow: RUE 2003), p. 20.

22 Igor Ivanov, *Diplomaticheskii vestnik*, February 2003.

23 Vladimir Lukin, in *Schengen: Novyi bar'er mezhdu Rossiei i Yevropoi?*, p. 36; Margelov's remarks are quoted in *Itar-Tass Weekly News*, 21 September 2002.

24 'Referendum v otdel'noi vzyatoi strane', *Zavtra*, No. 38, 17 September 2003.

25 Discussion in *Schengen: Novyi bar'er mezhdu Rossiei i Yevropoi?*, p. 43; Nadezhda Arbatova, 'Rasshireniye ES na vostok' (note 18 above).

26 Nadezhda Arbatova, discussion in Chizhov, *Bezvizovyi rezhim mezhdu Rossiei i ES*, p. 35 (note 21 above).

27 Richard Wright, in ibid., pp. 8–14.

28 EU–Russia Summit, Moscow, 10 May 2005, Conclusions, Annex 2, Road Map for the Common Space on Freedom, Security and Justice, p. 21, *http://europa.eu.int/comm/external_relations/russia/summit_05_05/finalroad maps.pdf#fsj*, accessed 20 July 2005.

29 The EU and Kaliningrad, Communication from the Commission to the Council, COM (2001) 26 Final. Brussels, 17 January 2001. *http://europa.eu.int/comm/*

external_relations/north_dim/doc/com2001_0026en01.pdf, accessed March 2005.

30 Philip Hanson, 'Making a Good Entrance', in Alexander J. Motyl, Blair A. Ruble and Lilia Shevtsova, eds, *Russia's Engagement with the West: Transformation and Integration in the Twenty-First Century* (Armonk NY: M. E. Sharpe, 2005), pp. 142–3.

31 Kaliningrad: Transit, Communication from the Commission to the Council, COM (2002) 510 Final, Brussels, 18 September 2002; 'Joint Statement on Transit between the Kaliningrad Region and the Rest of the Russian Federation', Brussels, 11 November 2002, *www.europa.eu.int/comm/external_relations/russia/summit_11_02/js_kalin.htm*, accessed 16 December 2003.

32 Igor Leshukov, *Moscow Times*, 9 September 2002.

33 Timofei Bordachev, 'Rossiya i Yevropeiskii Soyuz: konets i novoye nachalo', *Carnegie Moscow Center Briefing Papers*, Vol. 6, No. 10, October 2004, p. 2.

34 'Declaration of the movement "Russia without Putin"', *Zavtra*, 27 January 2004.

35 'Kaliningrad – perekrestok vozhdelenii', *Sovetskaya Rossiya*, No. 124, 11 October 2003.

36 See N. V. Smorodinskaya's comments in Russia in a United Europe Committee (RUE), *Kaliningrad: Yevromost ili Yevrotupik* (Moscow: RUE, 2002), p. 45. See also Sergei Kortunov, 'Kaliningrad: gateway to wider Europe', *Russia in Global Affairs*, Vol. 3, No. 1, January–March 2005, pp. 53–66.

37 Likhachev, 'Rossiya i Yevropeiskii Soyuz', p. 36 (note 4 above).

38 Philip Hanson, 'Making a Good Entrance' (note 30 above), and Sergei Karaganov, *Rossiskaya Gazeta*, 2 April 2005.

39 Aleksei Likhachev, 'Russia's economic interests in a United Europe, *International Affairs* (Moscow), No. 5, 2004, p. 77.

40 A Northern Dimension for the Policies of the Union. Communication from the Commission to the Council, COM/98/0589, 25 November 1998. *http://europa.eu.int/comm/external_relations/north_dim/doc/com1998_0589en.pdf*, accessed 1 July 2005.

41 Christopher S. Browning, 'The region-building approach revisited: the continued othering of Russia in discourses of region-building in the European North', *Geopolitics*, Vol. 8, No. 1, Spring 2003, p. 50.

42 The action plans can be found at *http://www.europa.eu.int/comm/external_relations/north_dim/ndap/06_00_en.pdf* and *http://www.europa.eu.int/comm/external_relations/north_dim/ndap/com03_343.pdf*, accessed 1 July 2005.

43 Yu. S. Deryabin, '"Severnoye izmereniye" ES: problemy i perspektivy', Leont'evskiye chteniya, Vypusk 1, 2002. *http://www.journal.leontief.net/rus/deryabin.html*, accessed 13 April 2005.

44 Vladimir Ryzhkov, 'Introduction', in Russia in a United Europe Committee, *Severnoye izmereniye': ideya i real'nost'* (Moscow: RUE, 2002), and see the remarks of specialists in the discussion.

45 Statement by Yevgeny P. Gusarov, Deputy Minister for Foreign Affairs of the Russian Federation, at the 3rd Summit of the Baltic Development Forum, 2000, *http://www.cbss.st/documents/cbsspresidencies/10russian/3bdf/dbaFile262.html*, accessed 13 August 2005.

46 Viktor Khristenko, Deputy Prime Minister, speech to the Northern Dimension Forum in Lappeenranta, Finland, 22 October 2001, in *Results of the Northern*

Dimension Forum in Lappeenranta 22–23/10/2001 (Helsinki: Prime Minister's Office; Publications, 2001), p. 20.

47 Hiski Haukkala, 'The Northern Dimension of EU Foreign Policy', in Oksana Antonenko and Kathryn Pinnick, eds, *Russia and the European Union* (London: Routledge, for the International Institute for Strategic Studies, 2005), pp. 35–50.

48 See, for example, Paweł Kowal, ed., *EU Eastern Dimension – A Real Chance or Idée Fixe of Polish Policy?* (Warsaw: Centre for International Relations, 2002). For Russia's likely response, see Andrey Makarychev, 'Europe's Eastern Dimension: Russia's reaction to Poland's initiative', *PONARS Policy Memo*, 301, November 2003.

49 Vadim Kononenko, 'What's New About Today's EU–Russia Border', *UPI Working Papers*, No. 50, Finnish Institute of International Affairs, 2004.

50 Alexander Sergounin, 'Regionalization around the Baltic Sea Rim: Perceptions of Russian Elites', in *The Regional Dimension of the Russian–Baltic Relations* (St Petersburg: Centre for Integration Research and Projects, 2004), pp. 119–33.

51 Wyn Rees, 'The External Face of Internal Security', in Christopher Hill and Michael Smith, eds, *International Relations and the European Union* (Oxford: Oxford University Press, 2005), p, 218.

52 Agreement on Partnership and Cooperation (PCA), *Official Journal of the European Communities*, OJ L 327, 28/11/1997.

53 See Nuclear Safety in Central Europe and the New Independent States, *http://europa.eu.int/comm/external_relations/nuclear_safety/intro/nis.htm*, accessed 3 September 2005.

54 Common Strategy of the European Union, OJ L 15, 24/06/1999; Medium-Term Strategy, 'Strategiya razvitiya otnoshenii Rossiiskoi Federatsii s Yevropeiskim Soyuzom na srednesrochnuyu perspektivu (2000–2010 gg)', *Diplomaticheskii vestnik*, No. 11, 1999, pp. 20–28; Russia: Country Strategy Paper 2002–2006, *http://europa.eu.int/comm/external_relations/russia/csp/02–06_en.pdf*, accessed 2 May 2005.

55 Sandra Lavenex, 'EU external governance in "wider Europe"', *Journal of European Public Policy*, Vol. 11, No. 4, 2004, p. 688.

56 Ibid., p. 689.

57 Four road maps were envisaged, for a Common Economic Space, a Common Space of Freedom, Justice and Home Affairs, a Common Space of External Security, and a Common Space on Research, Education and Culture. Environmental issues were incorporated into the road map for the Common Economic Space. See Final Road Maps, *http://europa.eu.int/comm/external_relations/russia/summit_05_05/index.htm#fsj*, accessed 3 April 2005.

58 Olga Potemkina, 'Russia's engagement with Justice and Home Affairs: a question of mutual trust', *CEPS Policy Brief*, No. 16, March 2002, p. 4.

59 Oksana Antonenko, 'Russia and EU Enlargement: From Insecure Neighbours to a Common Space of Security, Justice and Home Affairs', in *Russia and the European Union*, pp. 67–101 (note 47 above).

60 E. Kuznetsova, 'Will the road maps lead Russia to Europe?', *International Affairs* (Moscow), No. 4, 2005, p. 70.

61 Common European Union strategy towards Russia in the area of justice and home affairs, *http://europa.eu.int/comm/justice_home/fsj/external/russia/fsj_external_*

russia_en.htm, accessed 25 September 2005.

62 *Itar-Tass Weekly News*, 14 April 2003.

63 Vladimir Rushailo, Secretary of the Russian Security Council, quoted in ibid., 30 April 2003.

64 Georgy Kunadze, 'Why provoke conflicts?', *New Times*, August, 2005.

65 *Itar-Tass Weekly News*, 23 May 2005.

66 Ibid., 28 February, 2005

67 Kuznetsova, 'Will the road maps lead Russia to Europe?', p. 69 (note 60 above).

68 Konstantin Kosachev, Press Conference, *Itar-Tass Weekly News*, 8 July 2005, and EU–Russia Relations, *http://europa.eu.int/comm/external_relations/russia/intro/index.htm*, accessed 3 August 2005.

69 See, for example, Nadezhda Arbatova, 'Yeshche raz o Rossii i "Bol'shoi Yevrope"', *Nepriskosnovennyi zapas*, No. 4, 2003, and Andrei Zagorski, 'Russia and the Shared Neighbourhood', in Dov Lynch, ed., *What Russia Sees*, Chaillot Paper, No. 74, January 2004, pp. 74–5.

70 Nadezhda Arbatova, ed., *How to Deepen Cooperation Between Russia and the EU*, Second Annual Report of the International Committee 'Russia in the United Europe', Moscow, 2003, *http://www.rue.ru/Riz_wer_Dokl_03.pdf*, accessed 15 September 2005.

71 Zagorski, 'Russia and the Shared Neighbourhood', p. 75 (note 69 above).

72 Potemkina, 'Russia's Engagement with Justice and Home Affairs', p. 5 (note 58 above).

73 See Bordachev, 'Rossiya i Yevropeiskii Soyuz', p. 2 (note 33 above), and the comments by Viktor Cherkesov, head of the Russian State Drug Control Committee, *Itar-Tass Weekly News*, 29 October 2003.

74 Vladimir Chizhov, 'European Union: a partnership strategy', *International Affairs* (Moscow), No. 6, 2004, p. 79.

75 Ania Krok-Paszkowska and Jan Zielonka, 'The European Union's Policies', in *Russia's Engagement with the West*, p. 160 (note 30 above).

76 See, for example, *Parlamentskaya gazeta*, 30 March 2000.

77 *Diplomaticheskii vestnik*, No. 6, 2001, p. 80.

78 See his declaration to the European Parliament Development Committee, IP/02/1655, 12 November 2002, *http://europa.eu.int/comm/external_relations/news/patten/ip02_1655.htm*, accessed 14 October 2005.

79 'Copenhagen prefers Chechens to Putin', *gazeta.ru*, 28 October 2002, *http://www.gazeta.ru/2002/10/28/Copenhagenpr.shtml*, accessed 14 October 2005.

80 *Itar-Tass Weekly News*, 3 December 2002; 28 November 2003.

81 Communication from the Commission to the Council and the European Parliament on relations with Russia, COM (2004) 106, *http://europa.eu.int/comm/external_relations/russia/russia_docs/com04_106_en.pdf*, accessed 30 June 2005.

82 *Itar-Tass Weekly News*, 4 September 2004.

83 Sergei Lavrov, 'In the face of a Common Threat', *Diplomatic Yearbook 2004*. See Russian Ministry of Foreign Affairs Press Release, Russia, European Union Human Rights Consultations in Luxembourg, 397–02–03–2005, 2 March 2005.

84 See, for example, the European Parliament's resolution on the EU–Russia summit in November 2004, P6_TA(2004)0099, *http://www.europarl.eu.int/omk/sipade3?PUBREF=-//EP//NONSGML+TA+P6-TA-2004-0099+0+*

DOC+WORD+Vo//EN&L=EN&LEVEL=1&NAV=S&LSTDOC=Y&LSTDOC =N, accessed 12 October 2005.

85 Yuri Borko, 'Rethinking Russia–EU relations', *Russia in Global Affairs*, No. 3, July/ September, 2004, p. 169.

86 See, for example, I.D. Ivanov, 'Rasshireniya ES: chto zhdet Rossiyu?', *Rasshireniya ES: ugroza ili shans dlya Rossii?* (Moscow: RUE, 2002), pp. 7–14, and the following detailed discussion about the economic consequences of enlargement.

87 See, for example, Joint Statement by V. V. Putin, President of the Russian Federation, G. Persson, President of the European Council, assisted by J. Solana, Secretary-General of the EU Council/High Representative for Common Foreign and Security Policy, 17 May 2001, *http://www.delrus.cec.eu.int/en/news_423.htm*, accessed 27 October 2005.

88 Maksim Medvedkov, 'Dlya Rossii v rasshirenii ES est' i dostoinstva i nedostatki', *Yevropa*, No. 1 (35), January 2004, pp. 7–9. *http://www.delrus.cec.eu.int/em/39/ eu35.pdf*, accessed 10 October 2005. See also the report produced by the Russian National Investment Council with the support of the Ministry of Foreign Affairs, 'The Effect of the EU Enlargement on Russia's Economy', Moscow, 2004. *http:// www.europe2020.org/en/section_voisin/doc/EU_eng.pdf*, accessed 10 October 2005.

89 The list is set out in ibid, pp. 48–9; Chizhov's statement can be found in Press release 161–30–01–2004, Ministry of Foreign Affairs of the Russian Federation, and the EU response is in 2563rd External Relations Council meeting – Brussels 23.02.2004, Press: 49 No. 6294/04. *http://ue.eu.int/ueDocs/cms_Data/docs/press- Data/en/gena/79150.pdf*, accessed 10 October 2005.

90 *Izvestiya*, 26 February 2004, and *Moscow Times*, 25 February 2004.

91 Protocol to the Partnership and Cooperation Agreement, Brussels, 27 April 2004, *http://www.europa.eu.int/comm/external_relations/russia/russia_docs/protocol_ 0404.htm* and Joint Statement on EU Enlargement and EU–Russia Relations, 27 April 2004, *http://www.europa.eu.int/comm/external_relations/russia/russia_docs/ js_elarg_270404.htm*, accessed 10 October 2005.

92 The Treaty's provisions focus on the protection and promotion of foreign energy investments, based on the extension of national treatment, or most favoured nation treatment (whichever is more favourable); free trade in energy materials, products and energy-related equipment, based on WTO rules; freedom of energy transit through pipelines and grids; reducing the negative environmental impact of the energy cycle through improving energy efficiency; and mechanisms for the resolution of disputes. See *The Energy Charter Treaty and Related Documents* at *http://www.encharter.org/upload/9/ 12052067451575115819204971474353213193519086021f2543v3.pdf*, accessed 17 May 2006.

93 *EU–Russia Trade Relations*, p. 8, *http://trade.ec.europa.eu/doclib/docs/2006/may/ tradoc_113440.pdf*, accessed 17 May 2006; see also Aksar Gubaidullin and Nadia Kampaner, 'Gaz v Yevrope: est' li alternativa?', *Rossiya v global'noi politike*, No. 1, January/February 2006.

94 Debra Johnson, 'EU–Russia Energy Links', in Debra Johnson and Paul Robinson, eds, *Perspectives on EU–Russia Relations* (London: Routledge, 2005), pp. 175–93. Since there is less prospect of the EU diversifying its energy supplies than of Russia diversifying its markets, James Hughes calls the Russia–EU

relationship one of 'asymmetric interdependency'. See James Hughes, 'EU Relations with Russia: Partnership or Asymmetric Interdependency?', in Nicola Casarini and Constanza Musu, eds, *The EU's Foreign Policy in an Evolving International System: The Road To Convergence* (Basingstoke: Palgrave, forthcoming).

95 European Union–Russia Energy Dialogue, *http://ec.europa.eu/energy/russia/overview/index_en.htm*; accessed 17 May 2006.

96 Russia–EU Energy Forum, *http://www.energyforum.co.uk/index.php?lang=en*; accessed 17 May 2006.

97 *Itar-Tass Weekly News*, 2 January 2006.

98 Aksar Gubaidullin and Nadia Kampaner, 'Gaz v Yevrope: est' li alternativa?' (note 93 above).

99 *Itar-Tass Weekly News*, 3 January 2006.

100 Hughes, 'EU Relations with Russia' (note 94 above). The Russia–Ukraine gas dispute also raised doubts about what President Putin meant by energy security, an issue that he had just listed as first on his agenda for Russia's G-8 chairmanship, which commenced at the beginning of 2006.

101 *Russia and the European Union*, p. 40 (note 14 above), and Dmitri Trenin, *Nezavisimaya gazeta*, 9 February 2004.

102 Dmitri Trenin, 'Rossiya v "Shirokoi Yevrope", Carnegie Moscow Center Briefing, October 2002 and 'Identichnost' i integratsiya: Rossiya i Zapad v XXI veke', *Pro et Contra*, Vol. 8, No. 3, 2004, p. 12.

103 See the discussion in 'The world we're in', *International Affairs* (Moscow), No. 4, 2004, pp. 117–30.

104 Trenin, 'Identichnost' i integratsiya', p. 20 (note 102 above).

105 Timofei Bordachev and Tatyna Romanova, 'Russia's choice should provide for liberty of action', *Russia in Global Affairs*, Vol. 1, No. 2, 2003, p. 69.

106 Timofei Bordachev and Arkady Moshes, 'Is the Europeanization of Russia over?', *Russia in Global Affairs*, Vol. 2, No. 2, 2003, p. 91.

107 Timofei Bordachev, 'Rossiya i Yevropeiskii Soyuz: konets i novoye nachalo', Carnegie Moscow Center Briefing, October 2004.

108 Konstantin Khudoley, 'Russia and the European Union: New Opportunities, New Challenges', in Arkady Moshes, ed., *Rethinking the Respective Strategies of Russia and the European Union*, Special FIIA/Carnegie Moscow Center Report, 2003; see also *Otnosheniya Rossii i Yevropeiskogo Soyuza: sovremennaya situatsiya i perspektivy. Situatsionnyi analiz pod rukovodstvom S.A. Karaganova* (Moscow, 2005), p. 18. See Chapters 1 above and 4 below for more on the ENP.

109 Some 80 per cent of the experts who participated in a 2005 report on the current state of Russia–EU relations apparently agreed that membership was feasible within 15–20 years. See *Otnosheniya Rossii i Yevropeiskogo Soyuza*, p. 7 (note 108 above). From the list of participants, it is clear that a number of them can be categorized as pragmatic nationalists. The majority, however, agreed that membership in the medium term was inconceivable.

110 Nadezhda Arbatova, 'Russia–EU quandary 2007', *Russia in Global Affairs*, Vol. 4, No. 2, April/June 2006, p. 101.

111 Ibid.; see also *Russia and the Enlarged European Union: The Arduous Path Toward Rapprochement* (Moscow: RUE, 2004).

112 Khudoley, 'Russia and the European Union'; *Otnosheniya Rossii i Yevropeiskogo*

Soyuza, p. 17 (both note 108 above).

113   Chizhov, *Itar-Tass Weekly News*, 4 December 2004.

114   Communication from the Commission to the Council and the European Parliament on relations with Russia, COM(2004) 106, p. 2 (note 81 above).

115   *Russia and the Enlarged European Union*; *Otnosheniya Rossii i Yevropeiskogo Soyuza*, p. 2 (notes 1111 and 108 above).

116   Vladimir Lukin in *International Affairs* (Moscow), No. 1, 2005, p. 58.

117   *Rasshireniya ES: ugroza ili shans dlya Rossii?* (Moscow: RUE, 2002), pp. 17–18.

118   *Otnosheniya Rossii i Yevropeiskogo Soyuza*, pp. 21–2 (note 108 above).

119   Timofei Bordachev, 'Toward a strategic alliance', *Russia in Global Affairs*, Vol. 4, No. 2, April/June 2006, p. 115.

120   *Otnosheniya Rossii i Yevropeiskogo Soyuza*, p. 8 (note 108 above).

121   Rolf Shuette, 'EU–Russia Relations: Interests and Values – A European Perspective', *Carnegie Papers*, No. 54, December 2004, pp. 1–2.

122   Karen Smith, 'Enlargement and European Order', in *International Relations and the European Union*, p. 286 (note 51 above).

123   *Otnosheniya Rossii i Yevropeiskogo Soyuza*, p. 19.

124   Commission of the European Communities, Communication from the Commission to the Council and the European Parliament, 'Wider Europe – Neighbourhood: A New Framework for Relations with our Eastern and Southern Neighbours', COM (2003), Brussels, 11.3.2003.

125   Vladimir Chizhov, 'European Union: a partnership strategy', *International Affairs* (Moscow), No. 6, 2004, p. 85. For details of the European Neighbourhood Policy, see Commission of the European Communities, Communication from the Commission, European Neighbourhood Policy Strategy Paper, COM (2004) 373, Brussels, 12 May 2004.

126   *Otnosheniya Rossii i Yevropeiskogo Soyuza*, p. 4.

127   Timofei Bordachev, 'Russia's European Problem: Eastward Enlargement of the EU and Moscow's Policy, 1993–2003', in Antonenko and Pinnick, *Russia and the European Union*, p. 61 (note 47 above).

128   Marek Menkiszak, *Russia vs the European Union: A 'Strategic Partnership' Crisis*, Warsaw, CES Studies, January 2006, p. 41.

4   RUSSIAN SECURITY ENGAGEMENT WITH THE EUROPEAN UNION

1   For further discussion of Russia–EU soft security cooperation, including the issues of organized crime, nuclear safety, environmental protection and drug trafficking, see Andrew Monaghan, *Russian Perspectives of Russia–EU Security Relations*, Conflict Studies Research Centre, Defence Academy of the UK, August 2005, pp. 5–9, 12–13.

2   For the background on Russian interaction with and perception of the Western European Union, see Dmitry Danilov and Stephan De Spiegeleire, *From Decoupling to Recoupling: A New Security Relationship between Russia and Western Europe?*, Chaillot Paper No. 31 (Paris: Institute for Security Studies, Western European Union, April 1998.

3   Clelia Rontoyanni, 'So far, so good? Russia and the ESDP', *International Affairs*, Vol. 78, No. 4, 2002, p. 816.

4 Vladimir Baranovsky, *Russia's Attitudes Towards the EU: Political Aspects* (Kauhava: Ulkopoliittinen instituutti and Institut für Europäische Politik, 2002), pp. 107–9. Vladimir Baranovsky, 'Common European Security and Defence Policy: Horizons of the Russian Perception', in Vladimir Baranovsky and Alexandre Kalliadine, eds, *Russia: Arms Control, Disarmament and International Security* (Moscow: IMEMO, Russian Academy of Sciences, 2002), pp. 36–7.

5 Baranovsky, *Russia's Attitudes Towards the EU*, pp. 105–6.

6 Dmitri Trenin, 'A Russia-within-Europe: Working Towards a New Security Arrangement', paper prepared for the Sixth Meeting of the European Security Forum, Brussels, 14 January 2002, pp. 1–4.

7 Nadezhda Arbatova, 'Novaya strategiya bezopasnosti ES', *Sovremennaya Yevropa*, Vol. 16, No. 4 (October–December 2003), p. 67.

8 Aleksei Arbatov, in N. Arbatova, ed., *Yevrobezopasnost': est' li v ney mesto dlya Rossii...'* (Moscow: Committee 'Russia in a United Europe', 2002), pp. 15–17.

9 Alexei Arbatov, 'Pod odnim zontikom', *Nezavisimaya gazeta*, 7 April 2003.

10 Yuri Borko, 'Rethinking Russia–EU relations', *Russia in Global Affairs*, Vol. 2, No. 1, July/September 2004, p. 171.

11 N. Zaslavskaya, 'Yevropeyskaya politika v oblasti bezopasnosti i oboronoy: otnosheniya ES i NATO', in S. Tkachenko, ed., *Bezopasnost' v regione Tsentral'noy i Vostochnoy Yevropy: rol' Rossii i NATO* (St Petersburg: Iskra, 2001), pp. 67–9. Dmitri Danilov, 'The EU's Rapid Reaction Capabilities: A Russian Perspective', paper delivered at the IESS/CEPS European Security Forum, 10 September 2001, p. 2.

12 Sergei Karaganov, 'Russia, Europe, and new challenges', *Russia in Global Affairs*, Vol. 1, No. 1, January/March 2003.

13 Sergei Karaganov, director of the Council on Foreign and Defence Policy, in Arbatova, *Yevrobezopasnost'*, p. 42 (note 8 above).

14 N. Kovalev, 'Concerning a Common European Space in the Struggle against Terrorism and Organized Crime', in N. Arbatova, ed., *Vozmozhno li Pravovoe Prostranstvo mezhdu Rossiey i Yevropeyskim Soyuzom?* (Moscow: Committee 'Russia in a United Europe', 2004), pp. 12–14.

15 Interviews, Moscow, 22 and 26 March 2004.

16 Interview of internal security official, Moscow, 25 March 2004.

17 Vladimir Baranovsky, 'Russian Views on NATO and the EU', in Anatol Lieven and Dmitri Trenin, eds, *Ambivalent Neighbors: The EU, NATO and the Price of Membership* (Washington DC: Carnegie Endowment for International Peace, 2003), p. 293.

18 Colonel-General Leonid Ivashov, head of the Russian Defence Ministry's administration for cooperation with foreign armies, *Monitor*, Jamestown Foundation, Vol. V, No. 238, 23 December 1999.

19 Colonel Vladimir Dvorkin, director of the Centre on the Problems of Strategic Forces, in N. Arbatova, ed., *Rossiya i ES: brat'ya po oruzhiyu?* (Moscow: Committee on 'Russia in a United Europe', 2003), pp. 8–12, 17.

20 Meeting with foreign military attachés, Itar-Tass, Moscow, 15 December 2004, BBC Mon Alert FS1 FsuPol grh/sku. This meeting occurred after the EU turned down a Russian draft for expanding military contacts and proposed instead that bilateral programmes should be implemented stage by stage, depending on the progress of the ESDP.

21 Russian Public TV, 3 October 2001, BBC Mon FS1 FsuPol gar.

22 For a proposal by a Western specialist for a Russia–EU 'High-Level Group on Wider Security', initially focusing on peace support and then expanding its remit to include other security questions, see Dov Lynch, *Russia Faces Europe*, Chaillot Paper No. 60 (Paris: Institute for Security Studies, European Union, May 2003), pp. 91–3.

23 Joint Statement of EU–Russia summit, St Petersburg, 31 May 2003; 9937/03 (Presse 154). On the Russian side Presidential Assistant Victor Ivanov will supervise the common space on freedom, security and justice, while Foreign Minister Sergei Lavrov will supervise the common external security space. Remarks by Putin at the Russia–EU summit, 21 May 2003, Ministry of Foreign Affairs, *http://www. ln.mid.ru*. For the road maps on the common spaces, see *http://europa.eu.int/comm/ external_relations/russia/summit_05_05/index.htm*.

24 The analysis in this section benefits considerably from Lynch, *Russia Faces Europe*, pp. 66–72 (note 22 above); Dov Lynch, 'Russia's strategic partnership with Europe', *The Washington Quarterly*, Vol. 27, No. 2, Spring 2004, pp. 108–11. For a summary of the agenda to realize the common space in the field of external security, see the joint declaration 'on strengthening dialogue and cooperation on political and security matters (Annex IV)', Rome, 6 November 2003, Daily News Bulletin, Russian Ministry of Foreign Affairs, *http://www.ln.mid.ru*.

25 For example, 'Joint statement on the Middle East', at the 10th EU–Russia summit, 11 November 2002, *http://www.europa.eu.int/comm/external_relations/russia/ summit_11_02/js_meast.htm*.

26 See talks between Foreign Minister Ivanov and the EU troika, 23 January 2003; Interfax, Moscow, 24 January 2003, BBC Mon FS1 FsuPol pl/jg.

27 Interfax, Moscow, 5 October 2001, BBC Mon FS1 FsuPol 11.

28 Council of the European Union, 'Presidency Report on European Security and Defence Policy', Brussels, 22 June 2002, 10160/2/02 REV COSDP 188, Annex IV.

29 Vladimir Chizhov, 'Russia–EU cooperation: the foreign policy dimension', *International Affairs* (Moscow), Vol. 51, No. 5, 2005, p. 137.

30 Trenin, 'A Russia-within-Europe', p. 4 (note 6 above). For a good analysis of Russian perspectives on the factors undermining effective EU–Russia cooperation over crisis management, see Andrew Monaghan, 'Does Europe exist as an entity for military cooperation? Evolving Russian perspectives, 1991–2004', *Connections: The Quarterly Journal*, Vol. III, No. 2, June 2004, pp. 56–60.

31 For a positive assessment of this proposal, see Andrew Monaghan, 'The disasters and catastrophes alternative: Russia–EU security relations', *European Analysis*, 2004, *www.europeanalysis.org.uk*.

32 See interview of Anatoly Safonov, Putin's special representative on issues of international cooperation in the fight against terrorism, RIA news agency, Moscow, 9 November 2004, BBC Mon FS1 FsuPol sz.

33 'Russian-EU talks boost cooperation', *Monitor*, Jamestown Foundation, Vol. VII, No. 183 October 2001), p. 5. See Joint Statement on the Fight against Terrorism, issued from EU–Russia summit on 11 November 2002, *http://europa.eu.int/comm/ external_relations/russia/summit_11_02/js_terr.htm*. For a good analysis of the extent of cooperation in curbing terrorist financing and in information and intelligence-

sharing over terrorism, see Domitilla Sagramoso, *Russia's Western Orientation after 11th September: Russia's Enhanced Cooperation with NATO and the European Union* (Rubbetino, Rome: Centro Militare di Studi Strategici, 2004), pp. 28–38.

34 Vassily Likhachev (Russia's permanent representative to the EU during 1998–2003), 'Russia and EU: proficiency essential', *Russia in Global Affairs*, Vol. 2, No. 2, April–June 2004, p. 104. Anti-terrorism is understood as action against terrorism activities before they occur, while counterterrorism is active measures to respond immediately to terrorist attacks.

35 Alexander Yakovenko, 14 October 2004, Russian Foreign Ministry, *http://www.ln.mid.ru*. The EU response to the Beslan crisis is presented by Chris Patten, EU Commissioner for External Relations, 'The tragedy in Beslan and the fight against terrorism', Speech/04/398, European Parliament Plenary, Strasbourg, 15 September 2004; Foreign Minister Bernard Bot, President of Council of Ministers of the European Union, 'Why Russia and the EU need one another', 19 October 2004, *http://www.eu2004.nl*.

36 See Burkhard Schmidt, ed., *EU Cooperative Threat Reduction Activities in Russia*, Chaillot Paper No. 61 (Paris: Institute for Security Studies, European Union, June 2003), especially pp. 46–8.

37 Multilateral Nuclear Environment Programme in the Russian Federation, signed on 21 May 2003 in Stockholm; see *http://www.europa.eu.int/comm/external_relations/north_dim/ndep.index.htm*.

38 Statement by Russian Deputy Prime Minister Ilya Klebanov, Itar-Tass, Moscow, 14 December 2000, in *BBC Summary of World Broadcasts. Former Soviet Union*, SU/4025 B/3.

39 See Arbatova, ed., *Rossiya i ES: Brat'ya po Oruzhiyu?* (note 19 above).

40 Earlier Russian responses to the ESDP are well analysed in Mark Webber, 'Third party inclusion in European Security and Defence Policy: A case study of Russia', *European Foreign Affairs Review*, Vol. 6, No. 4 (Winter 2001), pp. 407–26; Dieter Mahncke, 'Russia's attitude to the European Security and Defence Policy', *European Foreign Affairs Review*, Vol. 6, No. 4, Winter 2001, pp. 427–36; Clelia Rontoyanni, 'So far, so good? Russia and the ESDP', pp. 813–30 (note 3 above).

41 Timofei Bordachev, 'Europe's Russia Problem: Immediate Concerns and Long-term Perspectives', in Iris Kempe, ed., *Prospects and Risks beyond EU Enlargement* (Opladen: Leske and Budrich, 2003), p. 92.

42 Tuomas Forsberg, 'Russia's Role in the ESDP', in Esther Brimmer, ed., *The EU's Search for a Strategic Role: ESDP and its Implications for Transatlantic Relations* (Washington DC: Center for Transatlantic Relations, 2002), p. 92.

43 Lynch, 'Russia's strategic partnership with Europe', p. 112 (note 24 above); Lynch, *Russia Faces Europe*, pp. 76–7 (note 22 above).

44 Itar-Tass, Moscow, 23 April 2004, BBC Mon FS1 FsuPol mjm/iu.

45 Meeting in Novo-Ogarevo, attended by the author with other Western specialists and journalists, 6 September 2004.

46 See Sophia Clement-Noguier, 'Russia, the European Union and NATO after September 11', in Alexander Motyl, Blair Ruble and Lilia Shevtsova, eds, *Russia's Engagement with the West: Transformation and Integration in the Twenty-First Century* (Armonk NY: M. E. Sharpe, 2005), p. 252.

47 *A Secure Europe in a Better World – The European Security Strategy* (approved by

the European Council: Brussels, 12 December 2003); *http://ue.eu.int/uedocs/cmsU-pload/78367.pdf*.

48 Communication from the European Commission to the European Council and the European Parliament, *Wider Europe – Neighbourhood: A New Framework for Relations with our Eastern and Southern Neighbours*, COM (2003) 104, Brussels, 11 March 2003.

49 Speech in Berlin, 23 February 2003, Russian Foreign Ministry, 376–23–02–2004, *http://www.ln.mid.ru*.

50 Vladimir Chizhov, 'European Union: a partnership strategy', *International Affairs* (Moscow), Vol. 50, No. 6, 2004, p. 87.

51 See 'The EU's Relations with Moldova – An Overview', at *http://www.europe.eu.int/comm/external_relations/moldova/intro*.

52 For possible requirements of such a common position on the Moldovan conflict, see Lynch, *Russia Faces Europe*, pp. 96–103 (note 22 above); Dov Lynch, 'The Russia–EU Partnership and the Shared Neighbourhood', Report of EU Institute for Security Studies, July 2004, p. 3, *http://www.iss-eu.org/new/analysis/analy090.html*.

53 See Dov Lynch, 'Shared neighbourhood or new frontline? The crossroads in Moldova', *Russie.Nei.Visions* (Paris: IFRI, April 2005), No. 2, pp. 7–11.

54 For criticism of the EU approach towards Moldova at this time as primarily an experiment in EU–Russia cooperation for conflict settlement in Europe, see *Eurasia Daily Monitor*, Jamestown Foundation, Vol. 2, No. 28, 9 February 2005; Vol. 2, No. 74, 15 April 2005.

55 *http://europa.eu.int/comm/external_relations/russia/summit_05_05/index.htm*, p. 42.

56 Interfax news agency, Moscow, 12 May 2005, BBC Mon FS1 FsuPol ws/pl/of.

57 After joint Moldovan and Ukrainian requests for the EU to support the creation of effective border monitoring and customs arrangements on the Moldova–Ukraine border in December 2005, an EU Border Assistance Mission (BAM) for this border, including the Transdniestria section, was inaugurated. See *Eurasia Daily Monitor*, Vol. 2, No. 190, 13 October 2005; Vol. 2, No. 225, 5 December 2005.

58 These options are analysed in Dmitry Polikanov, 'Transdniestria, Abkhazia, Chechnya: Pros and cons of the EU intervention', *Connections: The Quarterly Journal*, Vol. III, No. 2, June 2004, pp. 33–8.

59 Russian specialists argue that a common Russia–EU political platform and a common action plan should precede any consideration of instruments for joint Russia–EU post-conflict stabilization or peace support missions in CIS conflict zones, even if the EU contribution is only a civilian mission. Discussions in the Institute of Europe, Moscow, 1 November 2005.

60 Dmitry Danilov, 'Russia–EU Cooperation in the Security Field: Trends and Conceptual Framework', in Hanna Smith, ed., *Russia and its Foreign Policy: Influences, Interests and Issues* (Saarijärji: Kikimora Publications, 2005), p. 121. For an argument that the EU is in fact unlikely to act as a revisionist force at the expense of Russia in the 'shared neighbourhood', see Andrei Zagorski, 'Russia and the Shared Neighbourhood', in Dov Lynch, ed., *What Russia Sees*, Chaillot Paper No. 74 (Paris: Institute for Security Studies, European Union, January 2005), pp. 73–7.

61 Dov Lynch, 'The EU: Towards a Strategy', in Dov Lynch, ed., *The South Caucasus: A Challenge for the EU*, Chaillot Paper No. 65 (Paris: Institute for Security Studies,

European Union, December 2003), pp. 171–96.

62 Report by Imedi TV, Tbilisi, 2 March 2005, on Foreign Minister Salome Zour-abichvili's visit to Brussels, BBC Mon FS1 FsyPol sz/ibg; Interfax news agency, Moscow, 3 March 2005, BBC Mon FS1 FsuPol kg/skh.

63 Interfax news agency, Moscow, 10 May 2005, BBC Mon FS1 FsuPol kt/iz.

64 Thomas Gomart, *Enlargement Tests the Partnership Between the EU and Russia* (Swindon: Conflict Studies Research Centre, Defence Academy of the United Kingdom, August 2004), pp. 4–5; Andrey Makarychev, 'Europe's Eastern Dimension: Russia's reaction to Poland's initiative', PONARS Policy Memo, No. 301, November 2003, p. 3.

65 Makarychev, 'Europe's Eastern Dimension', p. 2.

66 Timofei Bordachev and Arkady Moshes, 'Is the Europeanization of Russia over?', *Russia in Global Affairs*, Vol. 2, No. 2, April 2004, p. 92.

67 Ibid., p. 98.

68 The EU sought to monitor the implementation of these regulations through an EU Border Assistance Mission. *Eurasia Daily Monitor*, Vol. 3, No. 58, 24 March 2006.

69 On these issues, see Frank Morgese, 'Border Security Implications for Dual Enlargement: A Comparison of Russia and Ukraine', in Graeme Herd and Jennifer Moroney, eds, *Security Dilemmas in the Former Soviet Bloc* (London: Routledge-Curzon, 2003), pp. 80–93.

70 Itar-Tass, Moscow, 10 December 2004, BBC Mon FS1 FsuPol vpa/jg.

71 Statement by Putin at annual new conference, RTR Russia TV, Moscow, 23 December 2004, BBC Mon FS1 MCU 241204 yk/mcu.

72 Ukraine has already participated in two ESDP missions in the Balkans and agreed in June 2005 to cooperate with the GALILEO European satellite navigation system.

73 Centre TV, Moscow, 18 December 2004, BBC Mon FS1 MCU 211204 rj/pf.

74 Konstantin Kosachev, 'Russia between European choice and Asian growth', *International Affairs* (Moscow), Vol. 52, No. 1 (2006), p. 6.

75 An example was the formation of the Russian–French Council for Security Cooperation in 2002, the essence of which continues in French talk of their 'unique' dialogue with Moscow over 'the European security structure'. French Foreign Minister Michel Barnier, AFP news agency, Paris, 21 January 2005, in BBC Mon EU1 EuroPol kk.

76 During Putin's presidency such meetings have been held in April 2003 in St Petersburg, in September 2003 in New York, in August 2004 in Sochi, and with the additional participation of Spain in March 2005 in Paris.

77 Divisions within Europe – the 'old' and the 'new' Europe debate – complicate Russian policy, especially when US policy appears aimed at politically elevating the role of former communist countries that have been on the European geographic periphery at the expense of nations that have been at the European core. See Andrey Makarychev, 'Russia between "old" and "new" Europe: new policy articulations', PONARS Policy Memo 333, November 2004, pp. 1–5.

78 In January 2005 Defence Minister Ivanov observed that cooperation with the EU in the field of defence and security remained 'in the embryonic stage, far lower than the level of our relations with individual NATO countries, with China or with India'. Itar-Tass news agency, Moscow, 14 January 2005, BBC Mon FS1 FsuPol lb.

5 RUSSIAN SECURITY ENGAGEMENT WITH NATO

1 For an overview of this issue, see Ingmar Oldberg, *Membership or Partnership: The Relations of Russia and its Neighbours with NATO and the EU in the Enlargement Context* (Stockholm: Swedish Defence Research Agency, October 2004).

2 Speech by Russian Deputy Minister of Foreign Affairs Vladimir Chizhov, 'Russia's vision of a European Security Policy partner: ESDP, NATO or somebody else?', Berlin, 23 February 2003, Russian Foreign Ministry, *http://www.mid.ru*.

3 Vladimir Baranovsky, *Russia's Attitudes Towards the EU: Political Aspects* (Kauhava: Ulkopoliittinen instituutti and Institut für Europäische Politik, 2002), pp. 76–8.

4 Speech by Defence Minister Sergei Ivanov, London, 13 July 2004, at *http://www.ln.mid.ru/Brp_4.nsf/arh/*. See also Ekaterina Kuznetsova, 'NATO: new anti-terrorist organization?', *International Affairs* (Moscow), Vol. 50, No. 3, 2004, pp. 22–6.

5 Itar-Tass news agency, Moscow, 11 January 2005, *BBC Summary of World Broadcasts. Former Soviet Union*, *http://www.bbc.monitoringonline.com* (henceforth BBC), Mon FS1 FsuPol gyl.

6 Sergei Yastrzhembsky, Itar-Tass news agency, Moscow, 30 January 2003, BBC Mon FS1 FsuPol jg/ar.

7 Interview in *Komsomols'kaya pravda*, 26 October 2004, BBC Mon FS1 FsuPol ps.

8 In an interview at the end of 2005 Sergei Ivanov made this clear: 'Let's look at the regions which currently are NATO's top priorities. All of them are very far from the North Atlantic zone and even from Europe, I mean Great Europe including Russia. They are North Africa, Sudan, Iraq, Iran, Afghanistan.' Centre TV, Moscow, 3 December 2005, BBC Mon FS1 MCU 051205 im/ak.

9 Aleksei Bogutarov, *Nezavisimaya gazeta*, 28 June 2004, p. 2.

10 Dmitri Vassiliev, 'The views of the Russian elite toward NATO membership', *PONARS Policy Memo*, No. 126, April 2000, pp. 3–5, *www.csis.org/ruseura/ponars/policymemos/pm_0126.pdf*.

11 For a Russian evaluation of this debate, see Denis Alexeev, *NATO Enlargement: A Russian Outlook* (Camberley: Conflict Studies Research Centre, November 2004), pp. 2–9.

12 Vassiliev, 'The views of the Russian elite toward NATO membership', pp. 5–7 (note 10 above).

13 Interview on Channel One TV, Moscow, 4 April 2004, BBC Mon FS1 FsuPol lb/va/ad; statement at Davos World Economic Forum, RIA Novosti 22 January 2003, *CDI Russia Weekly*, *http://www.cdi.org/russia/23jan04–17.cfm*.

14 Itar-Tass, Moscow, 4 December 2003, BBC Mon FS1 FsuPol gar/kt.

15 Interview conducted in the Kremlin, 7 July 2004.

16 Joint session of Rogozin's committee and the Political Committee of the NATO Parliamentary Assembly, in the Duma, Itar-Tass, Moscow, 22 March 2002, BBC Mon FS1 FsuPol ws/kdd.

17 Russia TV, 14 May 2002, BBC Mon FS1 FsuPol II.

18 Sergei Markov, Director of the Institute of Political Studies, 'NATO bez nas ne oboidetsya', *Nezavisimaya gazeta*, 2 August 2002.

19 Sergei Markov, 'NATO is unprepared for modern challenges', *Rossiya*, No. 24, 1–7 July 2004, p. 2.

20 Sergei Karaganov, chairman of the foreign policy lobby the Council on Foreign and Defence Policy, 'Novye vyzovy bezopasnosti: Rossiya i zapad', *Sovremennaya Yevropa*, 1 (January/March), 2002, p. 43.

21 Interviewed in Dmitri Suslov, 'Robertson reports to Putin', *Nezavisimaya gazeta*, 14 May 2003.

22 Sergei Karaganov, 'Russia and the International Order', in Dov Lynch, ed., *What Russia Sees*, Chaillot Paper No. 47 (Paris: Institute for Security Studies, European Union, January 2005), p. 43.

23 Major-General (ret.) Pavel Zolotaryev, president of the Interregional Military Reforms Support Foundation, 'Moscow plus NATO', *Nezavisimoe voennoe obozrenie*. No. 2, 23 January 2004.

24 Valery Uskov, a representative of the main international cooperation agency of the Russian Ministry of Defence, at a joint meeting of committees of the NATO Parliamentary Assembly and the State Duma. Itar-Tass, Moscow, 10 April 2003, BBC Mon FS1 FsuPol nv/ll.

25 Interviews, 22–23 March 2004 in Moscow; 7 April 2004 in Glasgow.

26 Ekho Moskvy news agency, Moscow, 20 October 2001, BBC Mon FS1 MCU 201001 grh/bj.

27 Ekho Moskvy, Moscow, 27 September 2003, BBC Mon FS1 MCU 270903 la/er.

28 Interview, Moscow, 23 March 2004.

29 As noted by Kuznetsova, 'NATO: new anti-terrorist organization?', p. 24 (note 4 above).

30 Interview, Moscow, 22 March 2004.

31 For example, Vyacheslav Tetekin, *Sovetskaya Rossiya*, 6 April 2004, p. 3.

32 Interview, Moscow, 23 March 2004.

33 Resolution 'In Connection with NATO Enlargement', No. 1299, 31 March 2004, passed by 305 deputies in favour, 41 against; Itar-Tass, Moscow, 31 March 2004, BBC Mon alert FS1 FsuPol pl/mjm; Ekho Moskvy, Moscow, 31 March 2004, BBC Mon FS1 MCU 310304 rj/ak; *Rossiiskaya gazeta*, 1 April 2004, p. 3; *Izvestiya*, 26 March 2004, p. 3.

34 Andrei Lebedev, *Izvestiya*, 30 March 2004, p. 3.

35 Interviews, Moscow, 24–25 March 2004.

36 Statement in meeting with military attachés of foreign countries, Itar-Tass, Moscow, 30 January 2003, BBC Mon FS1 FsuPol sku/nv.

37 Interview by Mikhail Poluboiarov, 'Towards NATO', *Rodnaya gazeta*, No. 15, 16 April 2004, p. 5.

38 Colonel-General Leonid Ivashov, Vice-President of the Russian Academy for Geopolitical Problems (and formerly responsible for the Russian Ministry of Defence's international military cooperation), *Kommersant*, 5 December 2003; *Sovetskaya Rossia*, 5 March 2005.

39 'Welcome NATO!', *Nezavisimaya gazeta*, 9 April 2004, p. 2. For a more reasoned military analysis, see Major-General Vladimir Slipchenko, interviewed in 'NATO is the Americans' shop', Alexander Khokhlov, *Novoe Izvestiya*, 12 April 2004, pp. 1, 7.

40 Interviews, Moscow, 25–26 March 2004.

41 Interview, Moscow, 19 April 2004.

42 Interviews, Moscow, 22 March 2004.

43 Interfax and Itar-Tass, Moscow, 28 February 2003, BBC Mon FS1 FsuPol ps.

44 For brief 'optimistic' and 'sceptical' assessments of NRC cooperation, see Tuomas Forsberg, 'Russia's relationship with NATO: a qualitative change or old wine in new bottles?', *Journal of Communist Studies in Transition*, Vol. 21, No. 3, September 2005, pp. 341–5.

45 According to the initial agenda of the NRC, Foreign and Defence Ministers meet only once a year, although in spring 2003 Russia called for more frequent crisis meetings. See Foreign Minister Igor Ivanov, NTV Mir, 13 May 2003, BBC Mon FS1 FSUPol stu/lb.

46 Interview of Konstantin Totsky, Russia's Permanent Representative at NATO, to Itar-Tass news agency, 29 October 2003; Daily News Bulletin, Russian Ministry of Foreign Affairs, 30 October 2003, *www.mid.ru*. Totsky notes that the Russian negative view of the PfP programme was because Moscow had viewed it as a means to assist countries intending to join NATO, but that Russia was now aware that states which do not intend to join the Alliance – for example Sweden – are also actively using these programmes. In June 2005 a NATO Information Centre concerned with international security issues was opened in Volgograd.

47 Robert E. Hunter, Sergey Rogov, and Olga Oliker, *NATO and Russia: Bridge-building for the 21st Century* (Santa Monica: Rand, 2002), p. 7.

48 Interview of senior Russian diplomats, Russian Foreign Ministry, 23 March 2004.

49 First Deputy Chief of the Russian General Staff, Colonel-General Yury Baluevsky, Itar-Tass, Moscow, 12 March 2002, BBC Mon FS1 FsuPol stu/gyl.

50 Aleksandr Yakovenko, Russian Foreign Ministry spokesman, Itar-Tass, Moscow, 2 December 2003, BBC Mon DS1 FsuPol ch/sz.

51 Andrei Kelin, Deputy Director, European Cooperation Department, Russian Foreign Ministry, 'Russia–NATO: toward a new stage of interaction?', *International Affairs* (Moscow), Vol. 51, No. 1, 2005, p. 42.

52 The initial NRC cooperation programme was contained in a declaration by the NATO member states and Russia, 'NATO–Russia Relations: A New Quality', 28 May 2002, *http://www.nato.int/docu/basictxt/b020528e.htm*. For progress by mid-2003 in the various areas of cooperation specified in this programme, see the statement on the NRC meeting of Foreign Ministers on 4 June 2003, *http://www.nato.int/docu/pr/2003/p030604e.htm*. For a NATO assessment of achievements by early 2004, see General Harald Kujat, Chairman of NATO's Military Committee and of the NRC Military Representatives, http://*www.nato.int/docu/articles/2004/a040226a.htm*. A recent overall assessment is found in Richard Weitz, *Revitalizing US–Russian Security Cooperation*, Adelphi Paper No. 377 (London: International Institute for Strategic Studies, 2005), pp. 59–73.

53 Speech by Putin at the 29 January 2005 meeting of the Security Council, *http://www.kremlin.ru/eng/speeches/2005/01/29/1333_type82913_83188.shtm*.

54 This analysis draws on presentations by senior NATO officials at a number of seminars organized by Chatham House. See also analyses by Paul Fritch and John Colston in *Responding to Terrorism and Other New Threats and Challenges* (Moscow: International Centre for Strategic and Political Studies, Moscow, 2005). See also Colonel-General Yury Baluevsky, in *Krasnaya zvezda*, 6 November 2004.

55 See *http://www.nato.int/docu/basictxt/b041209a-e.htm*.

56 Statement by Army General Valentin Korabelnikov, head of the Main Intelligence Directorate (GRU) of the Russian General Staff; Interfax, Moscow, 2 December 2003, BBC Mon Alert FS1 FsuPol ch/jg.

57 RTR Russia TV, Moscow, 14 October 2004, BBC Mon FS1 FsuPol sz/gyl.

58 Statement by Defence Minister Sergei Ivanov at meeting of NRC Defence Ministers, Itar-Tass news agency, Moscow, 14 October 2004, BBC Mon FS1 FsuPol sz/kt.

59 Itar-Tass, Moscow, 26 October 2004, BBC Mon FS1 FusPol ydy/iz; Itar-Tass, 10 December 2004, BBC Mon FS1 FsuPol nv/vpa. Russian ships do not operate as part of NATO's Allied Naval Forces Southern Europe (NAVSOUTH), but jointly with them; see Chief of the General Staff of the Russian Navy, Admiral Viktor Kravchenko, Itar-Tass report, Moscow, 11 January 2005, BBC Mon FS1 FsuPol lb/se. For a Russian assessment of the wider context of such naval cooperation, see Captain V. Makeev, 'Voenno-morskoe sotrudnichestvo v bor'be s terrorizmom', *Voennya mysl'*, No. 10, October 2005, pp. 27–31.

60 See 'Exercise "Kaliningrad 2004"', *http://www.nato.int/docu/pr/2004/p04–09e.htm*.

61 Statement by Russian Minister for Civil Defence and Emergency Situations, Sergei Shoigu, Itar-Tass, Moscow, 1 July 2003, BBC Mon FS1 FsuPol gyl/sv.

62 Statement on 1 March 2005, 'Soft nuclear monitoring', Vladimir Ivanov and Mikhail Tolpegin, *Nezavisimaya gazeta*, 2 March 2005, p. 1.

63 Aleksandr Babakin, *Nezavisimaya gazeta*, 4 August 2004, pp. 1, 7.

64 For a Russian military assessment of the potential for such collaboration, see Colonel-General Yu. Baluevsky, First Deputy Chief of the General Staff, 'Rossiya i NATO: printsipy vzaimootnosheniy, problemy i perspektivy sotrudnichestva', *Voennaya mysl'*, 6, June 2003, pp. 12–17.

65 Sharyl Cross, *Russia and NATO toward the Twenty-first Century: Conflicts and Peacekeeping in Bosnia-Herzegovina and Kosovo*, NATO–EAPC Research Fellowship Award Final Report, NATO/Academic Affairs, 1999–2001, August 2001, p. 22. For a Russian assessment of the participation of Russian forces in KFOR, see Yu. Morozov, V. Glushkov, and A. Sharavin, *Balkany segodnya i zavtra: Voenno-politicheskie aspekty mirotvorchestva* (Moscow: Centre of Military Strategic Studies of the General Staff of the Russian Armed Forces/Institute of Political and Military Analysis, 2001), pp. 279–87.

66 Reports by Vladimir Urban, 'Moscow admits defeat in the Balkans', *Novye izvestiya*, 17 January 2003; and Vadim Soloviev, 'Russia retreats, NATO expands', *Nezavisimoe voennoe obozrenie*, 16 May 2003.

67 'General Totskiy: Russian Ambassador to NATO', *NATO Review*, Autumn 2003, p. 32. Lieutenant-General A. Voronin, 'Problemy i perspektivy strategicheskogo partnerstva Rossiya–NATO', *Voennaya mysl'*, No. 11, November 2005, p. 43.

68 See *www.mid.ru*, 24 September 2002.

69 Andrei Kelin, Deputy Director, Department of General European Cooperation, Russian Foreign Ministry, 'Attitude to NATO expansion: calmly negative', *International Affairs* (Moscow), Vol. 50, No. 1, 2004, p. 23.

70 Statement by Army General Yury Baluevsky, after attending a meeting of the Russia–NATO Council, Itar-Tass news agency, Moscow, 11 May 2005, BBC Mon FS1 FsuPol sku/alk.

71 Statement at informal NRC Meeting in Taormina, Italy, *Krasnaya zvezda*, 11 February 2006.

72 Statements by Sergei Ivanov; RIA news agency, Moscow, 14 October 2004, BBC Mon FS1 FsuPol sz/kt; Itar-Tass news agency, 10 December 2004, BBC Mon FS1 FsuPol nv/ws/lr; Itar-Tass, 10 February 2005, BBC Mon FS1 FsuPol mjm.

73 For a detailed Russian analysis of the issues surrounding joint peacekeeping in the Eurasian region, involving forces of the EU/NATO and of Russia/The Collective Security Treaty Organization, or a 'coalition of willing states', see Yury Morozov, *Joint Peacekeeping in the Eurasian Region: Structures and Prospects* (Camberley: Conflict Studies Research Centre, October 2004), pp. 1–11.

74 Voronin, 'Problemy i perspektivy strategicheskogo partnerstva Rossiya–NATO', p. 43 (note 67 above). Lieutenant-General A. Voronin is a member of an expert committee of the Committee on Defence and Security of the Russian Federation Council.

75 See U. Morozov, 'Prospects for elaboration of joint doctrines of peacemaking activities for Russia and NATO: Russia's possible role in NATO Rapid Reaction Forces', in Robert Hunter and Sergey Rogov, *Engaging Russia as Partner and Participant: The Next Stage of NATO–Russia Relations* (Santa Monica CA: RAND Corporation, 2004), pp. 46–50.

76 See Russian Foreign Ministry press release, 20 July 2004, *http://www.ln.mid.ru*; Alexander Yakovenko in *Rossiiskaya gazeta*, 6 April 2005, p. 8; Vladimir Socor, 'No discounts on Baltic security', *Wall Street Journal Europe*, 27–29 February 2004, p. A9. For a detailed Russian assessment of CFE Treaty limits on military equipment, see Vitaly Mikhailov, 'Adaptatsiya posle adaptatsii', *Nezavisimoe voennoe obozrenie*, No. 26, 2–8 August 2002.

77 'Ivanov says Russia may pull out of arms treaty', *Moscow Times*, 10 February 2004.

78 First Deputy Chief of the Russian General Staff, Colonel-General Yury Baluevsky, *Izvestiya*, 3 March 2004, p. 3.

79 Statement by Colonel-General Konstantin Totsky, director of the Federal Border Service, Interfax, 27 January 2003, BBC Mon FS1 FsuPol gc/eg.

80 Itar-Tass news agency, Moscow, 15 November 2005, BBC Mon FS1 FsuPol jg/ia.

81 See Steven E. Miller and Dmitri Trenin, eds, *The Russian Military: Power and Policy* (Cambridge MA and London: American Academy of Arts and Sciences, MIT Press, 2004), especially Chapters 3 and 5.

82 Manfred Diehl, 'The importance of democratic reform and control of the Russian armed forces for the successful development of military cooperation with NATO/EU and NATO/EU members', *European Security*, Vol. 12, No. 2, Summer 2003, p. 81.

83 See Roy Allison, 'Russia, Regional Conflict and the Use of Military Power', in Miller and Trenin, eds, *The Russian Military: Power and Policy*, pp. 121–56 (note 81 above). For a useful Russian analysis of the contrasting Russian and NATO approaches to military reform, see Vadim Soloviev, 'Krutoy povorot v voennom reformirovanii', *Nezavisimoe voennoe obozrenie*, No. 40, 15–21 November 2002.

84 Paul Fritch, in *Responding to Terrorism* (note 54 above).

85 Meeting on 6 September 2004, in Novo-Ogarevo, attended by this author.

86 RIA Novosti, 22 January 2004, *CDI Russia Weekly*, *http://www.cdi.org/russia/23jan04–17.cfm*.

87 But the Chief of General Staff of the Russian Armed Forces, Yury Baluevsky,

appears less adversarial than earlier incumbents in this post or most other senior General Staff officers. He has stated that a military confrontation between Russia and NATO is impossible, 'as there are no volunteers in NATO to die with us in a common embrace'; Interfax-AVN military news agency website, Moscow, 31 October 2005, BBC Mon FS1 FsuPol tm/pl, and *Rossiiskaya gazeta*, 1 November 2005.

88 *Aktual'nyye zadachi razvitiya Vooruzhennykh Sil Rossiiskoy Federatsii* (The priority tasks of the development of the armed forces of the Russian Federation), Russian Federation Ministry of Defence, 2 October 2003, *http://www.mil.ru/articles/article5005.shtml*. Interfax, Moscow, 2 October 2003, BBC Mon Alert FS1 FsuPol kp/jg. See Svetlana Babayeva, 'Reforms over', *Izvestiya*, 14 October 2003; Vladimir Mukhin, 'Russia defines a new defence orientation', *Nezavisimoe voennoe obozrenie*, No. 36, 10–16 October 2003. This threat to revise Russian principles of military planning 'if NATO is preserved as a military alliance with its existing doctrine' was repeated by the then First Deputy Chief of the Russian General Staff, Colonel-General Yury Baluevsky, the following spring; see *Izvestiya*, 15 April 2004. See also Matthew Bouldin, 'The Ivanov Doctrine and military reform: reasserting stability in Russia', *Journal of Slavic Military Studies*, Vol. 17, No. 4 (2004), pp. 619–41.

89 Alexei Arbatov, the then Deputy Chairman of the Duma Defence Committee, in Dmitri Suslov, 'Russia declares a Cold War on NATO, *Nezavisimaya gazeta*, 10 October 2003. For a Russian analysis of a NATO, attack on Russia, which would lead to a full NATO victory in three weeks, see 'Direction of the main strike', Mikhail Khodaryonov, *Voenno-promyshlenny kur'er*, No. 14, 14–20 April 2004, pp. 1–2. For another assessment that NATO represents the 'main potential military threat to Russia' that may lead to more serious military threats 'linked with the fact that NATO will turn the Baltic states and some CIS members states into a certain cordon around Russia', see Yevgeny Yelkin, senior expert at the Russian Ministry of Defence, 'Challenges and threats to Russian security', *Voenno-promyshlenny kur'er*, No. 6, 18–24 February 2004, pp. 1, 11. Alexander Goltz argues that 'Russian military authorities have primordially categorized the alliance as playing the role of a so-called "global adversary"', as this justifies the preservation of a mass mobilization army; 'Russia–NATO relations: between cooperation and confrontation', *Moscow Defence Brief*, No. 2, 2005, p.3.

90 Vladimir Mukhin, 'Russia–NATO confrontation only beginning', *Nezavisimaya gazeta*, 5 April 2004.

91 For example, Konstantin Sidkov, head of the General Staff's Centre for Military Strategic Research, in Alexander Golts, 'Taking aim at NATO', *Moscow Times*, 19 July 2005, p. 10.

92 Mikhail Khodaryonok, 'Response to NATO expansion', *Voenno-promyshlenny kur'er*, No. 13, 7–13 April 2004, pp. 1–2.

93 Colonel-General Leonid Ivashov, 'NATO grows like cancer', *Voenno-promyshlenny kur'er*, No. 11, 24–30 March 2004, pp. 1, 7.

94 Andrei Kelin, Deputy Director, European Cooperation Department, Russian Foreign Ministry, 'Russia–NATO: toward a new stage of interaction?', *International Affairs* (Moscow), Vol. 51, No. 1, 2005, p. 37.

95 Interfax-AVN military news agency website, Moscow, 14 October 2004, BBC Mon FS1 FsuPol sz/kt.

96 Statement by Putin during meeting with foreign specialists and media representatives, Novo-Ogarevo, 6 September 2004, attended by the author. However, the commander-in-chief of the Russian Air Force, General of the Army Vladimir Mikhailov, accepted that flights by NATO warplanes in the Baltic countries' airspace would not affect Russia's military security, since 'given the capabilities of modern offensive weapons, it doesn't make much difference how far the places are from the border'; *Rossiiskaya gazeta*, 30 March 2004, p. 7.

97 'We've been X-rayed', Vitaly Strugovets, *Russkii kur'er*, 25 February 2004, p. 5.

98 Interfax-AVN military news agency website, Moscow, 7 November 2005, BBC Mon FS1 FsuPol gb/lb. The new aircraft were F-16CJ planes.

99 Interfax news agency, Moscow, 6 February 2006, BBC Mon FS1 FsuPol tm/lb.

100 Interfax-AVN military news agency website, Moscow, 29 June 2004, BBC Mon FS1 FsuPol pl.

101 Interview of Konstantin Totsky, in Daily News Bulletin of the Russian Foreign Ministry, 30 October 2003, *www.mid.ru*. This idea has made little progress.

102 These assurances were recorded in a letter from the NATO Secretary-General to Russian Foreign Minister Lavrov before the NRC meeting on 2 April 2004, the same day as the ceremony in Brussels to admit new members to NATO. The letter also recorded that no nuclear weapons or stores to take them will be deployed on the territory of the new member states, and that Russia and the NATO states will accelerate the process of ratification for an adapted CFE Treaty. Russian Foreign Ministry spokesman Aleksandr Yakovenko, Channel One TV, Moscow, 4 April 2004, BBC Mon FS1 FsuPol lb/va/ad.

103 Kelin, 'Russia–NATO: toward a new stage of interaction?', p. 36 (note 94 above); Vladimir Ivanov, 'V "seruyu zonu" pribaltiki kradutsya yadernye teni', *Nezavisimoe voennoe obozrenie*, 22 October 2004.

104 *Profil*, No. 22, 13–19 June 2005.

105 Statement by Russian Foreign Ministry official, Interfax, Moscow, 20 March 2004, BBC Mon Alert FS1 FsuPol sgm/va.

106 Defence Minister Anatoliy Hrytsenko, TV 5 Kanal, Kiev, 29 October 2005, BBC Mon KVU 291005 ng.

107 See *Eurasia Daily Monitor*, Jamestown Foundation, Vol. 2, No. 197, 24 October 2005.

108 Andrei Kokoshin, chairman of the State Duma Committee for the CIS and Ties with Compatriots. RIA news agency, Moscow, 9 November 2005, BBC Mon FS1 FsuPol mr/iu.

109 Sergei Ivanov has noted that 'nobody has yet evaluated all the consequences of Ukraine's admission to NATO', although he predicts that 'If Ukraine joins NATO, the Ukrainian military-industrial complex will die sooner or later.' Interview on Centre TV, Moscow, 3 December 2005, BBC Mon FS1 MCU 051205 im/ak.

110 Statements by Konstantin Totsky, Interfax, 29 July 2005, BBC Mon FS1 FsuPol stu; Sergei Ivanov, Itar-Tass, 7 June 2005, BBC Mon FS1 FsuPol sgm.

111 See *Eurasia Daily Monitor*, Jamestown Foundation, Vol. 2, No. 112, 9 June 2005.

112 Kelin, 'Russia–NATO: toward a new stage of interaction?', p. 39 (note 94 above).

113 STA news agency, 27 May 2005, BBC Mon FS1 FsuPol va/gh.

114 Foreign Ministry spokesman Aleksandr Yakovenko, RIA news agency, Moscow, 19 April 2005, BBC Mon FS1 FsuPol mjm/sgm.

115   For example, Sergei Karaganov, *Den'*, Kiev, 13 April 2005, pp. 1, 3; BBC Mon KVU 140405 gk/ph.

116   Interfax-AVN military news agency website, Moscow, 12 April 2005, BBC Mon FS1 FsuPol ydy/mjm. On another occasion he suggested that CIS countries might become NATO members within 7–10 years, *Profil*, No. 22, 13–19 June 2005.

117   RIA Novosti, Moscow, 20 December 2005, BBC Mon FS1 FsuPol ch/ib.

118   Most of the following proposals are summarized from the report of a second track working group on NATO–Russia relations in 2002, which remain relevant in many respects; Hunter, Rogov, and Oliker, *NATO and Russia: Bridge-building for the 21st Century*, pp. 24–9 (note 47 above). These findings are also presented in 'Doklad rabochei gruppi po otnosheniyam Rossiya–NATO', *Nezavisimoe voennoe obozrenie*, 13 (283), 19–25 April 2002. Some additional ideas for NATO–Russia cooperation in Europe can be found in Hunter and Rogov, *Engaging Russia as Partner and Participant: The Next Stage of NATO–Russia Relations*, pp. 6–15 (note 75 above). However, this second report places relatively more emphasis on the potential for NATO–Russia cooperation beyond Europe and this agenda reflects American more than European NATO member priorities. For a rather similar Russian set of recommendations, see Igor Tarasenko, *Long-Term Possibilities for NATO–Russia Naval Security Cooperation*, NATO Defence College Occasional Paper No. 7 (Rome, June 2005), pp. 29–32.

119   On the problems in this area, which have confined practical military-technical cooperation to bilateral agreements between Russia and individual NATO member countries, see Vladimir Rubanov, 'On the cooperation with NATO in defence industry', *International Affairs* (Moscow), Vol. 50, No. 6, 2004, pp. 68–78. See also Weitz, *Revitalizing US–Russian Security Cooperation*, pp. 67–9 (note 52 above).

120   Dmitry Danilov, 'Russia and European Security', in Dov Lynch, ed., *What Russia Sees*, Chaillot Paper No. 74 (Paris: Institute for Security Studies, European Union, January 2005), pp. 81–2, 85–6.

121   For a more optimistic assessment, see Forsberg, 'Russia's relationship with NATO', pp. 346–8 (note 44 above).

122   For an assessment of this issue before the effects of the Iraq war on NATO and Russia–NATO relations, see Richard J. Krickus, *Russia in NATO: Thinking about the Unthinkable* (Copenhagen: Danish Institute of International Affairs, 2002).

123   Former NATO Secretary-General George Robertson noted that he 'would not rule out the possibility of Russia joining NATO in the future', when interviewed on the eve of his farewell visit to Moscow on 29–30 October 2003. Interfax, Moscow, 28 October 2003, BBC Mon FS1 FsuPol gyl/ak.

124   Interview in Moscow, 5 May 2004.

125   Itar-Tass news agency, Moscow, 31 October 2005, BBC Mon Alert FS1 FsuPol tm/iu.

126   Interfax, Moscow, 18 July 2002, BBC Mon Alert FS1 FsuPol gyl/sku. But he does not rule out the possibility of accession, noting at the 42nd Munich Conference on Security Policy that 'Russia is not yet thinking about itself applying to join NATO but, as they say, never say never'; RIA Novosti, Moscow, 5 February 2006, BBC Mon FS1 FsuPol mr/va.

127   James A. Baker III, 'Russia in NATO', *The Washington Quarterly*, Vol. 25, No. 1, Winter 2002, pp. 96–7.

128 CTK news agency, Prague, 28 May 2003, BBC Mon EU1 EuroPol dk.

129 Itar-Tass, Moscow, 25 October 2004, BBC Mon FS1 FsuPol sz/ydy.

130 'Yelena Klitsunova and Leonid Karabeshkin, 'Russia–NATO: common threats, similar problems', *Nezavisimoe voennoe obozrenie*, No. 37, 17–23 October 2003, pp. 1–2.

131 Baker III, 'Russia in NATO, p. 102 (note 127 above).

132 In an expression of this 'democratic peace' argument, NATO Secretary-General Jaap de Hoop Scheffer has emphasized that the potential of NATO–Russia partnership depends on political dialogue, that there should be 'common under-standing of the fact that long-term stability can be ensured only by means of an effective democratic system of government'; *Nezavisimaya gazeta*, 10 February 2006.

133 *NATO's New Role in the NIS Area: Final Project Report*, Centre for Eastern Studies (CES), Warsaw, May 2005, *http://www.osw.waw.pl/en/epub/projekt/050414.htm*, p. 42. CES is a Polish governmental analytical centre.

134 Tarasenko, *Long-Term Possibilities for NATO–Russia Naval Security Cooperation*, pp. 28–9 (note 118 above).

6 RUSSIA AND 'EUROPE': THE PUBLIC DIMENSION

1 Issues of this kind are examined in relation to the 1999/2000 elections in Stephen White, Neil Munro and Richard Rose, 'Parties, Voters, and Foreign Policy', in Vicki L. Hesli and William M. Reisinger, eds, *The 1999–2000 Elections in Russia: Their Impact and Legacy* (Cambridge and New York: Cambridge University Press, 2003), pp. 51–72. A more comprehensive study is available in William Zimmerman, *The Russian People and Foreign Policy. Russian Elite and Mass Perspectives, 1993–2000* (Princeton NJ: Princeton University Press, 2002); it is in effect extended in the same author's 'Slavophiles and Westernizers redux: contemporary Russian elite perspectives', *Post-Soviet Affairs* Vol. 21, No. 3, July–September 2005, pp. 183–209.

2 Calculated in respect of GDP expressed in terms of purchasing power parity and foreign trade turnover in 1999, as reported in *Rossiiskii statisticheskii ezhegodnik. 2003: statisticheskii sbornik* (Moscow: Goskomstat Rossii, 2003), pp. 670, 690.

3 Sarah Oates, 'Party Platforms: Towards a Definition of the Russian Political Spectrum', in John Lowenhardt, ed., *Party Politics in Post-Communist Russia* (London and Portland OR: Frank Cass, 1998), pp. 76–97.

4 For an overview, see Stephen White, 'The Political Parties', in White, Zvi Gitelman and Richard Sakwa, eds, *Developments in Russian Politics 6* (London: Palgrave and Durham NC: Duke University Press, 2005), Chapter 5.

5 'Predvybornaya programma politicheskoi partii "Edinaya Rossiya"', *Rossiiskaya gazeta*, 13 November 2003, p. 11.

6 'Za vlast' trudovogo naroda! Predvybornaya programma Kommunisticheskoi Partii Rossiiskoi Federatsii', *Rossiiskaya gazeta*, 11 November 2003, p. 10 (also in *Sel'skaya zhizn'*, 13–19 November 2003, p. 5; *Zavtra*, No. 47, November 2003, p. 2; and *Parlamentskaya gazeta*, 27 November 2003, p. 3).

7 'Izbiratel'nyi blok "Rodina (Narodno-patrioticheskii soyuz)": programmnye dokumenty', *Rossiiskaya gazeta*, 12 November 2003, p. 10.

8 'Programma Liberal'no-Demokraticheskoi Partii Rossii (LDPR), prinyata na

XIII s"ezda LDPR 13 dekabrya 2001 g. v g. Moskve', consulted at *www.cikrf.ru*.

9 'Predvybornaya programma Rossiiskoi demokraticheskoi partii "Yabloko"', consulted at *www.cikrf.ru*.

10 Consulted at *www.yabloko.ru*.

11 Consulted at *www.sps.ru*.

12 'Predvybornaya programma Politicheskoi partii "Soyuz pravykh sil"', consulted at *www.cikrf.ru*.

13 *Argumenty i fakty* 7/2004, pp. 4–9 (pp. 7–8). Putin's address was also carried in *Izvestiya*, 13 February 2004, pp. 1 and 4–5, and in *Rossiiskaya gazeta*, 13 February 2004, pp. 1, 3. Communist challenger Nikolai Kharitonov's manifesto 'Za rodnuyu zemlyu i narodnuyu volyu!' appeared in *Rossiiskaya gazeta*, 20 February 2004, pp. 10–11, and in *Parlamentskaya gazeta*, 4 March 2003, p. 3; the Liberal Democratic candidate Oleg Malyshkin's address 'O. A. Malyshkin: moya tsel' – blago i schast'e kazhdogo rossiyanina' appeared in *Rossiiskaya gazeta*, 27 February 2004, pp. 10–11; Sergei Glaz'ev explained 'Zachem ya idu na vybory' in *Rossiiskaya gazeta*, 25 February 2004, p. 10, and in *Parlamentskaya gazeta*, 27 February–4 March 2004, pp. 4–5; and Sergei Mironov published 'Predvybornaya programma Sergeya Mironova' in *Rossiiskaya gazeta*, 19 February 2004, pp. 10–11.

14 Samuel P. Huntington, *The Clash of Civilizations and the Remaking of World Order* (London: Simon and Schuster, 1996), pp. 139–40.

15 Kolosov and his colleagues, for instance, found that 'Europe', for ordinary Russians, was defined less in terms of geography than 'as a way of life, wealth, success, satisfaction, leisure, [and] cultural highlights'; see V. A. Kolosov, ed., *Mir glazami rossiyan: mify i vneshnyaya politika* (Moscow: Institut Fonda "Obshchestvennoe mnenie", 2003), p. 76. Andreev found similarly that Russians associated Western Europe with concepts such as 'prosperity', 'comfort', 'human rights' and 'civilization', but their own country with 'crisis', 'narcotics', 'patriotism' and 'moral decline'; see A. Andreev, 'Obraz Evropy v sovremennom rossiiskom obshchestve', *Mirovaya ekonomika i mezhdunarodnye otnosheniya* 5/2003, pp. 35–43 (p. 42). For a group of junior officers, interviewed for our own project in Vladimir, Europe represented 'money', 'prosperity', 'technology', 'clothes', 'cars', 'an enduring culture', and equally 'a culture that is an example for others'; but 'the West' meant 'enemy', 'America' and 'Berlin' as well as high cultural and technological levels.

16 See, for instance, Jill Krause and Neil Renwick, eds, *Identities in International Relations* (London: Macmillan, 1996); William Bloom, *Personal Identity, National Identity and International Relations* (Cambridge: Cambridge University Press, 1993); and Ilya Prizel, *National Identity and Foreign Policy: Nationalism and Leadership in Poland, Russia and Ukraine* (Cambridge: Cambridge University Press, 1998).

17 For some recent discussions, see, for instance, Debra Johnson and Paul Robinson, eds, *Perspectives on EU–Russia Relations* (London: Routledge, 2005).

18 See 'Russia–Europe: On the Eve of the Summit in Ireland', 24 March 2004, consulted at *www.wciom.ru*.

19 See 'Rossiya, Evrosoyuz, VTO', 20 November 2003, and 'Evropeiskaya integratsiya i Rossiya', 9 June 2005, consulted at *www.fom.ru*, accessed 15 February 2006.

20 The *Eurobarometer 2004.1: Public Opinion in the Candidate Countries* (Spring 2004, accessed at *europa.eu.int*) records that 43 per cent of respondents in the new member states were broadly favourable to their imminent membership, with 16 per

cent against; responses are no longer disaggregated in terms of the more specific implications of membership (p. C50).

21 Other inquiries have also found that Russian supporters of EU membership were 'represented in approximately the same proportions in all age and educational groups'; see 'Rossiya i Evropa glazami rossiyan', *Sotsiologicheskie issledovaniya* 5/2003, p. 42. A more detailed regression analysis, not reported here, found that male gender, older age and higher education were statistically significant in predicting support for membership at the 1 per cent level, and higher levels of self-perceived income at the 5 per cent level; these social characteristics, taken together, nonetheless explained no more than 8 per cent of the variation.

22 See, for instance, Stephen White, Richard Rose and Ian McAllister, *How Russia Votes* (Chatham NJ: Chatham House Publishers, 1997), Chapter 3.

23 Kolosov, ed., *Mir glazami rossiyan*, p. 116 (note 15 above).

24 Ibid., p. 125.

25 Ibid., p. 117.

26 R. V. Svetlov, *Druz'ya i vragi Rossii* (St Petersburg: Amfora, 2002), p. 110.

27 Kolosov, ed., *Mir glazami rossiyan*, p. 118.

28 Results of this kind have also been found in other investigations. According to the Levada Centre, for instance, 67 per cent of those who were asked in December 2004 (and 50 per cent of Ukrainians) regretted the demise of the Soviet Union (see *www.levada.ru/press/2004122904.html*).

29 In April 1999, 33 per cent of Russians felt 'good' about the United States, and 38 per cent did so in March 2003, but 68 per cent did so in January 2002 and 62 per cent in September 2004 ('Russia's place in the world', accessed at *www.russiavotes. org*). Fluctuations in Russian attitudes towards the US are considered in L. D. Gudkov, 'Otnoshenie k SShA v Rossii i problema antiamerikanizma', *Monitoring obshchestvennogo mneniya: Ekonomicheskie i sotsial'nye peremeny* 2/2002, pp. 42–8, and in T. Vorontsova and A. Danilova, eds, *Amerika: vzglyad iz Rossii: do i posle 11 sentyabrya* (Moscow: Institut Fonda "Obshchestvennoe mnenie", 2001).

30 As in the case of attitudes to European Union membership, attitudes to foreign countries varied relatively little by age, gender or other characteristics. Perceptions of the friendliness or otherwise of India and Finland, at one extreme, varied little in terms of the social attributes of those who held either view, apart from a slight tendency of the more prosperous to take a more benign view than the sample as a whole, and to be less undecided. At the other extreme, males were somewhat more likely than females to regard the United States as a hostile country; but age, for instance, made little difference, with the over-60s no more likely to see the US as a hostile country than the sample as a whole. Once again, there were modest effects for income, with those who regarded themselves as having a good standard of living somewhat more likely to think the US was a friendly country than others; but on the whole, what is most remarkable about these calculations is the extent to which perceptions of the outside world are almost entirely unaffected by age, gender, education, income or residence. Kolosov and colleagues (*Mir glazami rossiyan*, Appendix tables 4 and 5) (note 15 above) also found minimal variations – and none that was greater than 10 percentage points – across various social categories in the perceived friendliness or unfriendliness of these countries.

31 See Kolosov, ed., *Mir glazami rossiyan*', Appendix table 7 (note 15 above).

32 Similar findings have emerged from other investigations: for instance, a VTsIOM study in early 2004 found that 54 per cent thought Russia should cooperate most of all in its foreign policy with Western Europe, as compared with 30 per cent who thought there should be most cooperation with the United States ('International affairs', accessed at *www.russiavotes.org*).

33 See for instance 'Rasshirenie NATO', 14 April 2004; 58 per cent saw NATO as 'aggressive' and just 17 per cent as 'defensive' (consulted at *www.fom.ru*).

34 Speaking on a British television programme in early March 2000, Putin made clear for the first time that he did 'not rule out the possibility' of Russia joining NATO provided Russia's interests were taken into account and that it was a fully-fledged partner (*Kommersant*, 7 March 2000, p. 2). He made similar remarks to Russian journalists at the time, but added that the question of entry would depend on NATO's transformation into a predominantly political organization and would at all events not be a matter for the immediate future (*Ot pervogo litsa. Razgovory s Vladimirom Putinym* (Moscow: Vagrius, 2000), p. 159). This issue is discussed more fully in Chapter 5 above, pp. 124–6.

35 These findings parallel those of McAllister and White, who found that perceptions of security threats were 'more notable for the absence than the presence of strong patterns', and that 'social characteristics such as gender, age and education made relatively little difference' to support for NATO membership (Ian McAllister and Stephen White, 'NATO enlargement and eastern opinion', *European Security*, Vol. 11, No. 4, Winter 2002, pp. 47–58 (at pp. 52, 55)).

36 As many as 89 per cent, for instance, supported closer checks on identity, and 60 per cent were willing to agree that movement inside the country and across national boundaries should be restricted; 87 per cent were concerned that they or their relatives might themselves be victims of a terrorist attack (Levada Centre survey, 24–27 September 2004, n = 1601, consulted at *www.russiavotes.org* on 24 May 2006).

37 Richard A. Kruger, *Focus Groups: A Practical Guide for Applied Research*, 2nd edn (Thousand Oaks CA: Sage, 1994), p. 238.

38 Lia Litosseliti, *Using Focus Groups in Research* (London: Continuum, 2003), p. 27.

39 These were views that found many echoes within the presidential administration, which was also concerned by what appeared to be a global plan to undermine the Russian state and allow its peripheral areas to be taken over by neighbouring states. See Margot Light and Stephen White, 'Russia and President Putin: wild theories', *The World Today*, Vol. 57, No. 7, July 2001, pp. 10–12.

7 'RUSSIA *IN* EUROPE' OR 'RUSSIA *AND* EUROPE'?

1 For a moderate Russian analysis of likely Russian responses to prevent further 'colour revolutions' in the CIS, see Alexei Arbatov, *Nezavisimaya gazeta*, 13 May 2005, p. 1.

2 Sergei Karaganov interview in *Den'*, 13 April 2005, *BBC Summary of World Broadcasts. Former Soviet Union, http://bbc.monitoringonline.com* (henceforth BBC), Mon KVU 140405 gk/ph.

3 Interview in *Nezavismaya gazeta*, 31 May 2004; in *Moskovsky komsomolets*, 21

December 2004, in Igor Torbakov, 'Russia faces foreign policy debate for 2005', *Eurasia Insight*, 18 January 2005, *http://www.eurasianet.org*. Pavlovsky is the President of the Moscow-based Foundation for Effective Politics and a consultant who worked for Viktor Yanukovych's campaign team in Ukraine. See also Igor' Zadorin, ed., *Integratsiya v Yevrazii: narod i elity stran YeEP* (Mosow: Yevropa 2006); the latter is part of a new 'Euro-east' publications series.

4 Alexander Dugin, 'Proval yevropeyskoy konstitutsii: shans dlya Rossii', *Rossiiskaya gazeta*, 16 June 2005.

5 Karaganov interview (note 2 above); see also Konstantin Kosachev, *Nezavisimaya gazeta*, 28 December 2004.

6 Interview on RTR, Moscow, 27 November 2004; cited in Dov Lynch, ed., *What Russia Sees*, Chaillot Paper No. 74 (Paris: Institute of Security Studies, European Union, January 2005), p. 133.

7 *Eurasia Daily Monitor*, Jamestown Foundation, Vol. 2, No. 168, 12 September 2005.

8 Ibid., Vol. 2, No. 112, 9 June 2005.

9 For an analysis of the security, economic and legal implications of Ukraine's bid for NATO accession, see *NATO v Ukraine. Sekretnye materialy*, Moscow, 2006.

10 Article by Sergei Lavrov, 'Extending the framework of partnership', *Rossiyskaya gazeta*, 11 May 2005; meeting of Lavrov in State Duma, 12 May 2005. Interfax news agency, 12 May 2005, BBC Mon FS1 FsuPol ws/mjm; transcript of remarks by Lavrov after talks with EU Troika, 28 February 2005, *www.mid.ru*; Vladimir Chizhov, 'European Union: a partnership strategy', *International Affairs*, Vol. 50, No. 6, 2004, pp. 84–7.

11 *Russia and the West: Opportunities for a New Partnership*, Bergedorf Round Table, Potsdam, Berlin, Hamburg, 24–26 June 2005, p. 66. Chizhov spoke at this round table.

12 That this concept includes all of Russia was confirmed by Putin in May 2005, when he wrote of 'a single greater Europe from the Atlantic to the Urals, and on the Pacific Ocean', in *Le Figaro*, cited in Konstantin Kosachev, 'Russia between European choice and Asian growth', *International Affairs* (Moscow), Vol. 52, No. 1, 2006, p. 8. For a more developed view of the economic relations of Russia and the EU as formed around separate centres of gravity, with the two sides characterized by different geo-economic and geopolitical interests, see Yu. Shishkov, 'Rossiya v yevropeyskom ekonomicheskom prostrantstve: narastayushchee odnochestvo', in L. Glukharev, ed., *Yevropa peremen: kontseptsii i strategii integratsionnykh protsessov* (Moscow: Kraft, 2006), pp. 273–81.

13 Andrey Makarychev, 'Europe's Eastern Dimension: Russia's Reaction to Poland's Initiative', PONARS Policy Memo 301, November 2003, p. 2.

14 See statements by the Russian Foreign Ministry spokesman Mikhail Kamynin, RIA Novosti, 22 February 2006, BBC Mon FS1 FsuPol au/sz; by Sergei Lavrov, Channel One TV, 24 March 2005, BBC Mon FS1 MCU 240306 evg/rj.

15 Interview on *Ukrayinska Pravda* website, Kiev, 2 March 2006, BBC Mon KVU 090306 ng/ar.

16 Deputy Foreign Minister Vladimir Chizhov, *Izvestiya*, 25 February 2004, p. 2.

17 In May 2005, on the eve of the celebrations of the victory in the Great Patriotic War, Putin affirmed that 'The Russian nation has always felt part of the large

European family, and has shared common cultural, moral, and spiritual value Therefore, the Russian nation's democratic and European choice is entirely logical'; Konstantin Kosachev, 'Russia between European choice and Asian growth' *International Affairs* (Moscow), Vol. 52, No. 1, 2006, p. 8.

18 Rolf Schuette, *EU–Russia Relations: Interests and Values – a European Perspective* (Washington DC: Carnegie Endowment for International Peace, December 2004), Carnegie Papers No. 54, pp. 26–7.

19 Speech on 23 November 1981; L. Brezhnev, *Leninskim Kursom. Rechi, privetstviya, stat'i, Vospominaniya*, Vol. 9 (Moscow: Politicheskoy literatury, 1982), p. 323.

20 See Stephen White, Margot Light and Ian McAllister, 'Russia and the West: is there a values gap?', *International Politics*, Vol. 42, 2005, pp. 316–19.

21 Ibid., pp. 320–30.

22 Communication from the Commission to the Council and the European Parliament on Relations with Russia (COM (2004) 106), 9 February 2004, *http://europa.eu.int/comm/external_relations/russia_docs/com04_106_en.pdf*. For a Russian critique of this document for demanding that Russia adopt 'the same values that present-day Europe has developed over the past several decades in greenhouse conditions under the protection of the US', see Sergei Karaganov, in *Rossiiskaya gazeta*, 25 February 2004, pp. 1, 7.

23 See Karen Smith', 'The outsiders: the European neighbourhood policy', *International Affairs*, Vol. 81, No. 4, July 2005, pp. 757–73.

24 Schuette, *EU–Russia Relations*, p. 16 (note 18 above).

25 Communication from the Commission to the Council and the European Parliament on Relations with Russia (COM (2004) 106), 9 February 2004, *http://europa.eu.int/comm/external_relations/russia_docs/com04_106_en.pdf*.

26 Chris Patten, *Not Quite the Diplomat. Home Truths about World Affairs* (London: Allen Lane, 2005), pp. 177–8.

27 See Konstantin Kosachev, Chairman of the State Duma's Committee on International Affairs; Interfax, Moscow, 20 March 2005, BBC Mon FS1 FsuPol mr/skh.

28 See Andrew Monaghan, *Russian Oil and EU Energy Security* (Swindon: Conflict Studies Research Centre, UK Defence Academy, November 2005).

29 Kosachev, 'Russia between European choice and Asian growth', p. 5 (note 17 above).

30 Andrew Kuchins, 'From values to true dialogue', *The Moscow Times*, 22 June 2005, p. 10. EU documents that express support for democracy in Russia, unlike US statements, tend not to link this expressly to expectations that democratization will result in more peaceful policies. For an argument that a 'democratic peace' in the former Soviet Union is particularly vulnerable to national issues, as well as to the effects of concentration of political power in the hands of a narrow group of elites, see Bear Braumoeller, 'Deadly doves: liberal nationalism and the democratic peace in the Soviet successor states', *International Studies Quarterly*, Vol. 41, No. 3 (September 1997), pp. 375–402. For the research conclusion that states undergoing democratization are substantially more likely to participate in external wars than are states whose regimes remain unchanged or changed in an autocratic direction, see Edward Mansfield and Jack Snyder, 'Democratic transitions, institutional strength and war', *International Organization*, Vol. 56, No. 2, Spring 2002, pp. 297–337.

31 The texts of the road maps are available at *http://europa.eu.int/comm/external_relations/russia/summit_05_05/index.htm.*

32 Dov Lynch, 'EU–Russia Relations: Reconciling Inner and Outer Abroads?', unpublished paper presented to the European Institute of Public Administration, September 2005, pp. 6–7.

33 Michael Emerson, 'Four Common Spaces and the Proliferation of the Fuzzy', CEPS Policy Brief No. 71 (Brussels: Centre for European Policy Studies, May 2005), pp. 1–4.

34 *Russia and the Enlarged European Union: The Arduous Path Toward Rapprochement*, Committee 'Russia in a United Europe', Moscow 2004, pp. 45–54.

35 For a detailed assessment, see V. Inozemtsev and Ye. Kuznetsova, 'Rossiya: pochemy "dorozhnye karty" ne vedut v Yevropu?, *Sovremennaya Yevropa*, No. 4, 2005, pp. 64–79.

36 Dmitry Suslov, 'Road Maps to Europe?', 9 June 2005, *www.russiaprofile.org*; *Eurasia Daily Monitor*, Vol. 2, No. 94, 13 May 2005.

37 Sergei Medvedev, presentation at conference 'Assessing Russia's European choice', Finnish Institute of International Affairs, Helsinki, 11 November 2005. For a measured critique of the road maps, see Dmitry Danilov, 'Dorozhnye karty, vedushchie v nikuda', *Nezavisimaya gazeta*, 24 May 2005.

38 See Nadezhda Arbatova, 'Russia–EU quandary 2007', *Russia in Global Affairs*, Vol. 4, No. 2, April/June 2006, pp. 100–110; Timofei Bordachev, 'Toward a strategic alliance', *Russia in Global Affairs*, Vol. 4, No. 2, April/June 2006, pp. 117–23.

39 For a cautious Russian approach to the process of negotiating a 'PCA-2', see Vassily Likhachev (Deputy Chairman, Committee for International Affairs, Federation Council), 'Russia and the European Union', *International Affairs* (Moscow), Vol. 52, No. 2, 2006, pp. 102–14.

40 Dmitry Danilov, 'Obshchee prostranstvo vneshney bezopasnosti Rossii i ES: ambitsii i real'nost'', *Mirovaya ekonomika i mezhdunarodnye otnosheniya*, No. 2, 2005, pp. 35–47; Dmitry Danilov, 'Russia–EU Cooperation in the Security Field; Trends and Conceptual Framework', in Hanna Smith, ed., *Russia and its Foreign Policy: Influences, Interests and Issues* (Saarijärvi: Kikimora Publications, 2005), pp. 122–3. Danilov sets out a list of principles to be agreed on.

41 Timofei Bordachev, 'Russia's European Problem: Eastward Enlargement of the EU and Moscow's Policy, 1993–2003', in Oksana Antonenko and Kathryn Pinnick, eds, *Russia and the European Union: Prospects for a New Relationship* (London and New York: Routledge, 2004), pp. 62–4. However, for an argument that during the next 10–15 years Russia should prioritize infrastructure projects to expedite the integration process and 'facilitate the formation of communities of economic or social entities', see Arkady Moshes, 'Reaffirming the benefits of Russia's European choice', *Russia in Global Affairs*, Vol. 3, No. 3, July/September 2005, pp. 95–6.

42 For an ambitious proposal for such a Strategic Partnership Agreement, see Yuri Borko, 'Rethinking Russia–EU relations', *Russia in Global Affairs*, Vol. 2, No. 3, July/September 2004, pp. 168–78.

43 For a clear Russian exposition of options for cooperation in the fields of security and economics, see Yu. Borko and D. Danilov, *Rossiya–Yevropeyskiy soyuz: strategiya strategicheskogo partnerstva*, Reports of the Institute of Europe, Russian Academy of Sciences, No. 157, OGIN TD, Moscow, 2005.

44 Hiski Haukkala, 'The Relevance of Norms and Values in the EU's Russia Policy', UPI Working Paper, 52, Finnish Institute of International Affairs, Helsinki, 2005, p. 9.

45 The dilemma is elaborated well in Derek Averre, 'The EU–Russian Relationship in the Context of European Security', in Debra Johnson and Paul Robinson, eds, *Perspectives on EU–Russia Relations* (London and New York: Routledge, 2005), pp. 79–89.

46 Foreign Minister Sergei Lavrov in a report to the State Duma, Interfax, Moscow, 12 May 2005, BBC Mon FS1 FsuPol ws/mjm.

47 Interview of Jaap de Hoop Scheffer, in *Nezavisimaya gazeta*, 27 February 2004, p. 11.

48 In a similar vein, a Polish study identified three scenarios for the development of Russia–EU relations as follows. first, a *change in Russia* – a political breakthrough results in a rebirth of Russia's 'European project'; second, *pragmatization or stagnation*, by which the two parties develop pragmatic cooperation in selected fields and give up attempts to create a real 'common space'; and, third, *confrontation* – in response to crises and the EU's growing activity in its eastern neighbourhood, Russia launches a counteroffensive and limits it cooperation with the EU so that relations are restricted to a necessary minimum. The short-term forecast, at least to 2008, is for the second scenario, but looking more than ten years ahead it is argued that international trends will move Russia closer to the first scenario. *Russia vs. the European Union: a 'Strategic Partnership' Crisis*, Centre for Eastern Studies (CES) No. 22, Warsaw, January 2006, pp. 62–3, *www.osw.waw.pl*.

49 'Otnosheniya Rossii Yevropeiskogo Soyuza: sovremennaya situatsiya i perspektivy', Moscow 2005, report prepared by a scenario group, based on the situation analysis conducted at a workshop on 21 January 2005. The workshop was organized by the Institute of Europe of the Russian Academy of Sciences, the Institute of Strategic Studies and Analysis, the Aeroflot Joint Stock Company, the Council on Foreign and Defence Policy, and the Editorial Board of the magazine *Russia in Global Affairs*. See *http://www.svop.ru*; *http://www.globalaffairs.ru/numbers/12/3647.html*. See also the conclusion of Chapter 3 above.

50 For an argument that there should be a serious discussion over Russian accession to the EU and that Russia should adopt a model of development that does not exclude this possibility, see Dmitry Suslov, Deputy Director of Studies of the Council on Foreign and Defence Policy, 'Koloniya Yevropy ili ee chast'', *Nezavisimaya gazeta*, 23 May 2005.

51 Averre, 'The EU–Russian Relationship', p. 81 (note 45 above).

52 Interview in *Rossiiskaya gazeta*, 20 May 2005; and *http://en.rian.ru/world/20050520/40387988–print.html*.

53 See 'Otnosheniya Rossii i Yevropeiskogo Soyuza', p. 18 (note 49 above). The Norwegian model is supported by Timofei Bordachev, 'Russia and EU Enlargement: Starting the Endgame', in Esther Brimmer and Stefan Frohlich, eds, *The Strategic Implications of European Union Enlargement* (Washington DC: Center for Transatlantic Relations, Johns Hopkins University, 2005), pp. 167–8. See also Moshes, 'Reaffirming the benefits of Russia's European choice', p. 97 (note 41 above).

54 For one elaboration of such a treaty, see Bordachev, 'Toward a strategic alliance', pp. 116–23 (note 38 above).

55 Sergei Karaganov, 'Russia and the International Order', in Lynch, ed., *What Russia Sees,* p. 33 (note 6 above). See also Sergei Karaganov, 'Yevropeiskaya strategiya Rossii: noviy start', *Rossiya v global'noi politike,* Vol. 3, No. 2, March/April 2005, pp. 172–84; 'Rossiya i Yevropa: trudnoe sblizhenie', *Rossiiskaya gazeta,* 1 April 2005.

56 *Eurasia Daily Monitor,* Vol. 2, No. 123, 24 June 2005. Timofei Bordachev, 'EU Crisis: What Opportunities for Russia?', in Thomas Gomart and Tatiana Kastueva-Jean, eds, *Russie. Nei. Visions* (Paris: IFRI, 2006), pp. 63–9.

57 Bordachev, 'EU Crisis', p. 60 (note 56 above).

58 Alexander Dugin, 'Proval Yevropeiskoi konstitutsii: shans dlya Rossii', *Rossiiskaya gazeta,* 16 June 2005; see also *Rossiiskaya gazeta,* 21 June 2005; *Eurasia Daily Monitor,* Vol. 2, No. 123, 24 June 2005.

59 Vladimir Soloviov, 'Russia aspires to the role of NATO ally', *Kommersant,* 8 December 2005, p. 10. The existence of this discussion has not been confirmed by any official Russian sources.

60 Konstantin Kosachev, cited in 'Shanghai Cooperation Organization: The anti-NATO', *Nezavisimaya gazeta,* 27 October 2005, p. 3; also in Interfax new agency, Moscow, 26 October 2005, BBC Mon FS1 FsuPol sz/gb.

61 This is reflected in fundamentalist nationalist thinking. Leonid Ivashov envisages the SCO growing into an alliance with a military potential equal to NATO. Adranik Migranyan sees the task of the SCO as to squeeze out and restrict NATO's zone of responsibility. Interfax-AVN military news agency website, 26 October 2005, BBC Mon FS1 FsuPol sgm/gb.

62 RIA news agency, Moscow, 18 February 2005, BBC Mon FS1 FsuPol ch/stu.

63 Foreign Minister Sergei Lavrov, as cited in *Vremya novostei,* 24 June 2004, p. 5.

64 Jaap de Hoop Scheffer, interviewed in *Vremya novostei,* 6 August 2004, pp. 1, 5.

65 Dmitri Trenin, 'Russia's Security Integration with America and Europe', in Alexander Motyl, Blair Ruble, and Lilia Shevtsova, eds, *Russia's Engagement with the West: Transformation and Integration in the Twenty-First Century* (Armonk NY: M. E. Sharpe, 2005), p. 290. This chapter offers three options for Russian security integration with the leading Western states; the quote taken is from the most optimistic one that considers Russian modernization in conjunction with security integration with Europe and the Atlantic alliance.

66 Alexei Pushkov, producer and host of 'Postscript' (TV Centre), *Trud,* 9 June 2004.

Index

P. 176 — ↗ delve into symbol/terminology

whole concept of sovereign demonacy seems to be a reaction to normative pressures, etc — convergence of 'value' type stuff pushed by EU

→ see Economist world 2008

№30 : Strategy plays on people's troubled relationships with the past, their disillusionment vis-a-vis the chaos, instability of Yeltsin era frustration that things were not achieved & W. pursued non-conciliatory strategies & did things despite Russian opposition/concessions (so) — P ≠ choose authoritarianism, but

* Graham Timmins *